A READER

ECONOMICS

OF CRIME

SECOND EDITION

Neil O. Alper
Daryl A. Hellman

Professors of Economics
Northeastern University

Pearson
Custom
Publishing

Cover Photo © Sarah Putnum / The Picture Cube, Inc.

Printed in the United States of America

10

Please visit our website at www.pearsoncustom.com

ISBN 0–536–00246–0

BA 990750

PEARSON CUSTOM PUBLISHING
160 Gould Street/Needham Heights, MA 02494
A Pearson Education Company

CONTENTS

LIST OF AUTHORS

Gary S. Becker, Department of Economics, University of Chicago.

William J. Bowers, College of Criminal Justice, Northeastern University.

James M. Buchanan, Center for the Study of Public Choice, George Mason University.

Philip J. Cook, Institute of Political Sciences and Public Affairs, Duke University.

John J. DiIulio, Jr., Department of Politics, Princeton University.

Theodore N. Ferdinand, Center for the Study of Delinquency, Crime and Corrections, Southern Illinois University.

James Alan Fox, College of Criminal Justice, Northeastern University.

Richard B. Freeman, Department of Economics, Harvard University.

Daryl A. Hellman, Department of Economics, Northeastern University.

Mark H. Moore, John Fitzgerald Kennedy School of Government, Harvard University.

Karen Needels, Mathematica Policy Research, Inc.

Anne Morrison Piehl, John Fitzgerald Kennedy School of Government, Harvard University.

Glenn L. Pierce, Center for Criminal Justice Policy, Northeastern University.

Paul H. Rubin, Bureau of Economics, Federal Trade Commission.

Thomas C. Schelling, Department of Economics, University of Maryland.

Carl S. Shoup, Sandwich, New Hampshire.

Gordon Tullock, Department of Economics, University of Arizona.

Gary A Zarkin, Research Triangle Institute.

INTRODUCTION

This book of readings is designed to accompany *The Economics of Crime* by Daryl A. Hellman and Neil O. Alper. The readings are arranged to follow the organization of that text and are selected to complement the material presented there. The readings represent both theoretical and empirical studies that examine issues which are central to the economic approach to either understanding criminal behavior or to developing effective public policy for dealing with crime. All of the papers, however, are not written by economists, nor do they all appear in the economics literature. In the book, as in the field, much of the important work relevant to the Economics of Crime comes from related disciplines.

The readings selected for the book were published over roughly a 30-year period, from 1964 to 1996. Thus the readings cover the period over which the Economics of Crime was developing as a field, from its beginnings in the mid to late 1960s to the present. An excerpt from Gary Becker's seminal paper which appeared in 1968 and which is often credited as the real beginning of the field is included in the collection, not only because of the subject matter covered, but because of the importance of this particular article to the development of the Economics of Crime as a legitimate area of inquiry.

The first selection, "The Economics of Crime" by Paul Rubin, is intended to provide an introduction to the subject matter and an overview of many of the issues that are examined both in the Hellman text and in this book of readings. Rubin discusses the economic model of crime, the deterrent effect of punishment in general and capital punishment in particular, organized crime, and the efficiency of courts and corrections.

The next three papers form a set. They are all included to elaborate on a discussion of the dimensions of the crime problem. Each is an empirical investigation of how crime or arrest rates vary either over space or over time. The Fox and Hellman paper examines variability in campus crime rates for over 200 colleges and universities. They look at the relative "safeness" of the campus compared to the city or town in which it is located and the relative safeness of campuses compared with one another. One of their interesting conclusions is that the location of the campus (i.e., rural, suburban, urban) does not appear to make a difference. They then try to determine what factors are associated with varying crime rates across campuses. In doing so, this reading introduces us to various theories of criminal behavior.

The Ferdinand and Cook and Zarkin papers both examine crime patterns over time. Ferdinand examines arrest rates for various crimes in the city of Boston over an approximately 100-year period during which there is considerable instability, secular change and cyclical movement. Cook and Zarkin focus on variability of crime rates over the business cycle. In addition to providing interesting descriptions of crime patterns over time, these papers also serve to introduce hypotheses concerning causes of criminal behavior.

The first paper by Gordon Tullock, "Does Punishment Deter Crime?," examines an extremely important policy issue which is raised by the economic model of criminal behavior. Tullock describes the economic argument and summarizes much of the empirical evidence and tests of the economic model. Tullock's paper, however, was published in 1974 and, while a good summary then, his optimistic conclusion concerning tests of the economic model must be re-examined in light of subsequent research. Nevertheless, his paper is included here because of its readability and good summary of many of the issues.

The following paper by Tullock, "An Economic Approach to Crime," and the one by Shoup, "Standards for Distributing a Free Governmental Service-Crime Prevention," examine aspects of the optimum allocation of criminal justice resources. Tullock attempts to define an "optimum law" in two areas—motor vehicle offenses and tax evasion. He demonstrates the use of the economic approach in determining optimal law enforcement policy.

The Shoup paper examines a related issue—the optimal allocation of police resources over neighborhoods. His paper illustrates the potential conflict between the "efficiency" of minimizing a city-wide crime rate with the "equity" of providing equal possibilities of victimization across neighborhoods.

The following three selections, one by Ann Morrison Piehl and John J. DiIulio, one by Karen Needels, and one by Gary Becker, provide examples of economic analyses of the use of prisons and corrections. The Peel and DiIulio paper provides "a cost-benefit analysis of incarceration for male offenders. Based on a study of New Jersey offenders, they found that incarceration does pay, but not necessarily for all crimes. They recommend additional research to forge a "new intellectual consensus on crime policy" especially as it relates to incarceration.

Needels' paper examines the post-release labor market experiences of offenders in Georgia. Using information that covers 17 years of criminal activity and nine years of post-release earnings, she examines the impact of race, education, age and criminal history on the employment and earnings of ex-offenders.

Becker's piece is from his classic 1968 article. In this short discussion he uses economic reasoning to argue for the increased use of fines in place of traditional forms of punishment, such as incarceration. His discussion clearly illustrates the economic perspective, whether or not one agrees with his conclusion.

The rest of the readings in the book are included because they focus on particular types of crime or policy issues related to those crimes—crimes against property, crimes against persons, "victimless" crimes and organized crime. The paper by Freeman provides an overview of the impact of the changes in the labor market, especially for less skilled, young males in the U.S., on their criminal behavior. He also examines the public policy implications of these changes relevant to the labor market and the legitimate opportunities it provides, and incarceration.

The next three papers, all by Bowers and Pierce, focus on issues related to crimes against persons—capital punishment and gun control. The articles dealing with capital punishment address the question of the equitable and efficient application of capital punishment. "Arbitrariness and Discrimination under Post-*Furman* Capital Statutes" provides evidence that the implementation of a new, Post-*Furman*, generation of capital statutes still does not lead to an equitable application of the death penalty. Bowers and Pierce find this to be especially true with respect to the race of the offender and victim. The question of efficiency is addressed in "Deterrence or Brutalization: What Is the Effect of Executions?" Bowers and Pierce find evidence that executions lead to two additional homicides in the month following an execution, raising doubts about utilizing capital punishment as an efficient method of deterring homicides.

The third Bowers and Pierce paper, "The Bartley-Fox Gun Law's Short Term Impact on Crime in Boston," provides an excellent test of the predictability of the economist's model of criminal behavior. It examines the impact of a change in public policy that increases the criminal's cost of "doing business" on the market for crimes against persons. It is left to the reader to decide whether the model "passes or fails" the test.

The final two papers, by Schelling and Buchanan, apply economic analysis to organized crime. The one by Schelling is from the Presidential Crime Commission's Task Force Report on Organized Crime, issued in 1967, which has become a classic example of the economic approach to understanding criminal behavior and criminal organizations. The central question which he addresses is why some criminal activities, or markets, are "organized" while others are not. An understanding of the incentives and disincentives to large-scale organization can help in the design of appropriate public policies for dealing with organized crime. The Buchanan paper extends some of Schelling's arguments by asking whether or not there are possible advantages to society of having organized, or monopolized, criminal activity, rather than having competition.

In total, the collection of readings provides a sample of the kind of research being done by economists and other social scientists examining crime and the criminal justice system. The papers cover a diverse set of topics and include both theoretical and empirical work. In doing so, the readings demonstrate the methodology of economic inquiry, give a sense of how the economic approach compares with that of other social sciences, and introduces students to some of the theoretical and empirical tools used in economic research.

THE ECONOMICS OF CRIME

Paul H. Rubin

Until about 1968 most academic research on crime was done by sociologists. The basic premise of this work seems to have been that criminals were somehow different from noncriminals, and the major research consisted of searching for the ways in which criminals differed. There also was a reasonably widespread feeling that punishment did not deter crime. Therefore, the solution to crime was some sort of rehabilitation. This feeling was based partly on the idea of the difference between criminals and noncriminals and the corresponding feeling that criminals were not sufficiently rational to respond to incentives. It also was based partially on some empirical studies which purported to show that capital punishment did not deter murder.

In 1968 articles by economists dealing with crime began appearing.[1] Of particular importance was the article by Gary Becker. Becker essentially argued that criminals are about like anyone else—that is, they rationally maximize their own self-interest (utility) subject to the constraints (prices, incomes) that they face in the marketplace and elsewhere. Thus the decision to become a criminal is in principle no different from the decision to become a bricklayer or a carpenter, or, indeed, an economist. The individual considers the net costs and benefits of each alternative and makes his decision on this basis. If we then want to explain changes in criminal behavior over time or space, we examine changes in these constraints. The basic assumption in this type of research is that tastes are constant and that changes in behavior can be explained by changes in prices. Tastes are assumed to be constant because we have absolutely no theory of changes in tastes (sociology not withstanding), and therefore an explanation that relies on tastes is tautological—that is, such an explanation can explain anything and therefore is not useful for scientific purposes.

Becker, then, directed our attention to those factors which affect the costs and benefits of criminal action. The most important of these factors is the opportunity cost of time. If one is a criminal, one has less time to spend on legitimate activities; also, if convicted of crime and sentenced to jail, one is not able to pursue legitimate activities for the period of the sentence. There are several empirically observable

Reprinted with permission from *Business* Magazine (formerly *Atlanta Economic Review*), July–August 1978. Copyright © 1978 by the College of Business Administration, Georgia State University, Atlanta.

variables which can be used to measure cost of time. These are average wage rates; education, under the assumption that opportunity costs are higher for educated persons; unemployment, under the assumption that the unemployed have relatively low opportunity costs of time; race, because, perhaps as a result of discrimination, blacks tend to have relatively poor job opportunities and thus low opportunity costs; and age, because young persons also tend to have relatively low opportunity costs.

Another important variable is the benefit from engaging in criminal activity. For crimes against property (robbery, theft, burglary) the relevant variables would be economic—they would relate to the possible value of goods to be stolen. Empirically, it is more difficult to measure these variables. Measures of income inequality are often used, on the assumption that it is the existence of some poor persons (with low opportunity costs of time) and some rich persons (with something worth stealing) that leads to relatively high returns to criminal behavior. For crimes against persons (murder, rape, assault), we have no theory as to the value of such offenses, and hence no theory as to what would affect the returns from such crimes.

The major cost of crime, in addition to opportunity costs, is the cost of punishment. This is an expected cost, in the sense that there is no assurance that any given criminal will be caught and convicted. The expected cost of punishment is thus $E = pf$, where p is the probability of punishment and f is the cost of punishment if it is given. The theory is unambiguous in predicting that an increase in E will lead to a reduction in crime, that is, the economic theory of crime unambiguously predicts that punishment will deter crime. This is a necessary and obvious implication of the law of demand—as the price of something increases, people demand less of it, whether the good be apples or crimes. This argument applies to crimes against persons as well as crimes against property. We do not know why some individuals demand "assault upon their neighbor" any more than we know why some individuals demand "fresh peaches"; but we do know that if we increase the price of each good, people will demand less of it. It is relatively easy to obtain data on average time served by convicted felons and on percentage of crimes cleared. However, because many crimes are not reported, our measure of p is somewhat weak. There has been much debate in the literature as to whether p or f is more important in deterring crime; that is, we could, for example, catch one burglar out of

100 and sentence him to 20 years or catch one burglar out of 10 and sentence him to 2 years without changing E, and there is a debate about which policy is more efficient. Given the current data, it is difficult to answer this question, though many studies seem to indicate that, at current levels, a 1% increase in the probability of conviction is more likely to deter crime than a 1% increase in the sentence. Becker has shown that, if this is so, we must be operating in a situation in which crime does not pay (the expected value of crime is negative) so that only risk seekers will be criminals. We will not pursue this point further.

We thus have a theory of crime which indicates that crime rates will be negatively associated with opportunity costs and with probability and severity of punishment and will be positively associated with gains from criminal behavior. I have also indicated what sorts of empirical variables are avialable to measure the theoretical variables. There have been several empirical studies of this theory; we will now examine these studies.

Tests of Economic Theory

There have been many empirical tests of the economic model of criminal behavior. A summary of this evidence is provided by Gordon Tullock.[2] Perhaps the best and most careful work has been done by Isaac Ehrlich.[3] These studies are statistical in nature. A common method is to use state data and to use crime rates as the dependent variable and the variables discussed earlier as independent variables. The statistical technique used is some form of multiple regression.

The results of all of the studies that have been performed are consistent, and all agree with the theory. That is, in all cases, increased costs of crime in terms of higher sentences or higher probabilities of conviction are associated with reduced crime rates. In addition, lower opportunity costs of crime are associated with higher crime rates. Thus we may be fairly certain that there is some deterrent effect of punishment and that the economic model is a useful model for explaining the behavior of criminals. It also was found that such deterrence affects crimes against persons as well as crimes against property. Thus increasing the cost of crimes such as assault or rape will serve to reduce the incidence of such crimes. As mentioned previously, we do not know why such crimes occur, but the law of demand would imply that an increase in their costs would reduce the number of these crimes.

There are some aspects of criminal behavior that the model does not fully explain. In particular, even after adjusting for all economic variables, the number of blacks in a state and the number of teenagers are generally associated with higher levels of crime. One possible explanation for this finding is that measures such as average income do not fully reflect incomes of these groups; another possibility is that crime enforcement in black areas is relatively poorer than in other areas. Nonetheless, currently we do not have a satisfactory explanation of these behaviors in terms of the economic model.

It is sometimes argued that the economic model of behavior assumes rationality and the ability to perform sophisticated calculations and that criminals are irrational and unable to calculate, so this model would be worthless. Two answers to this criticism are possible. First, the model does not assume perfect knowledge or complete and correct calculations; rather, the results follow if potential criminals have some idea, for example, that judges are getting tougher. Thus the assumption is that people respond to directions of change in the relevant variables, not that they have complete knowledge of the magnitudes of these variables. The second answer is more powerful. If criminals behave as postulated in the model, then certain results will be observed. We test the model by observing whether the predictions are correct. If the predictions are borne out, as they are, then we may continue to use the model. Given our current state of knowledge, it probably is fair to say that the economic model of criminal behavior is the most useful in explaining and predicting criminal behavior; therefore, good canons of scientific inference indicate that we should continue to use this model.

The Case of Capital Punishment

Much of the sociological argument about the lack of a deterrent effect of punishment has come from studies of capital punishment. It has been argued that capital punishment did not deter murder (or other crimes) and that therefore punishment in general did not deter crime. We have seen here that a substantial amount of evidence has been accumulated that shows that, in fact, punishment does deter crime; but we have not discussed specifically the case of capital punishment.

In recent years, Isaac Ehrlich examined the issue of capital punishment.[4] If execution is a worse punishment than, for example, life imprisonment, capital punishment should deter crime. In a rather sophisticated study Ehrlich calculated on the basis of rational behavior that the relevant probability is the probability of execution given that one has been convicted of crime. In this study he then found that over time capital punishment was significantly and importantly related to deterrence for committing murder. The number of executions over time was negatively associated with the number of murders that occurred. This study was a time series study, which is to say Ehrlich looked at data over time in obtaining the result. In a recently published paper in the *Journal of Political Economy*, Ehrlich examined detailed cross-section data and came to essentially the same conclusion. In states where more persons were executed for committing murder, significantly less murders were committed. Thus it is fair to say that we now are reasonably confident that capital punishment in fact serves to deter the crime of murder.

How can we then explain the earlier results in which it was claimed that capital punishment had no deterrent effect? There are two answers to this question. First, many of these studies were anecdotal in nature. That is, they were based on stories such as "during hangings for pickpocketing, pickpockets were common in the crowd." But this kind of evidence cannot prove anything. The relevant question is how much pickpocketing there would have been had there not been execution for this crime. We need some sort of statistical study to determine the true form of the relationship. Many of the earlier sociological studies were statistical, but the statistics were not very sophisticated. Methods such as comparing homicide rates in two neighboring states, one with capital punishment and one without, were used. This kind of approach controls for some of the relevant variables, but not many. Age, economic opportunities, and other characteristics of people between even similar areas may differ. The kind of study done by Ehrlich, using multiple regression techniques, is able to compensate for most differences that are thought to be significant. The results of Ehrlich's studies are very strong in indicating a deterrent effect for capital punishment.

It is in the case of capital punishment that the noneconomist is most skeptical about the results of the economic model. It is commonly felt that murderers are totally irrational and cannot be deterred from their evil intent. However, many murders are committed during the commission of other crimes such as armed robbery, and armed robbers are not likely to be particularly emotional during the commission of the crime. In addition, it is not clear to me that a man who kills his wife during a domestic argument (a common form of murder) is totally indifferent to the likely penalty. If he knows that the maximum he will receive is seven years in prison, he may well behave differently than if he knows that he may be executed. But here again, the best answer is the evidence, and the evidence does seem to indicate that in fact capital punishment does deter murder.

Organized Crime

There have been some studies by economists applying economic tools to organized crime.[5] The basic tools used have been those derived from industrial organization, the branch of economics dealing with firms and their behavior in markets. Unfortunately, the data available for the testing of hypotheses about organized crime are almost nil, so that most of the work has been purely theoretical and speculative. Thus the results in this section must be considered more tentative than those in the earlier sections.

One way of viewing organized crime is as a network of firms providing goods and services. It is in fact important to note that most of those criminal activities that are considered organized—heroin, gambling, loansharking, perhaps prostitution—do in fact involve the sale of goods and services that individuals want to buy, and this activity is lacking in the coercive effect of normal crime. Organized criminal firms deal with each other and with the ultimate consumer who buys the goods and services.

Many criminal firms have some monopoly power in the provision of some good or service. It is likely that this monopoly is in dealing with other criminal firms, rather than in dealing with ultimate consumers. A useful framework in which to view organized crime is as a firm with monopoly power supplying some needed good to other criminal firms. That good which is probably most important is capital. Capital is needed by many criminal organizations. The nature of the heroin market is such that many shipments tend to be large and must be paid for in advance. This requires capital. Gambling also requires capital. Loansharking is by nature a capital-using enterprise. If the sources of this capital to criminal firms are limited, then those who are willing to supply the capital can charge interest rates sufficiently high so that the borrowers will earn only a normal return on their time and effort. (Of course this return will be adjusted for the risks involved.) Thus a criminal firm can lend money to a heroin importer and not itself deal with the heroin at all; the price charged for the loan will be high enough for the lender to make most of the profit in heroin importing. There may be some monopoly in the provision of other goods to the criminal firm: for example, "connections" in the form of access to and information about bribed officials. We might expect monopolistic criminal firms to behave in this way because it is less expensive to monopolize a stage of production that exhibits some economies of scale and because monopolization of one stage of production can extract most of the available profits in the industry.

Viewing criminal activity as being organized in firms also can help us understand the geographic scope of organized crime. Some people seem to believe that there is one huge criminal firm controlling all organized criminal activities in the country (or even in the world). This is unlikely to be so: we would not expect a wider scope for criminal activities than for comparable noncriminal activities. In fact, there is reason to expect that criminal firms would be more localized than noncriminal firms. One advantage to national scope for a noncriminal firm is the information conveyed in the trademark of the company; this advantage is not available to criminal firms. Thus, though certain aspects of crime may involve dealings among firms in different locations, it is in fact unlikely that "there is a Nation-wide crime syndicate known as the Mafia, whose tentacles are found in many large cities."[6]

One should also be skeptical of analyses that attribute all manner of activities to organized crime. It is sometimes alleged that the pornography market in Atlanta and other cities is under the control of the Mafia (or, currently, the Cosa Nostra). It is difficult to see why organized crime would find this a desirable investment outlet. In fact, if criminals want to invest in legitimate enterprises, they would probably find it desirable to choose less conspicuous activities.

Viewing organized crime as a monopoly has one other implication of some interest, first pointed out by James Buchanan. Monopoly restricts output and raises price, thus obtaining for itself some profits. If certain activities, such as gambling, are illegal because society has decided they are wrong, and if this activity is provided by a monopoly, then in fact we will have less gambling than if the activity were provided by purely competitive criminal firms. That is, less *organized* crime and less crime may not be the same thing. If we want less crime, one way of achieving this goal might simply be to allow the activity to become monopolized, allow the firm to decide how much to provide. In this view, activities of the police in enforcing monopolies for organized crime may in fact be socially productive; it may be worthwhile to have the police maintain a criminal monopoly because this will serve to reduce crime.

Policy   Implications

Deterrence. The strongest result coming from the economic theory is that punishment in the form of increased probability of arrest and length of sentence serves to deter crime. Thus the first policy question we must ask is how much deterrence there should be. In one sense this is a question that society must answer when it decides how much it wants to spend on resources devoted to crime prevention. Presumably, we could have as little crime as we wanted if we were willing to spend enough on police, courts, jails, and so on to make probabilities of arrest very, very high for most crimes. The example of the assassination of Martin Luther King or of President Kennedy indicates that if we are willing to spend enough money we can solve almost any crime that is committed. But of course in most cases it is not worth spending this much money. Presumably for society we should spend money on crime prevention to the point where a dollar spent on crime prevention buys as much satisfaction, or utility, as a dollar spent in any other direction. Thus the marginal analysis of efficiency applies to crime reduction as well as to any other goods.

Second, it appears that we can buy more crime prevention by simply increasing lengths of sentences and becoming much harsher in our punishment of criminals. But this is not so. As Stigler has pointed out, "Marginal costs are necessary to marginal deterrence."[7] If we want criminals to behave in certain ways we must structure their rewards and punishments in order to elicit this behavior. If the punishment for robbery becomes the same as the punishment for murder, then we may reduce the number of robberies but we will greatly increase the number of robberies in which the robber murders his victim. If the punishment for the theft of $50 is the same as the punishment for the theft of

$5,000, fewer gas stations but more banks will be robbed. Increasing punishments for crime may have very undesirable effects on the types of crime that people actually do commit. The so-called Lindbergh Law, which has made kidnapping a capital offense, may have served to reduce the number of kidnappings but also served to increase the number of times the kidnappers found it worthwhile to kill their victims.

Another question that we may ask is that of the "rights" of the accused. It is widely argued that various Supreme Court rulings during the 1950s and 1960s increased the rights of criminals and had the effect of increasing the amount of crime. To a certain extent this of course is true—if criminals must be given lawyers, then some criminals who would otherwise have been convicted will be able to escape punishment. On the other hand, some defendants who are falsely accused will also be able to escape punishment. The inescapable problem is basically one in statistical decision making. Anything that makes it more likely that a criminal will be convicted also makes it more likely that an innocent person will go to jail. Anything that makes acquittal of an innocent person more likely also makes acquittal of a criminal more likely. We must somehow reach a decision as to where we want the balance to be placed. (In reaching this decision it is important to note that convicting innocent persons of crime will have no deterrent effect. If we convict innocent persons we are letting criminals go, and this reduces the cost of committing a crime.) Although the Supreme Court may have increased the rights of those accused of crime, it is not clear that the Court has gone too far in this direction. We must balance the various costs and benefits at the margin, and there is no presumption that the policy procedure used before the court decisions was optimal. These are empirical questions, but they are very difficult to answer because of different values that individuals place on limiting police power or acquitting actual criminals.

For most crimes punishment is in the form of a jail term. However, this is rather inefficient. The criminal is unable to be productive while he is in jail, and he bears some cost while no one gains as a result. Thus it is more efficient to use monetary fines as a form of punishment than to use incarceration. The problem with using monetary fines is that most criminals do not have very much money. But whenever it is possible to use a fine, Becker's analysis clearly demonstrates that fines are more efficient than jail sentences because there is no social dead-weight loss from the use of a fine. In many so-called white-collar crimes fines are the standard method of punishment. Some people view this as a bias in our social system toward the wealthy, but it can be easily explained on the grounds that wealthy white-collar defendants are more likely to have the money to pay fines and the paying of a fine is more efficient. For any given jail sentence there would be some fine that would create an equivalent amount of disutility to the defendant but would not have the associated efficiency cost.

It is also worth considering capital punishment. Earlier we argued that evidence indicates that capital punishment does in fact deter murder. However, this in itself is not a sufficient argument for capital punishment. Many people believe strongly that the state should not execute people, and the argument that capital punishment deters murder cannot be used to destroy this moral belief. In deciding whether or not to have capital punishment it is nonetheless important that we do consider the evidence. We must know what kinds of decisions we are making. Ehrlich's first article was cited by the Supreme Court in its decision reinstituting the death penalty for murder. It is also important to note that evidence gathered in Ehrlich's study indicates that each execution in fact deters more than one murder. In one paper he indicated that between 7 and 17 murders were deterred by each execution, though this range is subject to some doubt. Again, this does not mean that we should adopt capital punishment, but it is an important consideration in making this decision.

The Courts. Most criminal cases do not go to trial. That is, most criminal cases are settled by some form of "plea bargaining." This is a situation is which, for example, the criminal accused of assault with a penalty of perhaps 10 years will plead guilty to a lesser crime such as disorderly conduct with a smaller penalty. Many persons view the existence of plea bargaining and the fact that most cases are settled through plea bargaining as an imperfection in our legal system.

Actually, if we assume rational behavior on the part of criminals and prosecutors, we would expect most cases to be settled by plea bargaining.[8] A court trial uses resources. The criminal must hire a lawyer and spend money in other ways on his defense. The prosecutor also must spend time and money to appear in court and argue his case. If the two parties can settle the case without going to court, there is some positive amount of money or resources they can split between themselves; going to court is essentially like participating in an unfair gamble. For this reason, if behavior is rational, we would expect most cases to be settled out of court and again this is what we observe. In fact, most civil cases also are settled out of court.

What determines the settlement? The main determinants are the estimates by the prosecutor and the defendant of the expected sentence if the case goes to court. If both parties are sure that the prosecutor could get a 10-year sentence, then perhaps the plea bargaining will involve an 8- or 9-year sentence. On the other hand, if both parties feel it likely that the defendant will be acquitted in the case of trial, then the plea bargaining will involve a rather low penalty and the defendant will get a rather low sentence as a result of the plea bargaining. Those cases in which the courts will be used generally will be cases in which there is disagreement on the part of the two parties as to what the sentence will be. Thus, if the prosecutor thinks the sentence will be 10 years and the defendant thinks the sentence would be 2 years, it may well be that there is no ground for bargaining and the two parties will end up going to trial and not settling. On the other hand, if they both agree as to probabilities of conviction or expected sentences, then a settlement becomes much more likely.

Other factors can also affect the likelihood of a plea bargain. As the sentence expected by both parties becomes smaller, the likelihood of a plea bargain becomes greater. As the cost of a trial becomes greater, the likelihood of a plea bargain becomes greater. Also, defendants who are spending time in jail while awaiting a trial are more likely to settle than are defendants who are released on bail awaiting trial. It is also true that the analysis of the decisions as to whether to settle or go to court is independent of the guilt of the defendant. An innocent defendant who is likely to be convicted would be rational to plead guilty to a lesser crime, and of course the guilty defendant who is likely to be acquitted would be unlikely to plead guilty.

Prisons. We may identify four possible functions of prisons: punishment of the guilty, isolation of the guilty so that while imprisoned they cannot commit additional crimes, rehabilitation, and deterrence.[9] Punishment is a moral issue; as an economist I have no particular expertise in discussing the morality of vengeance, and I will say no more about it. To the extent that many crimes are committed by professional criminals, each of whom commits many crimes, then incarceration of these individuals will in fact reduce crime. This issue also is relevant for a discussion of the bail system; one actual function of denial of bail (pretrial incarceration) is to keep suspects from committing crimes while awaiting trial. The last two purposes of prison—rehabilitation and deterrence—are of more interest.

The prevailing ideology in American criminal jurisprudence for many years has been that the purpose of prison should be to rehabilitate criminals. This is perhaps consistent with the view, mentioned earlier, that criminals are somehow different from others. If this is so, then a possible method of crime control is to remove this difference, perhaps by counseling or by psychiatric treatment of convicted criminals. In addition, training in marketable skills will increase legitimate opportunities for criminals and thus reduce the relative value of criminal activity. Unfortunately, rehabilitation does not seem to work. Most of the studies of rehabilitation indicate that it has virtually no effect on criminal behavior or on recidivism (the commission of crime by a released criminal). This failure has led to unfortunate results. Because it has been felt that the purpose of prison was to rehabilitate criminals and because prison does not do this, many judges seem to have felt that there was little purpose in sentencing criminals to jail terms. This behavior ignores the deterrence function of prison.

There are two logically distinct aspects of deterrence, but these separate categories have been confused by many analysts, with unfortunate consequences. Incarceration of a convicted felon may serve to deter him from commission of crimes in the future after he is released, or this incarceration may serve to deter others from becoming criminals. The first type of deterrence does not seem to occur; the second does. Judges and criminologists, however, observing the failure of the first type of deterrence as shown by high recidivism rates, have fallen into the error of assuming that deterrence does not work at all.

Some thought would convince us that we would not expect a convicted felon to be deterred from committing future crimes. If the economic model of crime is correct, a felon is an individual who has decided that he can maximize his utility by being a criminal. Presumably, he included in his calculations the probability that he would serve a jail sentence. He has now served a sentence. What has happened? First, he now has a "record" so that future noncriminal opportunities are less than they were before. Second, presumably he has learned some additional criminal skills from fellow inmates. Thus, if he decided before being convicted that crime was a rational choice, he is likely to make the same decision again—the costs of crime, in terms of forgone legitimate activities, are lower because of his criminal record, and the benefits are greater because of the criminal skills which were acquired while in prison. Thus, if the economic model is correct, for both reasons we would expect recidivism by rational criminals.

What of those who have not yet been convicted of crime? Here is where we would expect to find a significant effect of deterrence. In initially deciding whether to engage in criminal activity, the expected sentence is relevant; increasing this sentence then would serve to reduce the benefit of criminal activity. Thus it is primarily for those who are on the margin of becoming criminals that severity of punishment would serve as a deterrent.

The rehabilitation model is responsible for some other unfortunate aspects of criminal sentencing. In many cases, sentences vary widely for the same crime, depending on the characteristics of the criminal. In addition, many sentences are indeterminate—the felon is sentenced to jail until someone (probably the parole board) decides that he is rehabilitated. If we realized that in fact there is not much chance for rehabilitation, then this type of sentence would not occur; rather, each crime would have a relatively fixed sentence, and all those committing the same crime would serve about the same time. We might not even want to increase the average length of time served for given crimes; the argument here is for reducing the variance, rather than the average. As previously discussed, increasing the length of sentences is not necessarily a desirable policy.

The Case of Atlanta

What can be said about the special case of crime in Atlanta? Data for 1970 indicate first, that Atlanta had higher crime rates than the average for crimes against persons:[10] the national average was 360 crimes per 100,000 persons; for Atlanta, the figure was 392. Also, annually there were 3,176 crimes against property in Atlanta per 100,000 persons; nationally the average was 2,380. Economic factors do not seem to explain this discrepancy. Family income in Atlanta averaged $12,160 compared to an urban average of $11,599. The education level on average was the same in Atlanta as the national average. Also, unemployment of males was somewhat lower in Atlanta than nationally: 2.4% vs. 4%. Probability of conviction for crimes seems higher in Atlanta than elsewhere: 4% in Atlanta vs. 2%

nationally. (This figure, however, may be subject to some doubt. It refers to sentences of one year or more and thus may be biased if, for example, average sentences in Atlanta are higher than elsewhere.) For those who were sentenced to one year or more in Atlanta, the average sentence was 7.77 years served; comparable figures are not available nationally. On the other hand, the average age in Atlanta was lower than the national average (26.3 years in Atlanta, 28.1 for all urban areas), and there were more blacks in Atlanta (23% in Atlanta, 15% for all SMSAs). Finally, there were 1.24 police per 1,000 population in Atlanta and 2.3 police per 1,000 nationally. (One explanation of the positive association between race and crime is that the police may spend relatively less time in black areas; Atlanta's relatively low police force is consistent with this argument.) Thus we can explain, at least in part, Atlanta's higher than average crime rate in terms of the factors which the economic theory identifies as causative.

Footnotes

[1] Gary S. Becker, "Crime and Punishment: An Economic Approach," *Journal of Political Economy*, March 1968, pp. 169-217; Gordon Tullock, "An Economic Approach to Crime," *Social Science Quarterly*, June 1969, pp. 59-71; Gary S. Becker and William M. Landes, eds., *Essays in the Economics of Crime and Punishment* (New York, National Bureau of Economic Research, 1974); Lee R. McPheters and William B. Stronge, eds., *The Economics of Crime and Law Enforcement* (Springfield, Illinois, Charles C. Thomas, 1976); and Simon Rottenberg, ed., *The Economics of Crime and Punishment* (Washington, D.C., American Enterprise Institute, 1973).

[2] Gordon Tullock, "Does Punishment Deter Crime?" *The Public Interest*, Summer 1974, pp. 103-111.

[3] Isaac Ehrlich, "Participation in Illegitimate Activities: A Theoretical and Empirical Investigation," *Journal of Political Economy*, May 1973, pp. 521-565.

[4] Issac Ehrlich, "The Deterrent Effect of Capital Punishment: A Question of Life and Death," *American Economic Review*, June 1975,

pp. 397-417; and Isaac Ehrlich, "Capital Punishment and Deterrence: Some Further Thoughts and Evidence," *Journal of Political Economy*, August 1977, pp. 741-788. See also Peter Passell and John B. Taylor, "The Deterrent Effect of Capital Punishment: Another View," and the reply by Ehrlich, both in *American Economic Review*, June 1977, pp. 445-451 and 452-459.

[5] Thomas C. Schelling, "Economic Analysis of Organized Crime," in The President's Commission on Law Enforcement and the Administration of Justice, *Task Force Report: Organized Crime* (Washington, D.C., U.S. Government Printing Office, 1967), appendix D; James M. Buchanan, "A Defense of Organized Crime?" pp. 119-132, and Paul H. Rubin, "The Economic Theory of the Criminal Firm," pp. 155-166, both in Rottenberg, *The Economics of Crime and Punishment*.

[6] From Senate committee hearings, quoted in Gus Tyler, ed., *Organized Crime in America* (Ann Arbor, Michigan, University of Michigan Press, 1962).

[7] George J. Stigler, "The Optimum Enforcement of Laws," *Journal of Political Economy*, May 1970, pp. 526-536.

[8] William M. Landes, "An Economic Analysis of the Courts," *Journal of Law and Economics*, April 1971, pp. 61-107.

[9] The discussion is largely from James Q. Wilson, *Thinking About Crime* (New York, Basic Books, 1975).

[10] Data from *1970 Census of the Population, Characteristics of the Population, Georgia* (Washington, D.C., Bureau of the Census, 1973); and Federal Bureau of Investigation, *Uniform Crime Reports—1970* (Washington, D.C., U.S. Government Printing Office, 1971).

LOCATION AND OTHER CORRELATES OF CAMPUS CRIME

James Alan Fox
Daryl A. Hellman

Very little scholarly research has attempted to examine the determinants and correlates of crime on college and university campuses. That in 1980 the United States' 3,231 institutions of higher education had an enrollment of over twelve million students suggests that crime on campuses hardly presents an insignificant problem. Nevertheless, McPheters' (1978) analysis of 38 colleges remains the only effort to exploit empirically the campus crime and police data that have been made available in recent years in the FBI's *Uniform Crime Reports*. As McPheters points out, previous studies have approached the problem of campus crime from an administrative, or operational, perspective (see Iannarelli, 1968; Gelber, 1972). However, an understanding of the factors that influence campus crime rates, whether they be characteristics of the student body, structural features of the campus, administrative aspects of the university, or the location of the campus, should permit better control of campus crime. In addition, university campuses represent a rather unique arena in which to satisfy, more generally, the interest among social scientists in the correlates of crime. The relative homogeneity of the age distribution of the campus population, the required mobility of university students, and the well-defined nature of the university community are all characteristics unique to a campus setting. The campus is also an environment that can be subjected to alteration and control, thus affording an opportunity for social experimentation with respect to crime control.

Beyond adding to our understanding of the causes of crime in general and of campus crime in particular, an examination of campus crime rates can contribute to an understanding of the relationship between colleges and their surrounding areas. The extent to which a campus attracts or repels criminal activity relative to the town or city in which it is located has obvious implications for community relations and for the relative fiscal burdens on university and local police. Criminal spatial mobility across political jurisdictions and the consequent impacts on community welfare have been examined, both

Reprinted with permission from *Journal of Criminal Justice*, vol. 13; James Alan Fox and Daryl A. Hellman, "Location and Other Correlates of Campus Crime." Copyright © 1985, Pergamon Press Ltd.

theoretically and empirically (see Mehay, 1977; Hakim *et al.*, 1979; Fabricant, 1980; Hakim and Rengert, 1981). However, the so-called "crime spillover" issue has not been studied within the context of a college campus and its surrounding community, even though this situation offers some potential for a solution, to the extent that "in lieu of" payments are negotiated with the community.

The purpose of this article is twofold: (1) to examine the relative "safeness" of campuses vis-à-vis their communities and to determine whether this varies by location within and outside metropolitan areas; and (2) to investigate the correlates of campus crime with particular attention to the dimensions of the campus profile that encourage or discourage criminal activity. For these purposes a data set was employed combining crime, clearance, and police counts for 222 colleges and universities and their surrounding communities. Profiles were constructed of the geographic, socioeconomic, scholastic, and environmental features of the campuses.[1]

We begin with an overview of the campuses and present some descriptive statistics on campus characteristics and campus crime. We then examine the relative safeness of college campuses and the pattern of campus crime by location. Campus crime rates are compared with those of the city or town in which the campus is located, and geographic differences, both in relative safeness and in campus crime rates are tested. Finally, the correlates of campus crime are investigated, focusing on the identifiable dimensions of campus attributes and their association with the crime measure.

Crime on the Campus

The 222 colleges and universities represented in this sample had a mean enrollment of 13,000 students.[2] About 90 percent of the schools had some sort of graduate program: on the average, graduate students represented 17 percent of the student body. Ninety-two percent of the schools in the sample were public institutions, 5 percent were private and less than 4 percent were sectarian.

There was greater variety in the sample with respect to location: 78, or 35 percent, of the schools were located outside of an SMSA; 65, or 29 percent, were located in a suburban area or a minor city in an SMSA; and 79, or 36 percent, were located within a major city in an SMSA. In addition, schools were identified by whether or not the campus was located within one of the thirteen Standard Consolidated Statistical Areas (SCSAs); 183 (82 percent) were located outside of an SCSA, while 39 (18 percent) were within one.[3]

Rates of crime (per 1,000) were calculated by taking the ratio of offenses to full-time equivalent (FTE) student enrollment plus faculty and scaling by 1,000. The distributions of each crime type as well as offense aggregates are displayed in Table 1. Although violent offenses were rare on most campuses (indicated by both the low mean values and the extreme skewness), property offenses and the aggregate total yielded more symmetric distributions that permit analyses less vulnerable to outliers.

Table 1. Descriptive Statistics for Campus Crime Rates for 1979

Offense	Mean	Minimum	Maximum	Standard Deviation	Skewness
Criminal homicide	0.002	0.000	0.182	0.015	10.365
Forcible Rape	0.098	0.000	1.279	0.153	3.233
Robbery	0.117	0.000	2.111	0.225	4.613
Aggravated assault	0.567	0.000	7.002	0.809	3.667
Burglary	4.511	0.000	46.051	4.841	3.758
Larceny-theft	26.497	0.000	76.735	12.863	0.931
Motor vehicle theft	0.686	0.000	12.568	1.059	7.025
Violent crime	0.783	0.000	9.062	0.957	3.975
Property crime	31.694	0.494	92.026	14.985	0.960
Total Crime	32.350	0.494	92.304	15.324	0.959

NOTES: N=222. Rates per 1,000 students and faculty.

Relative Safeness of the Campus

Our analysis of crime on the university campus begins with an examination of the relative safeness of the campus compared to the community in which it is located. One hypothesis tested is that relative safeness varies with location, i.e., that in rural areas the campus represents a relatively attractive crime target compared to the surrounding community, while in large, urban areas the campus represents a relatively well-guarded fortress. If this hypothesis is correct, we would expect to see higher ratios of campus crime to community crime in rural areas than in urban areas. In fact, campus crime rates might exceed community crime rates in rural locations, while campus rates would be less than community rates in urban areas.

Crime rates were calculated for 175 of the cities and towns in which the campuses were located and for which crime data were available. The aggregate-location crime rate does not necessarily measure the crime rate in the appropriate comparison area. It is more accurate the more uniform the crime rate within neighborhoods in the locations, the smaller the location, and the larger the area of influence surrounding the community.

The mean total index crime rate per 1,000 residents in a location was 68.134; the lowest rate was 9.475, while the highest was 142.379. A comparison of campus with location crime rates indicates that, overall, the ratio of campus index crimes per 1,000 to location crimes was less than one (0.58). On the safest campus relative to its location, the crime rate was only 1 percent of the location rate. At the other extreme, the most "dangerous" school had a crime rate almost three times that of its community. In the total sample, 20 campuses had crime rates that exceeded the crime rate in the city or town in which they were located.[4]

An analysis of variance framework was used to investigate the pattern of relative safeness by location and to test for locational influence. The ratio in 1979 of the rate of total index crime on the campus to that in the location was examined for the 176 campuses for which both campus and location crime data were available.

Table 2 contains data on the pattern of the crime ratio by location, by both SMSA and SCSA. Each cell contains the number of campuses in each category, the mean ratio of campus to location crime for the category, and the standard deviation. As expected, the ratio of campus to community crime was highest in non-SMSA locations. The mean ratio for non-SMSA (and non-SCSA) locations was 0.80. This ratio decreased to 0.59 for SMSA suburban or minor city locations. Within this group there was virtually no difference between SCSA and non-SCSA locations. The crime ratio decreased to 0.43 for campuses in SMSA major city locations. Within this category, the mean ratio was only 0.31 for campuses in major cities in SMSAs that are part of an SCSA.

Table 2. Ratio of Campus Crime Rate to Community Crime Rate
by Location

		SMSA			
		Outside SMSA	SMSA Suburb or Minor City	SMSA Major City	
Outside	(n)	54	26	64	144
SCSA	(x)	0.80	0.60	0.45	0.61
	(SD)	0.51	0.38	0.24	0.41
SCSA					
Inside			19	13	32
SCSA		--	0.57	0.31	0.47
			0.43	0.12	0.36
		54	45	77	176
		0.80	0.59	0.43	0.58
		0.51	0.40	0.23	0.41

Source	df	SS[a]	MS	F
Between	4	4.6316	1.1579	8.150*
SMSA	2	3.5633	1.7817	12.538*
SCSA	1	0.0068	0.0068	0.045
SMSA x SCSA	1	0.0746	0.0746	0.525
Within	171	24.2944	0.1421	
Total	175	28.9260	0.1653	

[a]The decomposed variation does not sum to the between sum of
squares, because of imbalance in the layout.
*$p < .001$.

Thus the pattern of relative safeness by location is consistent with
expectations. Furthermore, an analysis of variance of crime ratio by
location type (bottom of Table 2) reveals that while the differences
between location type are significant, they are attributable primarily to
the SMSA classification.

The Pattern of Campus Crime by Location

While the ratio of campus crime to community crime displays a clear pattern by location, it is not possible to determine from the ratio whether this is due to a geographic pattern in campus crime rates, in community crime rates, or in some combination of the two. That is, an examination of the ratio does not resolve the question of the kind and extent of influence that location (e.g., urbanness) has on campus crime. A declining ratio of campus to location crime with increasing urbanness is consistent with various patterns of crime spillover, including no spillover at all. For this reason we dismantled the ratio and performed the same analysis, separately, on the campus crime rate and on the location crime rate.

Table 3 presents the pattern of campus crime rate by SMSA and SCSA classifications, along with an analysis of variance of the effect of location type. Interestingly enough, the location of a college appears to have no association with the campus crime rate.

This surprising result—that urban, suburban, and rural campuses have similar rates of crime, on the average—suggests either that there is no influence of the community on campus crime or that the influence of the community is uniform per capita across locational types. A uniform influence on measured crime, however, may be the result of differential impacts by location that are cancelled by variation in the employment of police. This possibility will be investigated when crime correlates are examined.[5]

Thus the locational pattern observed in the ratio of campus to community crime is due simply to a locational pattern in community crime rates. Campus crime rates are either immune from, or similarly affected by, in a quantitative sense, their environment, regardless of whether campuses are located in rural areas or in major cities. Unequal levels of police protection, however, may explain the latter.

To confirm the suggestion above, we performed an analysis (not shown) of community crime rates by location. The pattern revealed was, expectedly, an increasing rate of crime with increasing urbanness. On the average, crime rates were highest in major cities in SMSAs, particularly those in SCSAs. Tests of significance from an analysis of variance showed the SMSA classification to be significant at the 0.01 level and the SCSA effect to be significant at the 0.05 level.

Table 3. Campus Crime Rate by Location

		SMSA			
		Outside SMSA	SMSA Suburb or Minor City	SMSA Major City	
Outside	(n)	78	39	66	183
SCSA	(x)	31.27	33.43	34.03	32.73
	(SD)	13.17	16.42	16.33	15.05
SCSA					
Inside		26	13	39	
SCSA		—	33.04	25.69	30.59
			19.15	8.56	16.64
		78	65	79	222
		31.27	33.27	32.66	32.35
		13.17	17.42	15.60	15.32

Source	d f	SS[a]	MS	F
Between	4	911.9785	227.9946	0.970
SMSA	2	279.4061	148.7030	0.633
SCSA	1	2.3656	2.3656	0.101
SMSA x SCSA	1	404.7852	404.7852	1.723
Within		217	50,984.1956	234.9502
Total	221	51,896.1730	234.8243	

[a]The decomposed variation does not sum to the between sum of squares, because of imbalance in the layout.

The Pattern of Crime Mix by Location

The results above suggest that location has no differential influence on the rate of crime on the campus. It may be possible, however, that location affects the mix of campus crime. A recent article in *Newsweek* on campus crime describes the situation at the University of Southern California: "The USC campus is bordered by the low-income, high-crime area of south central Los Angeles, and violent crime on campus has increased 150 percent in the past four years" (Williams, 1982:82). Thus, while the influence of the community on campus crime may be uniform when measured by the total amount of index crime, the community may have a differential effect on individual crimes within the index, causing the mix of crime to vary with location. To the extent that violent crimes are less easily deterred by police, this hypothesis is consistent with the hypothesis that the uniform influence of location on crime is due to increased police protection on urban campuses.

Analysis of variance was used to test the effect of location on crime mix, which was defined as violent crime as a percentage of total crime. It should be noted, however, that the number of violent crimes on campuses is quite small (see Table 1). Thus the magnitude of the percentage is unstable, and the analysis of differences somewhat impeded.

Table 4 shows college crime mix by campus location. While the effect of SMSA classification is negligible, the SCSA classification is significant at better than the 0.01 level. Campuses located in SCSAs have significantly larger shares of violent crime, even though they do not have significantly higher crime rates.[6]

To complete the analysis of the influence of location on campus crime, we looked at the pattern of community crime mix by location. The results (not shown) of the analysis of variance of violent crime in the community as a percentage of total index crime indicated that both SMSA type and SCSA type are highly significant, alone. As a community becomes more urban, measured by either SMSA location or SCSA location, the mix of crime becomes more violent. On the average, violent crime is over 14 percent of total crime in SMSA major cities that are located in SCSAs and only about 5 percent in non-SMSA locations.

Correlates and Determinants of Campus Crime

The conclusion that the location of a college campus does not have a significant effect on the campus crime rate may be accounted for, in part, by the explanation that there are offsetting characteristics of urban schools and that urban schools protect themselves more, thereby reducing the impact of, or spillover from, the surrounding community. In this section, we examine the impact that other characteristics of the college or university, in addition to location, have on the campus crime rate.

Table 4. Campus Crime Mix by Location

		Outside SMSA	SMSA Suburb or Minor City	SMSA Major City	
Outside	(n)	78	39	66	183
SCSA	(x)	0.0205	0.0209	0.0230	0.0215
	(SD)	0.0220	0.0203	0.0220	0.0215
SCSA					
Inside		26	13	39	
SCSA	—	0.0429	0.0320	0.0393	
			0.0698	0.0200	0.0580
		· 78	65	79	222
		0.0205	0.0299	0.0245	0.0246
		0.0220	0.0476	0.0218	0.0317

Source	d f	SS[a]	MS	F
Between	4	0.0114	0.0029	2.937*
SMSA	2	0.0002	0.0001	0.119
SCSA	1	0.0075	0.0075	7.755**
SMSA x SCSA	1	0.0011	0.0011	1.111
Within	217	0.2110	0.0010	
Total	221	0.2224		

[a]The decomposed variation does not sum to the between sum of squares, because of imbalance in the layout.
*$p < .05$.
**$p < .01$.

Before looking at correlation coefficients, it is useful to consider, a priori, how various campus characteristics might be associated with crime. We combined thirty-three campus descriptors into eight groups:

police characteristics, financial characteristics, density measures, accessibility and visibility measures, community and cohesiveness measures, scholastic characteristics, student body demographic characteristics, and locational characteristics. Calendar type was included as a miscellaneous category. The variables selected for testing, and the grouping of the variables, reflect, and are consistent with, the economic theory of criminal choice.[7] At the same time, they permit the further testing of standard relationships cited in the geography-of-crime literature (i.e., the influence of size, density, and accessibility on crime) as well as an examination of the impact of social structure and processes on criminal behavior.

Our police input measures were restricted to police labor. These should have been supplemented with capital inputs, including security devices. To the extent that police inputs deter crime, we would expect increases in police per capita to reduce crime. However, the police also perform a detection function. In addition, the demand for police is likely to increase as crime increases. These well-known problems inhibit simple correlation analysis.[8] A police output measure, the clearance rate, was expected to be negatively correlated with campus crime.

Financial characteristics included faculty salaries, the cost of tuition and room-and-board, and the percentage of students receiving financial aid. To the extent that these are proxy measures for gains from crimes against property (which constitute 97.5 percent of campus crime), crime should increase with increases in the financial status of students (and faculty). On the other hand, if these measures are considered indicators of the income status of potential criminals, rather than potential victims, we would expect the opposite relationship. Measures of income discrepancy on campus (as well as relative to the community) would have been preferable but were unavailable. Up to a point, the student-aid variable may capture income discrepancy on campus.

Density characteristics included standard measures, such as students per acre and buildings per acre. Evidence from other settings suggests that crime increases with density, partly because density increases anonymity and, therefore, decreases the probability of punishment, and partly because increased density increases the availability of targets.[9] Our density characteristics also included measures that corrected for the density of crime targets, or gains from crime, per full-time equivalent student. These included the percentage of students who are full-time and the percentage of students who live on campus. The latter group, in addition to being on campus more and having a certain amount of requisite property, are also more likely to report a crime to campus, rather than to local, police (see also McPheters, 1978).

Accessibility and visibility measures included the number of buildings and the number of acres. The absolute size of the college (i.e., area) may contribute to the crime rate by providing visibility, as well as by providing space in which crime can occur. The age of campus structures was also included in this set of variables. The year in which the college was founded was used as a proxy for the age of buildings on the campus. Older buildings may be more difficult to secure and, thus, more accessible.

Various measures of cohesiveness or sense of community included: the student-faculty ratio, the percentage of freshmen who drop out, the percentage of students who graduate, the percentage of students in a fraternity or sorority, the percentage of students who are "in-state" and the type of institution (public or private/sectarian). These variables were included to test the influence of social organization. A strong community may inspire greater allegiance to the "social contract"; it may also better define "defensible space." On the other hand, the cohesion measure may be interpreted as a measure of the pressure toward social conformity, which can alienate some members of the community, resulting in various forms of deviant behavior, including crime.

A number of other descriptors included in the analysis are associated with scholastic quality, such as the percentage of graduate students, the competitiveness of the school (a numerical scale from Barron's guide), and the percentage of the faculty with the Ph.D. or other terminal degree. Apart from their associations with economic status, these descriptors also measure the social pressure to succeed. Student demographic characteristics included the percentage of male students, the percentage of foreign students, the percentage of students over 21 years of age, and the percentage of minority students.

Finally, a group of locational characteristics were defined, including an urbanness measure (see note 5) distance from the closest central city, the unemployment rate in the SMSA corrected for distance, and the population of the community in which the campus is situated. If the results obtained in this study are consistent with previous results, none of the locational characteristics should significantly correlate with the campus crime rate.

While one campus characteristic may be associated with more than one group, identification of the various descriptive dimensions does permit some sorting of the information. The groups, and the descriptors categorized within each group, are listed in Table 5. The appendix contains a definition of each of the variables. Table 5 contains the mean value of each characteristic in the sample and the simple correlation of each with the total campus crime rate in 1979. Next to each correlation coefficient is its level of significance, followed by the number of observations on which the correlation was based. Because of missing data in the sample, the number of observations varies from 176 to 222, depending on the descriptor.

Some general comments can be made about the correlations. First, these are simple correlations. The significant positive correlation between crime and police is as expected, as is the negative correlation between the clearance ratio and crime.[10] The financial characteristic that is significantly correlated with crime, i.e., cost, has a large, positive correlation coefficient, suggesting that it measures gains from crime. The positive, although less significant, sign of the financial-aid variable is consistent with the alternative interpretation of the financial variables. Perhaps, as we suggested above, financial aid measures income discrepancy.

The density measures, with the exception of students per acre, have significant positive correlations, as expected. The percentage of full-time students and the percentage of students on campus have particularly large and significant coefficients, The accessibility/visibility measures have the expected signs (in Table 5, higher values of EST mean younger campuses), although the number of acres is not significant.

With the exception of the in-state variable (percentage of students who are instate), greater values for the community cohesiveness measures are associated with higher campus crime rates. (In the sample, 204 out of 222 of the campuses are public.) Perhaps the variables included are not adequate measures of community, or alternatively, perhaps the community measures may indicate social pressures leading to deviant behavior by those who cannot conform. To the extent that these variables do measure community structure, they may be associated with greater measures of conformity—i.e., greater pressures toward academic and social success. The positive correlation between community and campus crime would then be consistent with "strain theory."

Table 5. Correlates of Campus Crime Rate, 1979

Variable	Mean	Correlation Coefficient	Two-Tailed Significance Level	n
Police:				
C79POLR	3.0	0.1359	0.023	218
POC79	0.1	-0.0261	0.355	206
Finances:				
SALARY	3.6	-0.0533	0.217	217
COST	2,769.0	0.3647	0.001	206
AID	50.1	0.0989	0.073	217
Density:				
FT	81.5	0.3123	0.001	208
PCTDORN	30.8	0.2402	0.001	220
STPACRE	43.6	-0.1171	0.042	219
BLDPACRE	0.2	0.0653	0.177	203
Accessibility/visibility:				
BUILDING	65.4	0.2987	0.001	206
ACRE	669.1	0.0735	0.139	219
EST	1,889.0	-0.1538	0.012	217
Community/cohesiveness:				
SFRATIO	17.5	-0.1442	0.016	222
DROPOUT	19.7	-0.1789	0.008	178
FINISH	53.3	0.1790	0.008	178
FRAT	9.8	0.1967	0.004	182
INSTATE	85.7	-0.3653	0.001	220
TYPE	1.1	0.2420	0.001	222
Scholastic:				
GRAD	16.8	0.0441	0.261	212
ACCEPT	76.2	-0.1922	0.002	216
METRIC	64.3	-0.0586	0.196	216
ADVST	28.8	0.2903	0.001	182
COMPLETE	3.1	0.3202	0.001	222
PHD	67.7	0.2348	0.001	214

Table 5 continued

Student body demographics:				
MALE	49.6	0.1162	0.047	207
FOREIGN	2.5	0.0397	0.286	204
AGE	37.6	-0.0765	0.177	149
MINORITY	13.1	0.0399	0.279	219
ENROLL	13,087.0	0.0423	0.268	217
Location:				
URBAN	194,479.0	-0.0575	0.201	215
DISTANCE	28.2	-0.0254	0.353	221
UNEMPD	1.7	-0.0177	0.403	196
LPOP	200,256.0	-0.0628	0.204	176
Miscellaneous:				
CAL	0.2	0.0711	0.146	222

The variables in the scholastic-quality group show the same general pattern, some more significantly than others. A higher quality of education is associated with higher crime rates. This may be because a higher-quality education generally costs more, so that quality is positively correlated with the economic status of the students and the value of campus assets (an economic explanation). Alternatively, the positive relationship between academic quality and campus crime could be interpreted as evidence of basic strain theory processes.

Among the student demographic characteristics, only the percentage of male students is significant and is positively correlated with crime. This is consistent with research findings based on other types of samples. The percentage of minority students, while positively correlated with crime, is not significant. Generally, the signs of the demographic correlations fit expectations. For example, while not significant, older student bodies are associated with less crime.

The effects of the locational variables are all insignificant, consistent with our earlier analysis. The calendar- type correlation (miscellaneous category) is the right sign (higher values of calendar type mean longer calendars), but not significant.

Table 6. Principal Components of Campus Profiles (Oblique Rotation)

Variable	Component 1 (Quality)	Component 2 (Urbanness)	Component 3 (Size)
	Pattern Matrix		
SALARY	0.10640	0.02273	-0.30762
COST	0.88726	0.17184	-0.06710
AID	0.08563	-0.43584	-0.23314
FT	0.32454	-0.59555	0.29149
PCTDORM	0.46575	-0.65461	-0.00814
STPACRE	0.26943	0.56980	-0.19642
BLDPACRE	0.44365	0.34456	-0.03959
ENROLL	-0.07970	0.42558	0.67314
BUILDING	0.14073	0.05181	0.75562
ACRE	-0.22166	-0.15366	0.62829
EST	-0.33442	0.24535	-0.34897
SFRATIO	-0.42321	-0.03433	0.17076
DROPOUT	-0.47763	0.16369	-0.08572
FINISH	0.56690	-0.34898	0.03508
FRAT	0.31013	-0.20613	0.35610
INSTATE	-0.73439	-0.03434	-0.09611
TYPE	0.80212	0.13261	-0.18771
ACCEPT	-0.58163	0.02193	0.11977
METRIC	-0.16659	0.23280	-0.02005
ADVST	0.46174	0.17296	0.11146
COMPLETE	0.69890	0.07841	0.25078
PHD	0.30375	0.33128	0.39302
MALE	0.00795	0.22965	0.55509
GRAD	0.14361	0.48892	0.20335
MINORITY	-0.18949	0.17326	-0.24992
FOREIGN	0.06672	0.25090	0.19187
AGE	-0.41861	0.52753	-0.07424
URBAN	0.18907	0.60834	-0.18263
DISTANCE	-0.12886	0.56105	-0.05832
UNEMPD	0.06821	0.67651	0.05806

Table 6 continued

Correlation Matrix

Component 1	1.00000	-0.01936	0.14223
Component 2	-0.01936	1.00000	0.00593
Component 3	0.14223	0.00593	1.00000

While the correlation coefficients contained in Table 5 are suggestive, greater information about campus crime correlates can be obtained by identifying the major dimensions of campus profiles, using principal components analysis, and then regressing campus rates on the principal components.

Each of the campus descriptors contained in Table 5, with the exception of the police variables, calendar-type variable, and population-of-the-community variable, were included in the principal components analysis. The results are contained in Table 6. The components identified are those for which the eigenvalue exceeded two. Limiting the analysis in this way resulted in three components, which we have identified as indicators of scholastic quality (component 1), urbanness (component 2), and size (component 3). Combined, the components account for 40 percent of the overall variance in the descriptors, with scholastic quality alone accounting for almost 18 percent. An oblique rotation of the components altered the factor pattern only slightly; the components remained uncorrelated except for a slight correlation (0.14) between scholastic quality and campus size.

The scholastic-quality component loads heavily and positively on the descriptors associated with high-quality schools, i.e., COST (0.89), percentage who graduate (FINISH, 0.57), and competitiveness (COMPETE, 0.70). It also displays large positive loadings for the percentage of students who live on campus (PCTDORM, 0.47) and for private/sectarian schools (TYPE, 0.80). Large, negative loadings are found for the student dropout rate (DROPOUT, -0.48), the percentage of students who are in-state (INSTATE, -0.73), and the percentage of students accepted (ACCEPT, -0.58).

The urbanness component displays large positive loadings on the number of students per acre (STPACRE, 0.57), the percentage of graduate students (GRAD, 0.49), the percentage of older students (AGE,

0.53), the urban index (URBAN, 0.61), and the central-city unemployment rate corrected for distance (UNEMPD, 0.68). Large negative loadings are found for the percentage of full-time students (FT, -0.59), the percentage of students who live on campus (PCTDORM, -0.65), and the distance to the nearest central city (DISTANCE, -0.56).

The final component, size, has large positive loadings on the number of buildings (BUILDING, 0.76), the number of acres (ACRE, 0.63), and the total enrollment of the school (ENROLL, 0.67). Somewhat curiously, it also displays a large positive loading on the percentage of male students (MALE, 0.56).

Table 7. Principal Components Regression

Variable	Simple r	Simple r^2	Regression Coefficient[n]
P1 (quality)	0.34	0.11	5.07[*]
P2 (urbanness)	-0.10	0.01	-1.76
P3 (size)	0.25	0.06	3.44[*]
Multiple	R = 0.41	$R^2 = 0.17$	

[n]Due to the statistical properties of principal components, each of the regression coefficients have standard errors of unity, and thus the regression coefficients are identical to their t-ratios.
[*]$p < .001$.

Results of the regression analysis of the three obliquely rotated components are shown in Table 7. As expected, both scholastic quality and size exert strong positive influences on the crime rate (simple correlations of 0.34 and 0.25, respectively) and yield significant regression coefficients (the artificial scale imposed by the components analysis prevents substantive interpretation of the numerical values of the coefficients). Also consistent with earlier results, the urbanness component reveals a trivial (simple $r^2 = 0.01$) correlation with crime and an insignificant regression coefficient. Overall, about 17 percent of the variation in crime rates is explained by the three components in combination.

The major finding of this study is that location has no apparent influence on campus crime rates, although it may have some effect on crime mix. It seems that at this point, college campuses may be isolated entities whose crime problems exist as functions of internal attributes, e.g., the quality, and thus economic status and social environment of the campus, as well as the size, and thus the accessibility, of the campus, rather than as functions of external features of the communities surrounding the campuses. For the most part, the results reported here indicate that college campuses are not unlike other communities with respect to the etiology of crime. An obvious supplement to the research approach used here would be a micro-analysis based on individual case reports from specific campuses, including arrest reports and detailed profiles of surrounding neighborhoods. Such an approach would resolve some of the issues that emerged from this macro-analysis and permit further tests of competing criminological theories.

A possible explanation for the surprising finding that location has no influence on campus crime rates may stem from McPheters (1978) risk trade-off notion: rural campus crime rates reflect the large percentage of students who live on campus, while urban campus crime rates reflect adverse urban influences, offset somewhat by the small percentages of resident students. However, some of the regression results we obtained (not shown here), which include both the percentage of on-campus students, and location measures in a crime rate equation, affirm the insignificance of the location factor and thus do not support the trade-off hypothesis.

Although the results are not reproduced here, an analysis of the strength of campus police force by location was, for the most part, consistent with the finding that location is unimportant in understanding the campus crime picture. There is slight evidence that in the larger metropolitan areas (SCSAs), campuses protect themselves a bit more. Generally, however, urban campuses do not protect themselves more than suburban or rural campuses; they may rely, instead, on urban police to supplement their protective capabilities. More research needs to be done on the employment of police, in general, and on the influence of location, in particular. At the same time, it would be useful to supplement police-labor data with security-equipment information that would permit an investigation of their complementarity/substitutability in production, as well as a more accurate measurement of the deterrent effect of police inputs. Again, this could be incorporated in a micro-study.

Finally, the intuition-contradicting finding that higher levels of police enforcement are associated with higher, not lower, rates of campus crime may simply reflect an unresolved simultaneity bias. That is, the simple correlation between campus crime rates and campus police strength confounds two opposite effects: campuses with large police forces presumably prevent crime on campus and campuses with severe crime problems enlist additional police in an attempt to combat the crime problem. We are currently developing a four-wave (1977-1980) panel model of the interrelation of campus crime, campus police strength, and campus clearance rates, in order to disentangle these mutual dependencies. The temporal dimension, which is the cornerstone of panel designs, will allow explicit isolation (through the cross-lag impacts) of, for example, the influence of crime on police and the influence of police on crime (see Greenberg and Kessler, 1981).

While this cautionary note concerning simultaneity bias renders the crime-police association reported here uninterpretable, the majority of this study's findings are unaffected by this bias, since they involve exogenous factors whose association with crime is solely (or largely) unidirectional. Thus, the results described here concerning the impact of campus size, quality, and, in particular, location would remain essentially unchanged in more complex models of campus crime that include police measures.

Acknowledgements

We wish to thank Diane Gorrow and Shannon E. Griffiths for their assistance in data collection. We are also grateful for the computer assistance given by Susan A. Spaar. Finally, we wish to acknowledge the thoughtful comments and suggestions of anonymous referees. Research for this paper was funded in part by a grant from the Northeastern University Research and Scholarship Development Fund. The order of the authors' names was determined by lottery.

Footnotes

[1] Crime and police data appear in the annual publication of the FBI, *Crime in the United States*; clearance data for the campuses were taken from FBI tapes of Return A submissions. The campus data were extracted from several published collegiate guides, primarily *Barron's Profiles of American Colleges*, and were supplemented with direct telephone contact. Community colleges and medical schools reporting to the FBI program were not included in the sample.

[2] Our original sample included 226 campuses, after removing community colleges and medical schools. Four of these 226 schools, however, do not offer a summer session and were dropped from the analysis. Lack of a summer session would produce lower crime rates, other things being equal, simply because students would spend less time on campus. Difference in calendar type could cause a similar, although less severe, problem, which is corrected in the analysis by the use of a dummy variable for calendar type. For summer sessions, it was preferable to drop the four observations.

[3] An SCSA is defined as two or more contiguous SMSAs, where: one of the SMSAs must have a population of at least one million; 75 percent of each of the SMSAs must be urban; and there must be substantial economic interdependence. The thirteen SCSAs are: Boston-Lawrence-Lowell, MA-NH; Chicago-Gary, IL-IN; Cincinnati-Hamilton, OH-KY-IN; Cleveland-Akron-Lorain, OH; Detroit-Ann Arbor, MI; Houston-Galveston, TX; Los Angeles-Long Beach-Anaheim, CA; Miami-Ft. Lauderdale, FL; Milwaukee-Racine, WI; New York-Newark-Jersey-City, NY-NJ-CT; Philadelphia-Wilmington-Trenton, PA-DL-NJ-MD; San Francisco-Oakland-San Jose, CA; and Seattle-Tacoma, WA.

[4] The 20 schools and locations were:
> Western Illinois, Macomb, Il
> Indiana University, Bloomington, IN
> University of Maine, Orono, Me
> MIT, Cambridge, MA
> Tufts University, Medford, MA
> University of Massachusetts, Amherst, MA
> Michigan State, East Lansing, MI

University of New Hampshire, Durham, NH
Ithaca College, Ithaca, NY
RPI, Troy, NY
SUNY, Potsdam, NY
Kent State, Kent, OH
Miami University, Oxford, OH
Oklahoma State, Stillwater, OK
Indiana University, Indiana, PA
West Chester State College, West Chester, PA
University of Richmond, Richmond, VA
Washington State University, Pullman, WA
West Virginia University, Morgantown, WV
University of Wyoming, Laramie, WY

[5] It might be argued that the insignificant effect of location is due to the discrete measurement of location type and that the classification does not account for the considerable variability of urban influence within classes. To test for this possibility, the campus crime rate was correlated with an "urbanness" measure defined as:

$$U = \frac{\text{Pop}\sqrt{p}}{d^2 + 1}$$

where Pop = population of the SMSA,
p = percentage of the SMSA contained in the closest central city, and
d = distance from the campus to the closest central city.

The results were insignificant.

[6] The analysis of campus and community crime was restricted to the 175 observations for which crime data were available both for the college and the community in which the college was located. We performed an analysis of campus crime rate and crime mix by location type for all 222 schools, to confirm our earlier conclusions about the influence of location. The results were consistent. Location type had no differential effect on campus crime rates, but had some apparent influence on crime mix. The latter effect was restricted to campuses located in SCSAs, where violent crimes are a significantly larger percentage of total index crimes.

[7] For the foundation of this theory, see Becker (1968).

[8] The general problem of simultaneity bias in previous deterrence research has been well noted by Blumstein, Cohen, and Nagin (1978), as well as by others, such as McPheters and Stronge (1974). For a discussion of the identification problem, in particular, see the paper by Fisher and Nagin in Blumstein, Cohen, and Nagin (1978).

[9] Cf. Greenwood and Wadycki (1973) and Wilson and Boland (1978).

[10] See note 8.

Appendix

Definition of Campus Descriptor Variables

ACCEPT	Percent of applicants accepted
ACRE	Size of campus in acres
ADVST	Percent of graduating students pursuing advances study
AGE	Percent of students over 21
AID	Percent receiving financial aid
BLDPACRE	Buildings per acre
BUILDING	Total number of major buildings on campus
CAL	Academic calendar type (0=semester; 1=quarter)
COMPETE	Degree of academic competitiveness (scaled 1-9, with 9 the most competitive)
COST	Tuition and room-and-board rates weighted by in-state/out-of-state student mix
C79POLR	1979 full-time campus police per 1,000 FTE students and faculty
DISTANCE	Distance from campus to closest SMSA central city
DROPOUT	Freshman dropout rate
ENROLL	Total student enrollment
EST	Year of founding
FINISH	Percent of students finishing
FOREIGN	Percent of foreign students
FRAT	Percent students in fraternity or sorority
FT	Percent full-time students (undergraduate only)
GRAD	Percent graduate students

INSTATE	Percent in-state students
LPOP	Community population
MALE	Percent male (graduate and undergraduate)
METRIC	Percent enrolled of those accepted
MINORITY	Percent minority students
PCTDORM	Percent of students living on campus
PCTCC	Percent SMSA population in closest central city
PHD	Percent faculty with Ph.D. or other terminal degree
POC79	Percent clearance of campus crime
SALARY	Faculty salary (1 = --\$; 2 = -\$; 3 = \$; 4 = +\$; 5 = ++\$)
SFRATIO	Student/faculty ratio
SMSAPOP	Total population of closest SMSA
STPACRE	Students per acre
TUITION	In-state, full-time tuition
TYPE	Institution type (1 = public; 2 = private/sectarian)
UNEMP	Unemployment rate for closest SMSA adjusted for distance = $UNEMP/(DISTANCE^2 + 1)$
URBAN	Urbanness index = $(SMSAPOP \times \sqrt{PCTCC} / (DISTANCE^2 + 1)$

References

Becker, G. (1968). Crime and Punishment: An Economic Approach. *J. Pol. Econ.* 76:169-217.

Blumstein, A.; Cohen, J.; and Nagin, D., eds. (1978) *Deterrence and Incapacitation: Estimating the Effects of Criminal Sanctions on Crime Rates*. Washington, D.C.; National Academy of Sciences.

Fabricant, R. (1980) Interjurisdictional Spillovers of Urban Police Services: Comment. *S. Econ. J.* 45:955-61.

Gelber, S. (1972) *The Role of Campus Security in the College Setting.* Washington, D.C.: U.S. Government Printing Office.

Greenberg, D.F., and Kessler, R.C. (1981). Panel Models in Criminology. In *Methods in Quantitative Criminology*, ed. by J.A. Fox. New York: Academic Press.

Greenwood, M.J. and Wadycki, W.J. (1973). Crime Rates and Public Expenditure for Police Protection: Their Interaction. *R. Soc. Econ.* 31: 138-51.

Hakim, S.; Ovadia, A.; Sagi, E.; and Weinblatt, J. (1979). Interjurisdictional Spillover of Crime and Police Expenditure. *Land Econ.* 55:200-13.

_____ and Rengert, G.F., eds. (1981). *Crime Spillover.* Beverly Hills, CA: Sage.

Iannarelli, A.V. (1968). *The Campus Police.* Hayward, CA: Precision Photo Form.

McPheters, L.R. (1978). Econometric Analysis of Factors Influencing Crime on Campus. *J. Crim. Just.* 6:47-52.

_____ and Stronge, W.B. (1974). Law Enforcement Expenditures and Urban Crime. *Nat. Tax J.* 27:633-43.

Mehay, S.L. (1977). Interjurisdictional Spillovers of Urban Police Services. *S. Econ. J.* 43:1352-59.

Williams, D.A., with Morris, H. and Contreras, J. (1982). Crime on Campus. *Newsweek*, January 25, 1982.

Wilson, J.Q. and Boland, B. (1978). The Effect of the Police on Crime. *Law Soc. R.* 12:367-90.

THE CRIMINAL PATTERNS OF BOSTON SINCE 1849

Theodore N. Ferdinand

There is a budding interest in the criminal patterns of other nations among American criminologists.[1] Different kinds of societies with different types of social organizations should, according to criminological theory, exhibit different patterns of criminality, and those who explore the criminality of other nations serve not only to broaden our knowledge of exotic forms of crime but also to confirm (or deny) our theoretical expectations regarding the relationship between social organization and crime. Both objectives, however, can be served not only by cross-cultural research but also be longitudinal studies of American communities. In' tracing the criminal patterns of these communities as they assumed an urban, industrial character, it should be possible to identify the characteristic influences of a maturing urban social structure upon the criminal behavior of its population.

In the United States, many of the best sites for such studies are found in New England where urban communities and institutions began to emerge in the seventeenth century, and where the history of their development through the eighteenth and nineteenth centuries has been carefully preserved in the form of detailed anecdotal accounts of the times and as the official records of a variety of municipal agencies. As yet, few criminologists have utilized the archives of great metropolitan centers as a basis for studying criminal patterns of behavior, but such investigations are much more convenient and can yield just as much information about the criminal patterns of pre-industrial communities as cross-cultural studies.[2]

One of the reasons criminologists have failed to carry out such investigations may be a widespread suspicion that municipal records, both past and present, are too inaccurate to be usable. No one argues that the police and court records of any period are above suspicion, but the inadequacies of certain portions of these records are not adequate grounds for rejecting the entire archives of a city. Many of the biases in such data can be detected through internal analysis; moreover, the farther back in time one pursues these records, the more accurate and precise they tend to become. It is well known, for example, that the police of

Reprinted with permission from the University of Chicago Press from Theodore N. Ferdinand, "The Criminal Patterns of Boston Since 1849," *American Journal of Sociology*, vol. 73, No. 1, July 1967. © 1967 by The University of Chicago.

small, cohesive communities are considerably more effective in detecting and solving crime than the police of large, urban communities.[3] And even the largest cities in New England today were merely villages of small cities during most of the eighteenth and nineteenth centuries.

In addition, the attitude in New England toward crime was considerably more severe throughout much of its early history than it is today, suggesting that the vigilance and perseverance of the police were much stronger in the eighteenth and nineteenth centuries than they are now. Similarly, the records of New England courts in the eighteenth and nineteenth centuries are remarkable for the consistence with which they describe the apprehension and disposition of the simplest larcenies and the mildest of assaults.[4] If the frequency with which these simple crimes were set down in the court records is any indication of the diligence with which they were pursued, the police must have been vigilant indeed.

The Archives of the Boston Police

The present study is based upon the arrest reports of the Boston police, which have been issued annually since 1849; and through them I shall examine the changing criminal patterns of Boston as it grew from a city of 136,000 in 1850 to a great metropolitan center in 1950 with a population of 801,000 in the central city.[5]

A longitudinal study of this type confronts a special difficulty. In addition to the actual changes in criminal activity that have occurred over the last century, the arrest trends also reflect changes in police practice as well as changes in the courts' definition and interpretation of the criminal code. There is some risk, therefore, of confusing basic changes in criminal activity with more superficial changes in the manner in which the police and the courts have apprehended and dealt with crime over the years.

This risk, however, is more serious for certain kinds of crimes than for others. For example, it is unlikely that there has been a significant change over the last hundred years in the way in which murder has been defined or murderers apprehended. Similarly, forcible rape, robbery, and burglary are sufficiently serious as crimes to forestall drastic changes in their definitions or arresting practices. Minor crimes, on the other hand, may have been handled quite differently by the police of different eras.

In the nineteenth century we have already seen that nearly every assault and larceny, no matter how slight, was dealt with in the same fashion as major crimes, that is, the offender was arrested and brought to court. Today, however, if the police in large urban centers were equally vigilant toward minor assaults and larcenies, the apparatus of justice would become completely inoperable. Other difficulties will be evident as we proceed with our analysis, but it must be remembered that all data contain comparable distortions and that these imperfections do not destroy the basic usefulness of our data. They simply make their interpretation somewhat more complex.

Codifying the Arrest Reports

Since there was considerable variation in the classificatory systems used by the Boston police over the years, it was necessary, first, to reduce the arrest reports to a consistent and manageable form before beginning their analysis. The most general such schema available is that developed by the FBI in its annual reports of major crime.[6] Seven major classes of crime—(1) criminal homicide, including murder and non-negligent manslaughter; (2) forcible rape; (3) robbery; (4) aggravated assault; (5) burglary; (6) larceny of $50 or over; and (7) auto thefts—are utilized by the FBI in its crime index. For several reasons, however, it was not possible to adhere precisely to this method of classifying crime.

First, the Boston police did not consistently distinguish between negligent and non-negligent manslaughter through the years; hence, a single category—manslaughter—is utilized here which includes both types. Second, it was not possible to differentiate aggravated assault from simple assault with any consistency in the Boston police records; consequently, all assaults were included in the same category. Third, in analyzing the Boston data, it was not possible to distinguish consistently between larceny of $50 and over and larceny of less than $50, as the FBI does. Consequently, all larcenies were thrown into the same category, and a third departure from the FBI schema was the result. Finally, the Boston police did not begin reporting auto theft as a distinct category until 1927, and for this reason it is not included at all in this report. Moreover, since auto thefts were not distinguished from other types of larcenies before 1927, any auto thefts that occurred prior to that year were included in the larceny totals. In all other respects, however, it was possible to conform to the schema developed by the FBI, that is, with regard to the crimes of forcible rape, robbery, and burglary.

Once the data of the original arrest reports had been coded in this fashion, the arrest rate for each crime was calculated by three-year periods to reduce the fluctuations that annual data generally show. Three times in the last century, however, the Boston Police Department was completely reorganized, and the arrest reports for these years changed so radically that they were incomparable with those of the other years. In 1854, for example, the police were consolidated with the watchmen and the constables, and the arrest report of that year covered only seven months. When the police department was reorganized again in 1879, the report for these three years were not comparable with the rest and could not be used. To compensate for these gaps in the data, therefore, it was necessary to use a five-year period in 1849-53, a four-year period in 1875-78, and a two-year period in 1883-84.

The Pattern of Major Crimes in Boston

The results of analyzing the original arrest reports in this fashion are presented in Figures 1 through 8. A glance at Figure 1 reveals that the aggregate crime rate in Boston has shown an almost uninterrupted decline from 1875-78 to the present era. The period immediately before the Civil War saw a high rate of major crime, but during and shortly after the Civil War, crime declined, only to rise to an all-time peak in 1875-78.[7] Since that time, the crime rate has declined steadily to a level about *one-third* that in 1875-78.

I shall have more to say about the trend in Boston's over-all crime rate later, but for the present it should be noted that both the dramatic upturn following the Civil War and the steady decline from a peak around 1875-78 were also experienced by other American cities. Powell documents a rapid rise in serious crime in Buffalo shortly after the Civil War, and Rosenbaum cites several contemporary reports which suggest that there was a similar rise throughout the Northeast.[8] Powell shows also that the peak in serious crime established just after the Civil War in Buffalo was followed by a long decline to the present, broken only by rises in the first decades of the twentieth century and in the 1930s.[9] And Willbach shows that Chicago and New York City also experienced a slow but steady decline in major crime rates in the first decades of the twentieth century.[10] It would appear, then, that the long-term trend in major crime in Boston confirms to the pattern exhibited by several other American cities during the same period.

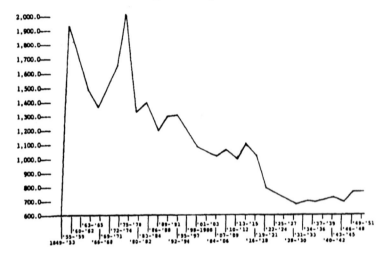

Figure 1. Rate of Major Crimes in Boston per 100,000 Population, 1949-1951

The reasons behind this long-term decline can only be guessed at without further information. The decline may mean, for example, that Bostonians have actually become less criminally inclined as the city grew into a metropolitan center, or it may mean that the city's courts and police have simply softened their approach to crime as the city developed.[11] An examination of the individual crimes described above should throw some light on this question and, accordingly, let us begin with a consideration of the trend in the murder rate over the last one hundred years.

Figure 2 reveals that the rate of murders in Boston has declined steadily if erratically over the last century. The highest rate occurred in 1855-59, and the lowest rate was registered in 1937-39. Since murder is one of the more serious crimes, it is unlikely that this decline can be attributed to a decrease in police vigilance in dealing with murderers. Today, metropolitan police departments are every bit as effective in solving murders as small-town departments. Moreover, it is difficult to relate the murder rate to specific events in the history of Boston. Neither great wars nor major depressions seem to have had any consistent effect upon the murder rate. During the Civil War the murder rate declined, but during the two world wars it increased slightly. Similarly, the depressions of 1873-78, 1893-98, 1919-21, and 1930-39 seem to have had no consistent influence. It would appear, therefore, that this steady decline reflects something more fundamental, that is, long-term shifts in the structure and organization of the city as it grew into a great metropolitan center.

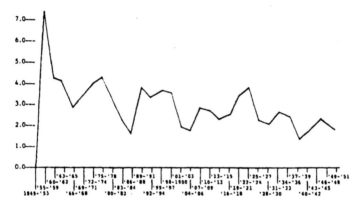

Figure 2. Murders per 100,000 Population in Boston, 1849-1951

The long-term trend of manslaughter, however, follows a quite different path. It is apparent from Figure 3 that the manslaughter rate in Boston remained relatively stable from 1849-53 to 1904-6. In 1907-9, however, it began a sharp rise to a new plateau, roughly *six times* the level throughout the nineteenth century. This new plateau persisted for nearly twenty years, from 1916-18 to 1934-36, when the manslaughter rate began to sink again to a level midway between the high and low levels of the hundred-year period.

There is good reason to believe that these fluctuations reflect primarily the introduction of the automobile in Boston around the turn of the century.[12] We cannot account for them in terms of changes in the statutes governing manslaughter, since the criminal code of Massachusetts from 1901 to the present shows only a minor reduction in the minimum term of imprisonment from three years to two and one-half years. Moreover, there are no close relationships between the manslaughter rate and such specific events as wars and depressions. Since it seems hardly likely that the mountainous rise in the twentieth century can be explained entirely in terms of changes in the police attitude and practice toward manslaughter as a crime, the rise in manslaughter rates during the first third of the twentieth century probably reflects to a considerable degree the introduction of the automobile during this period.

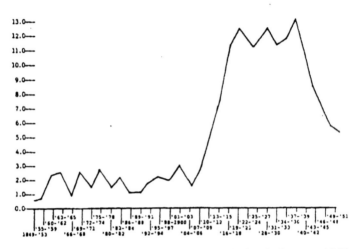

Figure 3.   Manslaughters per 100,000 Population in Boston, 1849-1951

It is more difficult, however, to explain the decline in manslaughter rates that began in 1934-36. Since this decline continued through the post-World War II period, it cannot be explained as a result of the decrease in cars on the road during the depression and World War II. Moreover, since the murder rate did not show a significant increase during this period, it is not likely that there was any tendency for the police to charge offenders with murder rather than manslaughter. It may be that the recent decline can be explained in terms of improved highways and an increasing skill and experience among the driving public, but before such a conclusion can be made with confidence, further information on this issue would be necessary.

The upward trend of forcible rape over the last century requires a somewhat more complicated explanation.[13] Beginning with the simplest factors first, it can be seen from Figure 4 that major wars and severe depressions have been associated with a decline in the rate of forcible rape. The Civil War and World War II were accompanied by minor declines in an otherwise upward tendency, and World War I saw a sharp drop in the rate, although the Spanish-American war was too short to have had any significant effect. The depressions of 1873-78, 1919-21, and 1930-39 all saw appreciable declines, with only the depression of 1893-98 showing an increase in rape. But even there the increase was slowed to some extent. Furthermore, it is clear from Figure 4 that the prosperous years of 1866-72, 1906-15, 1922-27, and 1940-51 witnessed sharp rises in the rate of forcible rape in Boston. Only during the prosperous years of 1880-92 did the rate fail to rise appreciably.[14]

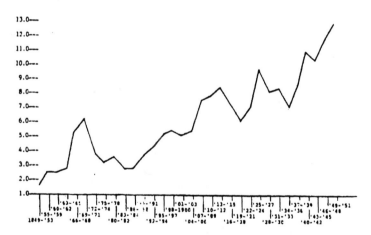

Figure 4. Forcible Rapes per 100,000 Population in Boston, 1849-1951

The relationship between forcible rape and wartime is easily explained. As the proportion of physically able men in the community declines during wartime, the rate of forcible rape declines accordingly. The relationship between rape and the economic cycle, however, is somewhat more difficult to explain. It may be that economic depressions have a psychologically depressive effect such that the individual becomes interested more in preserving and consolidating what he already has than in initiating new and risky adventures. During prosperity, however, his inhibitions may relax to some extent, and the individual becomes somewhat more daring.

There are two other general patterns that are also noteworthy in Figure 4. There can be no mistaking the persistent upward trend in the rate of forcible rape in Boston over the last century; the lowest rates are found at the beginning of the series, and the highest at the end. Moreover, there appears to be a distinct acceleration in the rise beginning about 1904-6. How might we interpret these two patterns?

The accelerated rise since 1904-6 coincides roughly with the introduction of the automobile and may reflect the influence of this invention upon sexual practices. Thus, as young couples found it easier to seclude themselves from the gaze of society, the incidence of every type of illicit sexual activity increased, including those based on force. The persistent upward tendency since the middle of the nineteenth century, however, may reflect a gradual expansion of the middle class in the social structure of Boston and the accompanying rise in the status of women. As a greater proportion of the population came to adhere to a middle-class style of life, the likelihood that a rape would be brought to the attention of the police and the offender arrested probably also increased. Even today, a middle-class girl if much more likely to complain to the authorities when she is molested by her escort. Thus as far as forcible rape is concerned, it appears that such specific events as economic prosperity and peace have reinforced the general upward trend established by broad social structural changes and the introduction of the automobile among the people of Boston.

With robberies, quite the opposite seems to have been the case. A glance at Figure 5 shows that the long-term tendency in robberies has been generally downward, with extraordinary events superimposing dramatic increases on this downward trend from time to time. Thus, the rate of robberies declined on average from the Civil War to a low in 1901-3. World War I was accompanied by a new high in 1916-18, and after a precipitous decline in the 1920s, the Great Depression saw another new high in 1931-33. The long-term decline set in again after this high, but World War II in turn witnessed a reversal of the trend for several years. Nevertheless, after the war, the general decline again reappeared. Thus, it would seem that the social dislocations of wars and depressions have encouraged a high rate of robberies, whereas broader, more enduring structural changes have contributed to a continuous erosion in the rate of robberies in Boston.

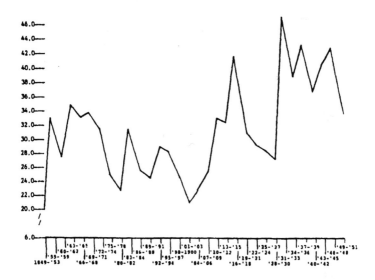

Figure 5. Robberies per 100,000 Population in Boston, 1849-1951

The same general pattern has also been found in Chicago and New York. Willbach's data over the twenty-year period indicates both cities experienced their highest rate of robberies in 1931-33.[15]

Burglaries, according to Figure 6, have shown much the same tendency as robberies. Superimposed upon a generally declining trend are several unusually high peaks that stem apparently from a series of extraordinary, nationally generated events. Severe depressions, for example, have been accompanied consistently by a high rate of burglary. The highest burglary rate for the entire time span was realized near the end of the Great Depression in 1937-39, and the second highest point occurred near the end of the severe depression of 1873-78. Unlike robberies, however, burglaries have not increased during wartime; indeed, the burglary rate in Boston has declined consistently during all three of the major wars in the last century.

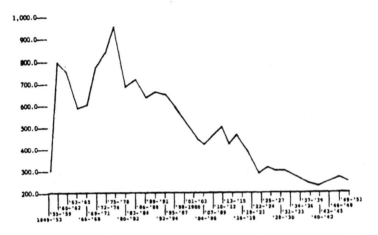

Figure 6. Burglaries per 100,000 Population in Boston, 1849-1951

The long-term trend of assaults in Boston, as revealed in Figure 7, exhibits an especially interesting pattern. It appears as if two distinct curves with entirely different characteristics are joined in 1925, one stretching from 1855-59 to 1922-24 and the other running from 1925-27 to 1949-51. The first exhibits a marked responsiveness to such events as major wars and severe depressions, while the second shows very little sensitivity to either. The highest rate of assaults occurred during the depression of 1873-78, but the Great Depression had scarcely any effect. Similarly, the Civil War and World War I were accompanied by distinct drops in the rate of assaults in Boston, but World War II saw little change. In other words, the rate of assaults in Boston seems to have been especially responsive to conditions in the community before 1925, whereas after that date even the most severe dislocations Boston has ever experienced produced little if any reaction.

This rather peculiar pattern probably reflects basic changes in the manner in which the Boston police have dealt with assaults over the last century. If during the nineteenth and early twentieth centuries the police were especially persistent in pursuing those who committed all kinds of assaults, the assault rate would have been expecially sensitive to changing conditions in the community. Simple assault embraces a wide variety of acts and involves a relatively large portion of the population. Because it is diffused so widely throughout the community, we might expect that a momentous event, for example, a major war or severe depression, would have a considerable impact upon the rate of this crime. Moreover, in the early period when all assaults were being pursued diligently, simple assaults probably comprised the bulk of offenses in this category. Consequently, in the nineteenth century the overall assault rate was responsive to the stream of historical events in the community.

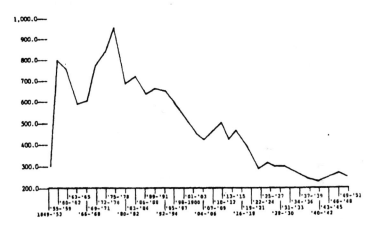

Figure 7. Assaults per 100,000 Population in Boston, 1849-1951.

During the modern era, however, the police have been forced to relax their vigilance toward minor crime, and accordingly, in recent years they have been making proportionately fewer arrests for minor assault. In effect, this means that today aggravated asault is making a greater contribution to the overall assault rate. But if aggravated assault, like murder, is relatively insensitive to the flow of events in the community, the responsiveness of the assault rate to wars and depressions should be considerably less today than it was in the nineteenth and early twentieth centuries, as it is.

There is no basis upon which a direct evaluation of the diligence of the Boston police in the nineteenth century might be made, but I have already remarked on the thoroughness with which the simplest assaults and larcenies were handled by the Boston Police Court in the early part of the nineteenth century. If these practices continued throughout the nineteenth century, it would seem that a high proportion of those involved in assaults and larcenies were, indeed, arrested during that period. By way of comparison, however, in the six-year period from 1960 to 1965, the Boston police solved 56.6 per cent of the aggravated assaults brought to their attention and of the larcenies reported, they solved only 42.7 per cent.[16] These figures are roughly comparable with the experience of other metropolitan police departments, but they suggest that the nineteenth-century Boston police need not have had a very high arrest percentage to have created the kind of inconsistent pattern described above.

Coming back to the data at hand, it is clear from Figure 8 that larcenies followed much the same pattern as assaults. Here again we find two distinct curves: first, an early one displaying a marked sensitivity to community events, followed by a curve showing little response at all. The only difference is that the shift from one type to the other seems to have occurred somewhat earlier, that is, by 1886-88. Thus, before 1886-88 the Civil War was accompanied by a dramatic drop from an all-time peak in 1855-59, which in turn was followed by a sharp rise during the depression of 1873-78. After this early period of rather wide fluctuations, however, World Wars I and II produced only a slight decline, and the Great Depression of 1930-39 brought about only a minor increase in the rate of larcenies. This last is especially interesting in view of the fact that robberies and burglaries both established all-time peaks during the Great Depression. The conclusion that larcenies are not being diligently investigated and solved in the modern era seems inescapable.

An Interpretation of Boston's Criminal Pattern

In terms of this analysis, then, two broad types of factors seem to affect the criminal patterns of a community. On the one hand, we have those specific factors like wars and economic depressions that have a fleeting, though powerful effect upon the criminal patterns of a community; and, on the other, we have those secular factors like an expanding middle class that consist of gradual, enduring changes in the social structure and organization of the community. The latter occur so slowly that their impact in any one year is scarcely noticeable, but their cumulative effect through the years is likely to change fundamentally both the rate and the pattern of criminal activity in the community.

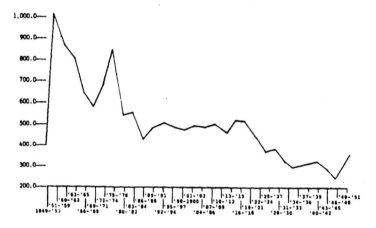

Figure 8. Larcenies per 100,000 Population in Boston, 1849-1951

Among the specific factors, the economic cycle is perhaps most powerful. Robberies, burglaries, larcenies, and assaults have all shown an inverse relationship to the level of economic activity in the Hub during the last century, while forcible rape has varied directly with the economic fortunes of Boston.[17] Major wars seem to have had a depressive effect upon major crime in Boston; forcible rape, burglary, assault, and larceny all have declined rather consistently whenever Boston became involved in a major war. Only murder and manslaughter have shown little sensitivity to the influences of the economic cycle or wars.

Quite independent of these specific factors, several of the crimes examined here have shown tendencies that may well reflect basic, secular shifts in the social structure of Boston. We have already mentioned the automobile as a factor in the rise in manslaughter and forcible rape, but there are several other social changes that must have had a profound effect upon the criminal patterns of Boston as it moved into the twentieth century.

First, the mechanisms of social control in a metropolis are much less personal and, therefore, much less effective in preventing deviancy of all kinds, and in a metropolis there is a much greater spirit of independence and personal freedom.[18] Second, the metropolis nearly always harbors a well-organized underworld in which a wide variety of criminal activities are pursued, including those involving the most serious kinds of crimes. These two changes alone would tend to produce increases in the rates of most crimes as a small city grew into a great metropolis, although it must be noted that few members of organized crime are ever arrested for their misdeeds.

Several other structural changes have probably influenced the crime rate in the opposite direction. Most American cities have grown in size primarily by assimilating large numbers of peoples who initially at least had little familiarity with urban manners and institutions. For example, Boston was inundated in the nineteenth century, first, by the starving yeomen of Ireland and, then, by the impoverished peasants of Sicily and southern Italy.[19] These immigrants and the city suffered grievously in the process. There can be little doubt that the gradual adjustment of the descendants of the Irish and Italian immigrants to the urban patterns of Boston has resulted over the years in a gradual reduction in the city's crime rate.

And by the same token, the fact that the city, like most American communities, has enjoyed a gradually rising standard of living during nearly the entire period of this study must have had a significant effect upon its crime rate.[20] The rising standard of living of Bostonians was probably accompanied by a relative stabilization of their employment and ultimately of their community life as well. Hence crimes usually associated with economic distress and social disorganization have declined in proportion to other types of crime, while sexual crimes, which are probably more common among the higher economic classes, have increased to some extent.

Taking into account all types of structural change, then, we can see that there have been counterbalancing pressures on the crime rate as Boston grew from a small city into a large metropolis. The fact that the crime problem has declined on balance leads me to suspect that, in the long run, those forces tending to diminish crime in Boston have been more powerful, although of course, there is no way of evaluating this view more precisely with the data at hand. This issue can only be settled conclusively when, perhaps, twenty or thirty similar studies of other cities have been performed. At that point, the specific relationship between crime rates and single factors like social control and the broader relationship between social organization and criminal patterns can be more precisely determined.

Some Conclusions

In conclusion, then, I have examined the criminal patterns of Boston over the long term, and the results suggest that the patterns of deviant behavior in the community as measured by police arrests depend basically upon three factors: the attitude and effectiveness of the police; the occurrence of momentary events in the community that have the effect of disturbing and dislocating the established social routines; and the occurrence of enduring changes in the structure of the community in response to qualitative changes in its function. The overall effect of both the momentary events and the more enduring changes in Boston's structure has been to encourage an intermittent but persistent downward tendency in the rate of every major crime except forcible rape and murder.

This downward drift, of course, stands in stark contrast to the popular belief that crime is growing more rampant and more serious every year. This belief has been fostered by the annual reports issued by the FBI, where appalling increases in crime and delinquency are monotonously recorded. The FBI has been issuing these reports only since 1930, and as Figure 1 indicates, the crime rate in Boston has, indeed, risen slightly since then. But even if we assume that the *long-term trend* in Boston and other major metropolitan centers has been downward, we need not conclude that there is a basic contradiction between these data and the trends traced by the annual reports of the FBI. The migration pattern of this nation over the last one hundred years has been from areas of low crime rates, that is, rural areas and small towns, to areas of high crime rates, that is, large urban centers; and a chronic increase in the crime rate in the entire society is not inconsistent with a steady decrease in the crime rates of its large cities.[21]

Footnotes

[1] See, in particular, Paul Tappan, *Comparative Survey of Juvenile Delinquency* (New York: United Nations, Department of Economic and Social Affairs, 1958); Tsung-yi Lin, "Two Types of Delinquent Youth in Chinese Society," in Marvin K. Opler (ed.), *Culture and Mental Health* (New York: Macmillan Co., 1959); Walter A. Lunden, Statistics on Delinquents and Delinquency (Springfield, Ill., Charles C. Thomas, 1964); E. Jackson Bauer, "The Trend of Juvenile Offenders in the Netherlands and the United States," *Journal of Criminal Law, Criminology, and Police Science*, LV (1964), 359-69.

[2] For a recent longitudinal study of a major American city, see Elwin H. Powell, "Crime as a Function of Anomie," *Journal of Criminal Law, Criminology, and Police Science*, LVII (June, 1966), 161-71. An early study of Boston's criminal patterns was performed by Sam Bass Warner, but he used court prosecutions from 1883 to 1932 as his basic data, not police arrest records (see his *Crime and Criminal Statistics in Boston* [Cambridge, Mass.: Harvard University Press, 1934]). In a related study, Leonard V. Harrison examined the arrest records of the Boston police from 1855 to 1932, and although he was concerned with only a few crimes, where his findings are comparable, they agree with my own (see his *Police Administration in Boston* [Cambridge, Mass: Harvard University Press, 1934]). Robert Topitzer has undertaken an analysis of the criminal patterns of an early period in the history of an American city (see his *Court Proceedings in the Social Order of Boston, 1703-1732* [unpublished Master's thesis, Northeastern University, 1967]). And finally, A.H. Hobbs compared the criminal patterns of eighteenth-century Philadelphia with those found in 1937 (see his "Criminality in Philadelphia," *American Sociological Review*, VIII [1943], 198-202).

[3] The FBI has found that the police of small communities consistently solve a higher percentage of their more mild offenses than their metropolitan colleagues (see, e.g., *Uniform Crime Reports* [Washington, D.C.: Federal Bureau of Investigation, 1964], Table 8, p. 95).

[4] A preliminary analysis by the author of the records of the Boston Police Court for the year 1823 reveals many larcenies of less than fifty cents and a comparable number of assaults involving no more than throwing snowballs or spitting at an individual.

[5] Although the city of Boston had a population of 801,444 in 1950, a better measure of its metropolitan character is the population of its Standard Metropolitan Statistical Area, i.e., 2,410,372.

[6] *Uniform Crime Reporting Handbook* (Washington, D.C.: Federal Bureau of Investigation, 1965), pp. 10-38.

[7] The arrest reports of the years 1849-53 almost certainly underestimate the amount of crime in Boston because the police of that period shared the peace-keeping function with a force of constables in the daytime and watchmen at night. In all likelihood, the arrest reports of the police do not include arrests made by the constables or the watchmen during this period.

[8] Powell, *op. cit.*, p. 164; and Betty B. Rosenbaum, "The Relationship between War and Crime in the United States," *Journal of Criminal Law, Criminology, and Police Science*, XXX (1930-40), 726-29.

[9] Powell, *op. cit.*

[10] Harry Willbach, "The Trend of Crime in Chicago," *Journal of Criminal Law, Criminology, and Police Science*, XXXI (1940-41), 726; and his "Trend of Crime in New York City," *ibid.*, XXIX (1938), 72.

[11] It would appear that these changes do not simply represent fluctuations in the intensity of police coverage in Boston. From 1855-59 to 1864-68, there was a decline in the rate of major crime of 29.8 per cent, while the number of policemen per 1,000 population was nearly stable at 1.67. Similarly, from 1866-68 to 1872-74, the rate of major crime increased by 21.1 per cent while the number of policemen per 1,000 was increasing from 1.67 in 1867 to 1.83 in 1873 for an increase of only 9.6 per cent (see Edward H. Savage, *Police Records and*

Recollections [Boston: Jackson, Dale & Co., 1873], pp. 95, 98, and 104-6).

[12] Warner noted the same peculiar pattern in manslaughters in Boston, and since he found that they paralleled prosecutions for motor-vehicle deaths, he concluded that the rise in manslaughters reflected primarily the growing use of autos in the Hub (cf. Warner, *op. cit.*, pp. 20-23). It is interesting to note, moreover, that from 1905 to 1920 the number of motor vehicles registered in the United States increased by a factor of 117.2, while in 1935 there were only 2.9 times as many motor vehicles registered as in 1920 (see Alfred D. Chandler, *Giant Enterprise: Ford, General Motors, and the Automobile Industry* [New York: Harcourt, Brace & World, 1964], p. 4).

[13] In 1893, the age of consent in Massachusetts was advanced by statute from ten to sixteen. This means, in effect, that those who were performing sexual intercourse with females between the ages of eleven and sixteen with their consent were guilty of rape after 1893 but not before. Thus, from 1894 on, the rate of forcible rape was inflated to some degree by this statutory change. The continuing rise in the rate of this crime to the present day, however, *cannot* be a result of this single change.

[14] It is impossible to test the relationship between this crime and the economic cycle in Boston with quantitative data, since there are no reliable long-term data on economic activity in Boston. Data for the United States as a whole do exist going back well into the nineteenth century, but the relevancy of these data to the economy of Boston is not close. Hence, relating them to longitudinal crime rates seems unwise.

[15] Willbach, "The Trend of Crime in Chicago," *op. cit.*, p. 722; and his "The Trend of Crime in New York," *op. cit.*, p. 69.

[16] *The Boston Sunday Globe*, May 8, 1966, p. A-3.

[17] These results are generally consistent with those reported by Daniel Glaser and Kent Rice in their study, "Crime, Age, and Employment," *American Sociological Review*, XXIV, No. 5 (October, 1959), 683. See also William F. Ogburn and Dorothy S. Thomas, "The Influence of

the Business Cycle on Certain Social Conditions," *Journal of the American Statistical Association*, XVIII (September, 1922), 324-40.

[18] The best discussion of the relationship between mechanisms of social control and social organization is contained in Georg Simmel's "The Persistence of Social Groups," reprinted in Edgar F. Borgatta and Henry J. Meyer (eds.), *Sociological Theory* (New York: Alfred A. Knopf, Inc., 1959), pp. 373-75. Simmel also provides, perhaps, the deepest insight into the character of urban man (see his "The Metropolis and Mental Life," *Sociology of Georg Simmel* [New York: Free Press, 1950], pp. 409-24).

[19] Oscar Handlin reports that, in 1850, 35.0 per cent of the Boston population were foreign born. In 1855 the figure was 37.9 per cent, in 1865 it was 34.3 per cent, and in 1880 it was still 31.6 per cent (see his *Boston's Immigrants* [Cambridge, Mass.: Harvard University Press, 1959], pp. 243-44, 246, and 261). In 1960 the percentage of foreign born in Boston was 15.8 per cent.

[20] See Bernard Barber, *Social Stratification* (New York: Harcourt, Brace & Co., 1957), Chap. xvi, for a careful discussion of the changing class structure in America.

[21] To illustrate the validity of this conclusion, consider the following hypothetical example. Suppose we have a society of 1,000,000 in which 80 per cent of the population lives in villages where the crime rate is 40 per 1,000. The remaining 20 per cent lives in urban areas where the crime rate is 100 per 1,000. The crime rate for such a society would be 52 per 1,000. Now suppose the village crime rate remains at 40 per 1,000, the urban crime rate *drops* to 60 per 1,000, and the percentage in urban areas rises to 90 per cent of the total, which is still 1,000,000. The new crime rate for the society has risen to 58 per 1,000 even though the rate has fallen sharply in the cities.

CRIME AND THE BUSINESS CYCLE

Philip J. Cook
Gary A. Zarkin

The business cycle has a pervasive effect on the structure of economic opportunity and hence on behavior. The effect is reflected in social indicators as diverse as school enrollments, birthrates, and labor force participation.[1] It would be surprising indeed if crime rates were immune to general business conditions, and certainly the conventional wisdom asserts that "street" crime is countercyclical. A recession always provides police chiefs with a comfortable explanation for their failure to prevent increases in the crime rate.

Empirically minded criminologists are not so comfortable with the assertion that crime rates exhibit a countercyclical pattern. Some apparent exceptions to this claim come readily to mind, such as the reductions in FBI Index crime rates in 1982 (the year the worst postwar recession hit bottom) and the extraordinary increases in these crime rates during the 1960s, a period of sustained economic growth and declining unemployment. A recent feature article in the *Washington Post* quotes James Q. Wilson's judgment that "overall unemployment seems to bear little or no relationship to crime" and that "there's no basis for a prediction that a deepening or continuing of the recession will lead to increases in the crime rate."[2] Recent reviews by Long and Witte and Freeman also tend to undermine any claim of a strong relationship between crime and the business cycle.[3]

On the basis of the analysis reported in this paper, we conclude that these agnostics are being too cautious. For two important types of crimes, robbery and burglary, there is strong evidence of a countercyclical pattern. Recessions do indeed increase the rate at which these crimes are committed. Since World War II, a third crime type, auto theft, has exhibited a reverse pattern: recessions reduce the rate of auto theft. Finally, we find that criminal homicide rates are insensitive to business fluctuations. These conclusions are supported by both nonparametric and regression analysis of U.S. crime rates since 1933.

In the next section we review the literature and discuss a variety of possible linkages between crime and the business cycle. Section II presents a nonparametric analysis of crime patterns over the nine

Reprinted with permission from the University of Chicago Press from Philip J. Cook and Gary A. Zarkin, "Crime and the Business Cycle," *The Journal of Legal Studies*, vol. xiv (1), January 1985, 115-28. © 1985 by The University of Chicago.

complete business cycles since 1933. Section III develops a more powerful parametric method of analyzing these data, which is implemented in the subsequent section. In the final section we consider the implications of these results for macroeconomic stabilization policy.

I. Linkages Between Crime and Economic Conditions

The history of all advanced economies is characterized by secular economic growth overlaid by short-term cycles in economic activity. Secular economic development has been characterized by profound changes in the technology of both production and consumption, with far-reaching ramifications for almost every aspect of social organization and control. It seems likely that the important interrelationships between crime and secular economic growth (and its social correlates) are qualitatively different from the processes by which short-term fluctuations in economic activity influence crime rates. It may be, for example, that both secular economic growth and recessions (typically short periods of negative growth) generate increased criminal activities. Our only concern in this paper is the effect of short-term fluctuations in economic activity.

There are a number of possible linkages between business conditions and crime. Some of these possibilities are summarized under four headings below.

1. Legitimate opportunities. The quality and quantity of legitimate employment opportunities are procyclical. The relatively high unemployment rates and related problems associated with economic recession may promote crime by lowering the opportunity cost of time spent in criminal activity (or prison), or through a variety of psychological mechanisms. Brenner, for example, emphasizes unemployment-induced "stress" as a cause of violent crime, while other authors speak of "frustration."[4]

2. Criminal opportunities. Recessions may also discourage crime by reducing the quality of *criminal* opportunities, particularly for property crimes. Potential victims may have a greater propensity to defend their property against muggers, burglars, and thieves during hard times; demand for stolen merchandise may be reduced; or potential robbery victims may be carrying less cash.[5]

3. <u>Use of criminogenic commodities</u>.[6] Intoxication has long been thought to be an important cause of crime, particularly violent crime. If alcohol consumption and abuse tend to increase during good times, then so may the incidence of drunken fights. If handgun sales tend to increase during good times, then these fights may become more lethal.

4. <u>The criminal justice system response to crime</u>. Reduced state and local tax collections during recessions may result in reduced budgets for police and courts and a consequent reduction in the criminal justice system's capacity to contain crime. On the other hand, recessions may promote greater cooperation by victims (because the opportunity cost of their time is less), with a consequent increase in the capacity of the system to identify and prosecute criminals.

There are surely other plausible linkages between crime and the business cycle, but perhaps this list is sufficient to support two conclusions: There are no clear predictions about whether crime is likely to be procyclical, countercyclical, or both (depending on the type of crime); and any effort to develop an estimable model that attempts to incorporate all the important linkages between crime and economic conditions would be subject to pervasive errors in specification, which may obscure the "reduced form" relationship between crime and the business cycle. A simpler, better-focused empirical approach is likely to be more illuminating.

The relationship between general business conditions and crime has been a popular subject of study for empirical criminologists since the mid-nineteenth century.[7] Interestingly, a number of early studies correlate the price of some staple commodity (wheat, rye) with some measure of criminal activity—an approach which was motivated by reasoning similar to that underlying modern studies of heroin prices and crime. An early review of this literature by Van Kan concluded: "Crimes against property find in large measure their indirect causality in bad economic conditions; their direct causality in acute need and even more in chronic misery. . . . Material well-being generally exalts the vital instincts, increases alcohol consumption, and therefore increases crimes against morals. All our literature confirms this fact . . . As for the question of the extent of the influence of economic factors on offenses against persons, the answers are less uniform."[8] Whether or not Van Kan accurately characterizes the literature, his assertion that there are qualitatively different relationships between crime and business conditions, depending on the type of crime, is interesting.

A landmark in this literature is Dorothy Swaine Thomas' *Social Aspects of the Business Cycle*, published in 1927. Thomas related various detrended measures of crime with an indicator of business conditions for Britain, 1857-1913, and found that robbery and burglary rates had a strong negative correlation (-.44), larceny a somewhat weaker negative correlation (-.25), and crimes of violence against the person exhibited essentially no relationship (+.06). Henry and Short support Thomas' conclusions on robbery and burglary by showing large increases in these crimes between 1929 and 1933 for ten cities for which data were available.[9]

Recent time-series studies of crime and economic conditions have had a more ambitious agenda than older studies, seeking a multivariate explanation of crime movements that typically includes several measures of economic conditions, demographic variables, and in many cases one or more variables intended to measure the likelihood and severity of punishment. Perhaps the most notable of these studies is Kenneth Wolpin's, which analyzes British data for a number of crimes for the years 1894-1967 (exclusive of the war years).[10] Wolpin incorporates three variables to serve as indicators of general business conditions—unemployment rate, gross domestic product per capita, and weekly wage for manual manufacturing workers. The latter two variables are indicators of secular economic growth as well as business cycle indicators, so the interpretation of their coefficient estimates is ambiguous (compare the discussion above of the differences between business cycle effects and effects of secular economic growth).

Wolpin's findings on the relationship of unemployment rate, GDP per capita, and weekly wage to four crime types are summarized in Table 1.[11] The unemployment coefficient is statistically significant only for burglary. The message from the pattern of coefficient estimates on the other two variables is obscure at best. It may be that British crime rates exhibited a clear cyclical pattern during this period, but such a pattern cannot be inferred from a multivariate analysis of this sort.

Based on the reviews by Sellin and Long and Witte, and on our own reading of this literature, we conclude that robbery and burglary are countercyclical, with most of the disagreement in the literature concerning the magnitude of the effect. On the other, hand, there is rather sharp disagreement about the relationship between homicide (or, more generally, violent crime) and business fluctuations. Brenner is the most prominent advocate of the claim that recessions increase the criminal homicide rate[12] although his empirical work appears to be seriously flawed.[13] Henry and Short are equally confident (based on their analysis of between-war U.S. data) that the homicide rate is *pro*cyclical.[14] Other authors find no relationship.

Table 1. Signs of Coefficient Estimates Regression Analysis of Crime Rates in England and Wales, 1894-1967

	Burglary	Robbery	Auto Theft	Felonious Wounding
Unemployment	+*	+	+	-
GDP per capita	-	-	-*	-
Real wage	-	+*	-	+*

Source—Kenneth I. Wolpin, An Economic Analysis of Crime and Punishment in England and Wales, 1894-1967, 86 *Journal of Political Economy* 815, 826-7 (1978).

NOTE: Excludes war years. Auto theft estimates based on only twenty-seven observations.
*Coefficient estimate exceeds twice estimate standard error.

We now turn to our own analysis of U.S. crime data. Unlike other recent students of these data, we do not attempt to estimate the parameters of a fully specified model relating crime to various indicators of economic conditions (and other variables). This approach is not supported by either the available data or current knowledge concerning these relationships. In any event, our more modest objective is to determine whether and how short-term fluctuations in economic conditions have influenced each of four types of crime in recent U.S. history.

II. Nonparametric Evidence

There were nine complete business cycles, as defined by the National Bureau of Economic Research (NBER), between 1933 and 1981. Figure 1 depicts annual crime rates during this period for four of the crimes included in the FBI's index of serious crime: murder and nonnegligent manslaughter, robbery, burglary, and auto theft.[15] The peaks of the NBER "reference" cycles are also shown on this graph.

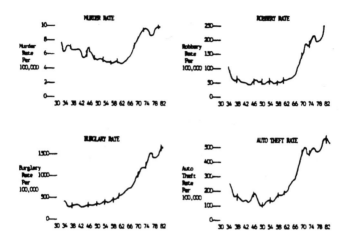

Figure 1

The intertemporal movements in these crimes are dominated by the long swings familiar to every student of crime: a downward drift from 1933 until the war and a sharp acceleration beginning in the mid-1960s with a peak in 1975. These gross movements in crime rates may obscure smaller patterns associated with the business cycle.

Our approach to sifting out effects related to the business cycle is to treat each cycle as a separate event, occurring in a unique context of criminogenic conditions, and, given this context, to assess the apparent effect of the postpeak slump on crime rates. This approach is made operational by calculating the average annual rate of growth in crime between each trough and subsequent cyclical peak and comparing this growth rate with the percentage change between the peak year and the subsequent year when the economy is slumping.[16] Table 2 reports these statistics. Consider, for example, the movement in the robbery rate during the business cycle that began in 1961 and peaked in 1969. Table 2 indicates that the robbery rate grew at an average of 12 percent per year during this period and 16 percent in the recession year of 1970.

Table 2. Crime Movements Over Nine Business Cycles

Reference Cycle Dates Trough	Peak	Interval Used in Calculations	Criminal Homicide Annual Growth Trough to Peak (%)	Next Year(%)	Robbery Annual Growth Trough to Peak (%)	Next Year(%)	Burglary Annual Growth Trough to Peak (%)	Next Year(%)	Auto Theft Annual Growth Trough to Peak (%)	Next Year(%)
3/33	5/37	1933-37	-2.4	-5.7	-13.2	-1.6	-6.9	.8	-10.0	-13.3
6/38	2/45	1938-45	-1.6	17.0	-1.6	9.8	.7	5.6	3.2	-9.7
10/45	11/48	1946-48	-6.7	-10.0	-6.6	5.8	-1.3	6.6	-15.7	-5.4
10/49	7/53	1949-53	-.9	-5.8	.0	4.7	2.4	6.4	6.8	-6.3
5/54	8/57	1954-57	-1.4	.0	-4.9	10.9	2.4	10.7	8.2	.5
4/58	4/60	1958-60	3.1	-6.0	4.5	-3.2	6.9	2.1	4.1	.4
2/61	12/69	1961-69	5.4	8.2	12.4	16.0	8.3	10.2	11.4	4.7
11/70	11/73	1971-73	4.5	4.3	-1.3	14.3	2.5	17.6	-1.9	4.4
3/75	1/80	1975-79	.3	5.2	-.7	14.8	-.4	11.3	1.5	-.8
Number of "pluses"+				4		8		8		2

*The unemployment rates in these trough and peak years are as follows:

Year	%	Year	%
1933-37	24.9-14.3	1961-69	6.7- 3.5
1938-45	19.0- 1.9	1971-73	5.9- 4.9
1946-48	3.9- 3.8	1975-79	8.5- 5.8
1949-53	5.9- 2.9		
1954-57	5.5- 4.3		
1958-60	6.8- 5.5		

+Number of cycles in which the growth in the crime rate from trough to peak was less than the rate of growth in the following year.

No attempt is made to explain why robbery was increasing throughout this cycle; the only interest is in comparing the relative magnitudes of these two percentages. The fact that robbery increased *more* quickly during the economic slump of 1970 than it had during the previous period of economic growth is interpreted as (weak) evidence that the robbery rate is countercyclical—recessions enhance the robbery rate.

The nine cycles together can be viewed as nine trials in a sort of natural experiment. Each trial yields a "plus" (if the postpeak increase exceeded the average increase from trough to peak) or a "minus" (in the reverse case) for each type of crime. If business conditions have no effect on crime, then either result is equally likely—the trial is somewhat analogous to flipping a fair coin. The fact that robbery and burglary have eight pluses out of nine trials is strong evidence that these crimes are countercyclical, since there is only a 4 percent chance that such an unbalanced result will occur by chance if the underlying probability is truly one-half and the trials are independent. Auto theft, with seven trials out of nine scoring a "minus," appears procyclical, although there is an 18 percent probability that such an imbalance would occur by chance. Criminal homicide, with four pluses and five minuses, appears insensitive to business conditions.

These nonparametric tests have the virtues of requiring few assumptions and being simple to calculate. On the other hand, this procedure does not produce an estimate of the magnitude of the effects, and it lacks statistical power. Furthermore, the assumption that the nine trials can reasonably be viewed as independent is questionable. A somewhat more elaborate procedure that remedies these problems is developed in the next section.

III. Regression Specification

We seek a simple procedure for estimating the strength of the relationship between short-term movements in economic conditions and resulting short-term movements in crime rates. The major challenge is to generate estimates that are free from the possible biases introduced by secular movement in the underlying causes of crime. (There may also be secular movement in the relationship between actual and recorded crime rates.)

The first task is to choose an indicator of economic conditions. Two indicators are widely used for this purpose: the civilian unemployment rate and the employment-population ratio. Both move nearly synchronously with fluctuations in business conditions.[17] We have elected to use both in our empirical work.

The simple correlations between these indicators and the four crime rates are reported in Table 3. During the postwar period both the unemployment rate and the employment-population ratio are highly positively correlated with each of the four crime rates. This result may seem mysterious, given that unemployment is countercyclical and employment procyclical. The explanation is that these correlations are dominated by the secular trends in these indicators, which have both been strongly upward during the last two decades—when crime rates were also trending upward.[18] The fact that the secular movements dominate the cyclical movements indicates the necessity of controlling for the former in order to estimate the influence of the latter.

Table 3. Economic Conditions and Crime: Correlations

| | Unemployment Rate | | Employment Ratio, |
	1933-81	1947-81	1947-81
Criminal homicide	.18	.49	.61
Robbery	-.02	.56	.60
Burglary	-.17	.60	.59
Auto theft	-.09	.46	.59

A simple method for eliminating secular movements in the crime rate and unemployment (or employment) rate is to write each of them as a ratio of the contemporaneous value to a moving average. The actual specification used in our analysis is as follows:

$$\log (C_t/\bar{\bar{C}}_t) = a + b \log (Q_t/\bar{\bar{Q}}_t) + e_t, \qquad (1)$$

where C_t = crime rate in year t; Q_t = employment rate in year t; e_t = residual "error" term, assumed to be generated by a first-order autocorrelation process with $Ee_t = 0$; $\bar{\bar{C}}_t$, $\bar{\bar{Q}}_t$ = moving geometric means centered on year t. This specification eliminates secular movements in crime rates caused by trends in crime reporting, demographic structure, "culture," public policy, and so forth. It also eliminates secular trends in the business conditions indicators, which in recent years have been caused by changes in demographic structure, earlier retirement, the changing role of women in the labor force, and so forth.[19]

IV. Regression Results

Equation (1) was estimated for the four types of crime, using both the unemployment rate and the employment-population ratio as indicators of economic conditions. Since a consistent series on the employment ratio was not available until 1947, the regressions using the employment ratio were only estimated for the period 1949-79.[20] The regressions using the unemployment rate were run both for this period and for the full period for which crime data are available (1935-79). Regressions were run using ordinary least squares and also using the estimated generalized least squares procedure in SAS (AUTOREG) to correct for a modest amount of first-order autocorrelation exhibited by the OLS residuals. (This correction had little effect on the estimates of either coefficients or standard errors.) All regressions were run twice, once using three-year moving averages and once using five-year moving averages as the denominators.

Our results are summarized in Table 4.[21] The intercept estimates are in every case a fraction of their estimated standard deviations, as would be expected and are omitted from Table 4.

Table 4. Summary of Coefficient Estimates

| | Unemployment Ratio | | | | Employment Ratio, 1949-79 | |
| | 1935-79 | | 1949-79 | | | |
	3 Years	5 Years	3 Years	5 Years	3 Years	5 Years
Criminal homicide	.05*	.05*	-.03	-.04	.66	.79*
Robbery	.16***	.16***	.17***	.16***	-2.79**	-2.45***
Burglary	.10***	.10***	.12***	.11***	-1.92***	-1.59**
Auto theft	-.04	-.04	-.09**	-.12***	1.79***	2.02***

NOTE: Estimates based on log-linear specification, corrected for first-order autocorrelation.
*Significant at .10 level.
**Significant at .05 level.
***Significant at .01 level.

The estimates of the unemployment coefficient are nearly identical for robbery (about 0.16) and for burglary (about .11), and all these coefficients are significantly different from zero. The results for the employment ratios for these two crimes also serve to support the obvious conclusion, that robbery and burglary rates are sensitive to fluctuations in economic conditions. Recessions appear to cause increases in these two crimes.

The magnitudes involved are not insubstantial. An increase in the unemployment rate from, say, 7 percent to 8 percent will result in a 2.3 percent increase in the robbery rate and a 1.6 percent increase in the burglary rate. Similar differences in these crime rates are associated with a reduction in the employment ratio of, say, 60 percent to 59.5 percent.

As shown in Table 4, the auto theft rate has been about as sensitive to short-term fluctuations in business conditions during the postwar period as burglary but in the opposite direction; recessions reduce the auto theft rate. Inclusion of the earlier period (1935-48) in the auto theft regressions dilutes this result somewhat, suggesting that the basic economics of auto theft has changed over this period.[22]

None of the homicide estimates is statistically significant at the 5 percent level, and all are very small in absolute magnitude. During the postwar period the evidence, if anything, suggests that homicide is slightly procyclical, but the evidence tilts the other way when the earlier data are included. Given that all the homicide elasticity estimates are so close to zero, there is little point in speculating about the observed pattern of results.

The general conclusions for these parameter estimates serve to support and strengthen the conclusions from the nonparametric analysis presented in Section II. Both types of analysis yield strong evidence that burglary and robbery are countercyclical and slightly weaker evidence that auto theft is procyclical. Homicide is insensitive to the business cycle.[23]

Given the variety of plausible linkages between business conditions and crime, it is not surprising that different types of crime respond in qualitatively different fashion to the business cycle. Perhaps the countercyclical nature of burglary and robbery reflects the relative importance of criminal supply-side influences for these crimes, whereas demand-side influences are more important for auto theft. We do not attempt an explanation for our results, but rather offer them as reliable grist for other theorists' mills.

V. Notes on Policy

There is overwhelming consensus that good times are better then bad times; a referendum on a credible proposal to eliminate recessions (without augmenting inflation, reducing economic growth, or installing a more pervasive government role in economic regulation) would win handsomely. We suspect that the popularity of such a proposal would be little influenced by a concern with crime, and for good reason. The major movements in crime rates during the last half century cannot be attributed to the business cycle. Recessions have caused relatively small increases in some types of crime (robbery, burglary) but have reduced auto theft and had negligible influence on murder rates. The effects of recession on other types of crime (child abuse, illicit drug use, price fixing, embezzlement) are unknown.

The criminogenic effects of secular economic growth may be larger than the effects of cyclical movements. Policies influencing investment and the rapidity of technical change may have a much greater influence on the nature and extent of crime over the long run than macroeconomic stabilization policy. However, such long-run effects are also much more difficult to assess using available data and statistical techniques. For now, we are content to offer clear answers concerning short-run fluctuations in economic conditions.

Footnotes

[1] See, for example, Linda N. Edwards, "The Economics of Schooling Decisions: Teenage Enrollment Rates," 10 *J. Human Resources* 155 (1975); M. Silver, "Births, Marriages, and Business Cycles in the United States," 73 *J. Pol. Econ.* 237 (1965); William P. Butz and Michael P. Ward, "The Emergence of Countercyclical U.S. Fertility," 69 *Amer. Econ. Rev.* 318 (1979); Jacob Mincer, "Labor Force Participation of Married Women: A Study of Labor Supply," in *Aspects of Labor Economics* (H. Gregg Lewis, ed., 1962); and Belton M. Fleisher and George Rhodes, "Unemployment and the Labor Force Participation of Married Men and Women: A Simultaneous Model," 58 *Rev. Econ. and Stat.* 398 (1976).

---

2 Nicholas D. Kristof, "Scholars Disagree on Connection Between Crime and the Jobless," *Washington Post*, August 7, 1982, p. A8, col. 3.

3 Sharon K. Long and Ann D. Witte, "Current Economic Trends: Implications for Crime and Criminal Justice," in *Crime and Criminal Justice in a Declining Economy* 69 (K.N. Wright ed. 1981); Richard B. Freeman, "Crime and Unemployment," in *Crime and Public Policy* 89 (James Q. Wilson ed. 1983).

4 M. Harvey Brenner, "Influence of the Social Environment on Psychopathology: The Historical Perspective," in *Stress and Mental Disorder* 161 (James L. Barrett, chief ed. 1979); Andrew F. Henry and James F. Short, Jr., *Suicide and Homicide: Some Economic, Sociological, and Psychological Aspects of Aggression* (1954); and Lynn A. Curtis, *Violence, Race, and Culture* (1975).

5 This change in the propensity for self-defense might result from victims' placing a lower implicit value on their time and/or safety from bodily harm during recessions than during good times.

6 This term was apparently coined by Mark H. Moore, "Controlling Criminogenic Commodities: Drugs, Guns, and Alcohol," in Wilson, *supra* note 4, at 125.

7 William A. Bonger, Criminality and Economic Conditions (1916); and Thorsten Sellin, "Research Memorandum on Crime in the Depression," *Social Science Research Council Bulletin* No. 27 (1937).

8 Joseph Van Kan, Les Causes Economiques de la Criminalité (1903), cited in Sellin, *supra* note 9, at 23.

9 Henry and Short, *supra* note 6, at 174.

10 Kenneth I. Wolpin, "An Economic Analysis of Crime and Punishment in England and Wales, 1894-1967," 86 *J. Pol. Econ.* 815 (1978).

11 Wolpin does not report results from criminal homicide.

[12] M. Harvey Brenner, "Estimating the Social Costs of National Economic Policy: Implications for Mental and Physical Health, and Criminal Aggression" (prepared for Joint Economic Comm., U.S. Congress, Oct. 26, 1976); Brenner, *supra* note 5; and *id.*, "Assessing the Social Costs of National Unemployment Rates" (formal statement submitted before Subcommittee on Domestic Monetary Policy of the Committee on Banking, Finance and Urban Affairs, August 12, 1982).

[13] Philip J. Cook and Gary A. Zarkin, *Homicide and Business Conditions: A Replication of Brenner's Analysis* (mimeographed, Duke University 1983).

[14] Henry and Short, *supra* note 6.

[15] These four crimes were chosen from among the seven included in the FBI Index. The other crimes included in the index are rape, aggravated assault, and larceny. In our judgment, the quality of the available data is likely to be higher for the four crimes we analyzed than for the other three.

[16] For the period under study, the median duration of the trough to peak period has been three years and nine months; the median duration of the downswing has been ten months (with a maximum of sixteen months).

[17] Carol Boyd Leon, "The Employment-Population Ratio: Its Value in Labor Force Analysis," 104 *Monthly Labor Review* 36 (2, 1981).

[18] The unemployment rate is defined as the fraction of all those who are employed or seek employment who are not employed. A person who chooses not to work or seek a job is considered "out of the labor force" rather than "unemployed." Thus it is logically possible for the number of people who are "unemployed" and the number "employed" to increase at the same time, and that in fact has been happening during the last two decades, in part due to the growing number of working women during this period.

[19] Leon, *supra* note 17.

---

[20] These 31 observations from 1949-79 required data from the thirty-five-year period 1947-81 when the five-year moving average was used.

[21] A complete set of results is available from the authors.

[22] For example, there may have been a trend away from "joyriding" and toward increased professionalization in auto theft, as a result of such factors as improved locks and increasing legal access by teenagers to autos. Professional-style thefts may be more sensitive than joyriding to the market for stolen cars. For an economic analysis of auto theft, see Walter Vandaele, "An Econometric Model of Auto Theft in the United States," in *Economic Models of Criminal Behavior* (J.M. Heineke ed. 1978).

[23] A further simple test of the relationship between crime and the business cycle is to correlate the annual rate of change for each crime rate with the annual rate of change of the unemployment rate. For the period 1947-81, the resulting correlation coefficients are as follows: -.22 (criminal homicide), .25 (robbery), .35 (burglary), and -.41 (auto theft). Of these, the burglary and auto theft coefficients are statistically different from zero at the 5 percent level of probability.

DOES PUNISHMENT DETER CRIME?

Gordon Tullock

Traditionally there have been three arguments for the punishment of criminals. The first of these is that punishment is morally required or, another way of putting the same thing, that it is necessary for the community to feel morally satisfied. I will not discuss this further. The two remaining explanations are that punishment deters crime and that it may rehabilitate the criminal. The rehabilitation argument was little used before about 1800, presumably because the punishments in vogue up to that time had little prospect of producing any positive effect upon the moral character of the criminal.[1]

But with the turn to imprisonment as the principal form of punishment—a movement which occurred in the latter part of the 18th and early part of the 19th century—the idea that the prison might "rehabilitate" the prisoner became more common. The word "penitentiary" was coined with the intent of describing a place where the prisoner has the time and the opportunity to repent of his sins and resolve to follow a more socially approved course of action after his release. The idea that prisons would rehabilitate the criminal and that this was their primary purpose gradually replaced the concept of deterrence as the principal publicly announced justification for the punishment system. I should like to defer discussing my views as to why this occurred until the latter part of this article, but here I should like to point out that, whatever the motive or the reason for this change, it certainly was not the result of careful scientific investigation.

So far I have been able to discover, there were no efforts to test the deterrent effect of punishment scientifically until about 1950. At that time, several studies were made investigating the question whether the death penalty deterred murder more effectively than life imprisonment. These studies showed that it did not, but they were extremely primitive statistically. This is not to criticize the scholars who made them. Computers were not then readily available, the modern statistical techniques based on the computer had not yet been fully developed, and, last but by no means least, the scholars who undertook the work were not very good statisticians. Under the circumstances, we cannot blame

Reprinted with permission of the author and publisher from *The Public Interest*, No. 36 (Summer, 1974), pp. 103-111. © 1974 by National Affairs, Inc.

them for the inadequacies of their work, but neither should we give much weight to their findings.

Moreover, even if it were the case that the death penalty did not deter murder, it would not automatically follow that deterrence does not work in general. The argument is frequently made that life imprisonment is actually a more severe punishment than the death penalty and it might turn out to be true—at least in the eyes of potential murderers. If this were the case, then one would anticipate that life imprisonment would have a greater deterrent effect than would execution. But in any event, the findings obtained in these early studies were largely the result of their very primitive statistical techniques.

Statistically testing deterrence is not easy because the prospect of punishment obviously is not the *only* thing that affects the frequency with which crimes are committed. The crime rate varies with the degree of urbanization, the demographic composition of the population, the distribution of wealth, and many other circumstances. Some statistical technique is necessary to take care of these factors—and such techniques are now available. Using multiple regression (or, in a few cases, a complicated variant on the Chi-Square test), it is possible to put figures on each of these variables into the same equation and to see how much they influence the dependent variable which, in this case, is the rate of a specific crime. Although there are difficulties, this procedure will give a set of numbers called coefficients that are measures of the effect of *each* of the purported causative factors on the rate of commission of the given crime. If punishment deters crime, it will show up in these figures as a coefficient that is both significant and negative. A number of other things in the equation may also show up as affecting the crime rate, but the purpose of this article is to discuss only whether *punishment* does or does not deter crime.

One of the basic problems with any kind of statistical research in the field of criminology is the appallingly poor quality of the data. Any study will have a great deal of what the statistician calls "random noise" in it. Most of the studies mentioned below use the FBI's *Uniform Crime Report* statistics, and almost all of the authors have made comments about how bad these statistics are. I am happy to say that the Law Enforcement Assistance Administration has begun a project aimed at a sharp improvement in crime statistics, and hence we can anticipate that such research will be a great deal easier in the future. All of the studies I will report are based on the earlier and poorer statistics, but in about a year or so there should be a new generation of studies drawing upon the much better data that will be available at that time.

The recent studies in deterrence come partly from economists and partly from sociologists. As an economist myself, I may be pardoned for starting with the economic studies, but I should say that, due to the long delay that intervenes between research and publication, it is not at all obvious which discipline actually had priority.

Most economists who give serious thought to the problem of crime immediately come to the conclusion that punishment will indeed deter crime. The reason is perfectly simple: demand curves slope downward. If you increase the cost of something, less will be consumed. Thus, if you increase the cost of committing a crime, there will be fewer crimes. The elasticity of the demand curve, of course, might be low, in which case the effect might be small, but there should be at least <u>some</u> effect.

Economists, of course, would not deny that there are other factors that affect the total number of crimes. Unemployment, for example, quite regularly raises the amount of crime and, at least under modern conditions, changes in the age composition of the population seem to be closely tied to changes in the crime rate. The punishment variable, however, has the unique characteristic of being fairly easy to change by government action. Thus, if it does have an effect, we should take advantage of that fact.

The 19th-century utilitarians had drawn this conclusion, and when economists in the 1950s and early 1960s began turning their attention to the problem of deterrence, this rather simple application of economic theory was one of the first things that occurred to them.[2] The first econometric test of this theoretical deduction from economics was performed by one of Gary Becker's graduate students, Arleen Smigel Leibowitz, in her Master's thesis.[3] The basic design of this research project was reasonably sophisticated, although, as can be seen below, it has been improved upon since then. Leibowitz used as her basic data the crime rate and the punishment for a number of different crimes in each state in the United States. She took into account both the severity of punishment (i.e., the average prison sentence) and the probability that punishment will actually be imposed (i.e., the percentage of crimes whose perpetrators are caught and sent to prison). A number of essentially sociological factors that might affect the crime rate were also included in her multiple regressions. Leibowitz's findings revealed an unambiguous deterrence effect on each of the crimes studied—that is, when other factors were held constant, the states which had a higher level of punishment showed fewer crimes. Such crimes as rape and murder were deterred by punishment just as well as (indeed, perhaps better than) burglary and robbery.

Another of Becker's students, Isaac Ehrlich, in his doctoral dissertation went over much of the same ground as Leibowitz but with a much more sophisticated and careful statistical methodology. The results, which are available in full text in his dissertation and in a somewhat abridged form in an article,[4] once again indicate that punishment does deter crime.·

Further work along the same general lines was carried out by Llad Phillips, Harold L. Votey, Jr., and John Howell. In general, these scholars used the same basic data and analytical methods as Leibowitz and Ehrlich, and confirmed their findings. More recently, this group of scholars has used the same data and similar methods in an effort to produce more detailed and specific results.[5] These studies, which are of great interest in themselves, are relevant to our present purpose only in that, as a sort of by-product, they contain further confirmation of the basic finding that punishment does deter crime. Further, Phillips has run a time-series test using national data in his multiple regression to supplement the cross-sectional tests on state data.[6] It also produced similar results. Last along this particular line, Morgan Reynolds in his doctoral dissertation has treated the same basic research design en route to some new results in another area.[7]

In addition to these studies using essentially the same data on crime and punishment in the 50 states, there are two important studies using different data. Michael Block compared the crime rates for Los Angeles police districts with the likelihood in each of these districts that offenders would be caught and sent to prison, and found a clear deterrence effect.[8] And R.A. Carr-Hill and N.H. Stern carried out a study using data drawn from England and Wales and, once again, determined that punishment does deter crime.[9]

Joseph Magaddino and Gregory Krohm, using California county data, have begun work which, from the results shown by their first regressions, apparently will lead to the same conclusion.[10] David Sjoquist and Phillips, Votey, and Donald Maxwell investigated somewhat different problems but their statistical outcomes provide further support for the deterrence theory.[11]

Finally, some students under my direction attempted to make a cost-benefit analysis of certain property crimes, primarily burglary, from the standpoint of the criminal—that is, they looked into the question of whether crime does pay. The data were particularly bad in this area, as the reader can well imagine, but they supported the conclusion that most people who took up the profession of burglary had made a sensible career choice. They did not make very much from burglary, but they were not very high-quality laborers and would have done as badly (or worse) if they had elected honest employment.[12] This is not of direct relevance to the deterrence hypothesis, but it does seem to indicate that at least some criminals make fairly rational decisions with respect to their careers, and hence that raising the price of crime would presumably reduce the frequency with which it is committed.

Recently this point of view has been questioned by a short study by Michael Sesnowitz.[13] (The article was commented upon by Krohm and a reply was made by Sesnowitz.[14]) Following an approach rather similar to that used by my students, Sesnowitz found that burglary did not pay in Pennsylvania. Basically, the difference between Sesnowitz's results and those which I would have expected comes from the fact that there are no data on the amount of time served by burglars in Pennsylvania who are sentenced to jail rather than prison. Sesnowitz assumed that the average jail sentence was the same as the average prison sentence for burglary (43 months). But since it is illegal in Pennsylvania for anyone to spend more than 23 months in jail (as opposed to prison), it is most unlikely that this is so; and if adjustments for this discrepancy are made, the results wind up rather similar to those obtained by my students. Incidentally, Pennsylvania apparently does have an exceptionally high punishment level for burglaries—and, correspondingly, an exceptionally low rate of burglaries, just as the deterrence hypothesis would predict.

So much for the economists; let us now turn to the sociologists. All the economists I have cited began their studies under the impression that punishment *would* deter crime. All the sociologists I am about to cite began under the impression that it *would not* and indeed, took up their statistical tools with the intent of confirming what was then the conventional wisdom in their field—that crime cannot be deterred by punishment. When they found out they were wrong, they quite honestly published their results, although they found it rather difficult to get their work accepted in the more conventional sociological journals.

The first of these sociologists was Jack Gibbs, who published a study in the *Social Science Quarterly* which indicated that punishment did indeed deter crime.[15] His statistical methods were basically rather different from those used by the economists—indeed, speaking as an economist, I would say they were more primitive; but the fact that the same conclusion comes from two different statistical techniques is further confirmation of its validity. The publication of this paper set off a spate of other papers by Louis Gray and David Martin, Frank Bean and Robert Cushing, and Charles Tittle.[16] All of these scholars took up their cudgels with the intention of demonstrating that Gibbs was wrong, and all ended up agreeing with him. In the process, they greatly expanded and improved upon his work. Moreover, they continued using statistical tools that were somewhat different from those that had been employed by the economists; hence, their work can be taken as an independent confirmation of the economists' approach.

The sociologists were very much interested in a problem that had also concerned the economists, but not so vitally. This is the question whether the severity of the sentence or the likelihood that it will be imposed is more important in deterring crime. In my opinion, this is not a very important question. Suppose a potential criminal has a choice between two punishment systems: One gives each person who commits burglary a one-in-100 chance of serving one year in prison,[17] in the other there is a one-in-1,000 chance of serving 10 years. It is not obvious to me that burglars would be very differently affected by these two punishment systems, although in one case there is a heavy sentence with a low probability of conviction, and in the other a lighter sentence with a higher probability of conviction.

I would suggest that the appropriate technique is simply to divide the average sentence by the frequency with which it is imposed, and to use that as the deterrent measure. Most of the sociologists and a good many of the economists mentioned above have attempted to determine which of these two variables is more important. Leaving aside my theoretical objections, I do not think the statistics are accurate enough for the results obtained from these tests to be of much value. Be that as it may, more often than not the researchers have found that the frequency with which the punishment is applied is of greater importance than its severity.

The first studies in this field, the ones I criticized at the beginning of my survey of the empirical literature, dealt with the death penalty.

Recently Ehrlich has returned to this problem and, by using a much more sophisticated method, has demonstrated a very sizeable deterrence payoff to the death penalty for murder.[18] His figures indicate that each execution prevents between 8 and 20 murders. Unfortunately, the data available for this study were not what one would hope for, so not as much reliance can be put upon his results as one normally would give to work by such a sophisticated econometrician. Earlier, and using a quite different set of statistics and a different method, I arranged to have a graduate student do a preliminary study of the same issue; his results showed that each execution prevented two murders. Here again, however, the data were bad and the methods were suitable only for a preliminary exploration.[19]

It should be emphasized that the question of whether the death penalty deters murder is a different one from the question of whether we wish to have the death penalty. One widespread minor crime is failing to return to the parking meter and put in a coin when the time expires. I take if that we could reduce the frequency with which this crime is committed by boiling all offenders in oil. I take it, also, that no one would favor this method of deterrence. *Thus, the fact that we can deter a crime by a particular punishment is not a sufficient argument for use of that punishment.*

In discussing the concept of deterrence, I find that a great many people seem to feel that, although it would no doubt work with respect to burglary and other property crimes, it is unlikely to have much effect on crimes of impulse, such as rape and many murders. They reason that people who are about to kill their wives in a rage are totally incapable of making any calculations at all. But this is far from obvious. The prisoners in Nazi concentration camps must frequently have been in a state of well-justified rage against some of their guards; yet this almost never led to their using violence against the guards, because punishment—which, if they were lucky, would be instant death, but was more likely to be death by torture—was so obvious and so certain. Even in highly emotional situations, we retain some ability to reason, albeit presumably not so well as normally.

It would take much greater provocation to lead a man to kill his wife if he knew that, as in England in the 1930s, committing murder meant a two-out-of-three chance of meeting the public executioner within about two months than if—as is currently true in South

Africa—there were only a one-in-100 chance of being executed after about a year's delay.[20]

Another example can be drawn from the American South. Before about 1950, there was a great deal of violence among blacks, particularly on Saturday nights. The local authorities took the view that this was an inherent matter of black character, and hence were reluctant to punish it severely. It has been pointed out that the reluctance of the police to punish such "black" traits was probably the principal reason for their existence. A black who slashed another black's face with a razor on Saturday night would probably merely be reproved by the police and, at most, would get a short term in jail. A white who did the same thing to another white would probably get several years in prison. The difference between the statistical frequency with which blacks and whites performed this kind of act is thus explicable in terms of the deterrence effect of punishment as it was then administered.

It should be noted that thus far I have said nothing whatsoever about how well-informed criminals or potential criminals are as to the punishments for each crime in each state. For punishment to have a deterrent effect, potential criminals must have at least some information about its likely severity and frequency. Presumably, the effect of variations in punishment would be greater if criminals were well-informed than if they were not. In practice, of course, potential criminals are not very well-informed about these things, but they do have some information.

Reports of crimes and punishments are a major part of most newspapers. It is true that most intellectuals tend to skip over this part of the newspaper, but the average person is more likely to read it than some things that appeal to intellectuals. And an individual who is on the verge of committing a crime or had already taken up a career of crime is apt to be much more interested in crime stories than is the average man. He should have, therefore, a rough idea of the severity of punishments and of the probability that they will be imposed. This information should affect the likelihood that he will choose to commit a given crime.

Nevertheless, the information that he will have is likely to be quite rough. Undoubtedly, if we could somehow arrange for people to have accurate information on these matters, we would get much better coefficients on our multiple regression equations for the deterrence effect of punishment. But since governments have a motive to lie—i.e., to pretend that punishment is more likely and more severe than it actually is—it is unlikely that we can do much about improving this information. Still, the empirical evidence is clear. Even granting the fact that most potential criminals have only a rough idea as to the frequency and severity of punishment, multiple regression studies show that increasing the frequency or severity of the punishment does reduce the likelihood that a given crime will be committed.

Finally, I should like to turn to the issue of why "rehabilitation" became the dominant rationale of our punishment system in the latter part of the 19th century and has remained so up to the present, in spite of the absence of any scientific support. The reasons, in my opinion, have to do with the fallacy, so common in the social sciences, that "all good things go together." If we have the choice between preventing crime by training the criminal to be good—i.e., rehabilitating him—or deterring crime by imposing unpleasantness on criminals, the former is the one we would *like* to choose.

The Reverend Sydney Smith, a follower of the deterrence theory, said a prison should be "a place of punishment, from which men recoil with horror—a place of real suffering, painful to the memory, terrible to the imagination . . . a place of sorrow and wailing, which should be entered with horror and quitted with earnest resolution never to return to such misery. . . ."[21] This is an exaggeration. Our prisons do not have to be that bad; the deprivation of liberty in itself may be a sufficiently effective punishment. But in any case, deterrence necessarily involves the deliberate infliction of harm.

If, on the other hand, we can think of the prison as a kind of educational institution that rehabilitates criminals, we do not have to consciously think of ourselves as injuring people. It is clearly more appealing to think of solving the criminal problem by means that are themselves not particularly unpleasant than to think of solving it by methods that are unpleasant. But in this case we do not have the choice between a pleasant and an unpleasant method of dealing with crime. We have an unpleasant method—deterrence—that works, and a pleasant method—rehabilitation—that (at least so far) never has worked. Under the circumstances, we have to opt either for the deterrence method or for a higher crime rate.

Footnotes

[1] Of course, they might prevent him from committing the crime by making it physically impossible. Cutting off both hands of a forger and hanging them about his neck probably had no effect on his desire to commit forgery, but certainly made it very hard to do.

[2] See Gary Becker, "Crime and Punishment: An Economic Approach," *Journal of Political Economy*, 76 (March/April, 1968), pp. 169-217. See, also, Gordon Tullock, "The Welfare Costs of Tariffs, Monopolies, and Theft," *Western Economic Journal*, 5 (June, 1967), pp. 224-32; and "An Economic Approach to Crime," *Social Science Quarterly*, 50 (June, 1969), pp. 59-71.

[3] Arleen Smigel Leibowitz, "Does Crime Pay: An Economic Analysis" (unpublished Master's thesis, Columbia University, 1965).

[4] Isaac Ehrlich, "Participation in Illegitimate Activities: An Economic Analysis" (unpublished Ph.D. dissertation, Columbia University, 1970); and "Participation in Illegitimate Activities: A Theoretical and Empirical Investigation," *Journal of Political Economy*, 81 (May/June, 1973), pp. 521-65.

[5] Harold L. Votey, Jr. and Llad Phillips, *Economic Crimes: Their Generation, Deterrence, and Control* (Springfield, Va.: U.S. Clearinghouse for Federal Scientific and Technical Information, 1969); Harold L. Votey and Llad Phillips, "The Law Enforcement Production Function," *Journal of Legal Studies*, 1 (June, 1972); Llad Phillips and Harold L. Votey, Jr., "An Economic Analysis of the Deterrent Effect of Law Enforcement on Criminal Activity," *Journal of Criminal Law, Criminology, and Police Science*, 63 (September, 1972); and Llad Phillips and Harold L. Votey, Jr., "The Control of Criminal Activity: An Economic Analysis," in *Handbook of Criminology*, ed. by Daniel Glaser (Chicago: Rand McNally & Co., forthcoming).

[6] Llad Phillips, "Crime Control: The Case for Deterrence," in *The Economics of Crime and Punishment*, ed. by Simon Rottenberg (Washington, D.C.: American Enterprise Institute for Public Policy Research, 1973), pp. 65-84.

[7] Morgan Reynolds, "Crimes for Profit: The Economics of Theft" (unpublished Ph.D. dissertation, University of Wisconsin, 1971).

[8] Michael Block, "An Economic Approach to Theft" (Stanford University, mimeographed paper).

[9] R.A. Carr-Hill and N.H. Stern, *An Econometric Model of the Supply and Control of Recorded Offenses in England and Wales*, rev. (University of Sussex: School of Social Science, 1972).

[10] Joseph P. Magaddino and Gregory C. Krohm (untitled paper, in progress).

[11] See David L. Sjoquist, "Property Crime and Economic Behavior: Some Empirical Results," *American Economic Review*, 83, no. 3 (1973); and Llad Phillips, Harold L. Votey, Jr., and Donald Maxwell, "Crime, Youth, and the Labor Market," *Journal of Political Economy*, 80 (May/June, 1972).

[12] William E. Cobb, "Theft and the Two Hypotheses," in *The Economics of Crime and Punishment*, ed. by Simon Rottenberg (Washington, D.C.: The American Enterprise Institute for Public Policy Research, 1973), pp. 19-30; Gregory C. Krohm, "The Pecuniary Incentives of Property Crime," *idem.*, pp. 31-34; and J.P. Gunning, Jr., "How Profitable is Burglary," *idem.*, pp. 35-58.

[13] See Michael Sesnowitz, "The Returns to Burglary," *Western Economic Journal*, 10 (December, 1972), pp. 177-81.

[14] Gregory C. Krohm, "An Alternative View of the Returns to Burglary," *Western Economic Journal*, 11 (September, 1973), pp. 364-7; and Michael Sesnowitz, "The Returns to Burglary: An Alternative to the Alternative," *idem.*, pp. 368-70.

[15] Jack Gibbs, "Crime, Punishment, and Deterrence," *Southwestern Social Science Quarterly*, 48 (March, 1968), pp. 515-30.

[16] Louis N. Gray and J. David Martin, "Punishment and Deterrence: Another Analysis of Gibbs' Data," *Social Science Quarterly*, 50

(September, 1969), pp. 389-95; Frank D. Bean and Robert G. Cushing, "Criminal Homicide, Punishment, and Deterrence: Methodological and Substantive Reconsiderations," *Social Science Quarterly*, 52 (September, 1971), pp. 277-89; and Charles R. Tittle, "Crime Rates and Legal Sanctions," *Social Problems*, 16 (Spring, 1969), pp. 409-23.

[17] This is actually somewhat higher than the risk that burglars now face in most parts of the United States.

[18] Isaac Ehrlich, "The Deterrent Effect of Capital Punishment: A Question of Life and Death." This is to be published in the *American Economic Review*.

[19] Since I cannot possible claim to have read everything that has ever been written on the subject, I have been conducting part of my research in this area by asking people who hear my speeches or read my papers to tell me if they know of any other articles or books in which the effectiveness of deterrence has been tested in a reasonably scientific manner. I have never received a positive response to this question, but I repeat it here.

[20] These figures are for blacks killing blacks, not for blacks killing whites, or, for that matter, for whites killing whites.

[21] Sydney Smith, *On the Management of Prisons* (London: Warde, Locke and Company, 1822), pp. 226, 232.

AN ECONOMIC APPROACH TO CRIME[1]

Gordon Tullock

Among the various approaches to the study of crime, the economic perspective has been one of the least developed and utilized.[2] The purposes of this article are to demonstrate the utility of the economic perspective and to present some simple computational tools in two areas of the law which the reader is likely to have fairly extensive personal experience—motor vehicle code violations and tax evasion. In the case of the former, we are not only fully experienced, but we also have a very good and clear idea in our minds of the consequences of the violation. While our knowledge and experience in regard to tax evasion are rather less than those concerning violations of the traffic code, most of us have at least contemplated padding our expenses on the income tax form, and we find very little difficulty in understanding why other people actually do it fairly regularly.

In addition to reader knowledge based on experience, there is a further advantage to discussing motor vehicle offenses and tax evasion. The customary element in such laws is extremely small. Most of our laws on crime came down from great antiquity and hence contain all sorts of quaint nooks and corners. The motor vehicle law is almost entirely a creation of the 20th century and is periodically changed quite drastically. Similarly, continuously changed by both legislative enactment and the actions of various administrative bodies. Thus, we do not have to deal with the weight of immemorial tradition when we turn to these problems.

Illegal Parking

To begin, let us consider the most common and simplest of all violations of the law, illegal parking. This is a new problem. In the days of yore, there were not enough idle vehicles to require special parking laws; when, however, common men began to buy automobiles, the number of vehicles was such that simply permitting people to park where they wished along the side of the street led to very serious congestion. The number of spaces was limited, and rationing on a first come, first served basis seems to have been felt to be unsatisfactory.[3]

Reprinted from *Social Science Quarterly*, vol. 50, No. 1, June 1969, pp. 59-71, by permission of the author and the University of Texas Press. © 1969 by the Southwestern Social Science Association.

In any event, the proper governmental bodies decided that there should be a "fairer" distribution of parking space, and it was decided that individuals should vacate spaces at some specified time, frequently an hour, after they occupied them.

The question then arose as to how to assure compliance. The method chosen was to fine noncompliance. The police were instructed to "ticket" cars which parked beyond the time limit, and the owners of the ticketed cars were then fined a small sum, say ten dollars. Thus, the individual could chose between removing his car within the prescribed period or leaving it and running some chance of being forced to pay ten dollars. Obviously, the size of the fine and the likelihood that any given car owner would be caught would largely determine how much overparking was done. The individual would, in effect, be confronted with a "price list" to overpark, and would normally do so only if the inconvenience of moving his car was greater than the properly discounted cost of the fine.[4]

Not all overparking is the result of a deliberate decision, however. Clearly a good deal of it comes from absentmindedness, and part is the result of factors not very thoroughly under control of the car owner. Nevertheless, we do not in general feel that the fine should be remitted. The absence of a criminal intent, or indeed of any intent at all, is not regarded as an excuse. When I was working in the Department of State in Washington, I served under a man who got several parking tickets a week. I think that I knew him well enough to be sure that all of these violations occurred without any conscious intent on his part. He would get involved in some project and forget that he was supposed to move his car. The District of Columbia was levying what amounted to a tax on him for being absentminded.

As far as I could tell, the police force of Washington, D.C., was not particularly annoyed with my superior. Apparently, they thought the revenue derived paid for the inconvenience of issuing tickets and occasionally towing his car away. Suppose, however, they had wanted to make him stop violating the parking laws. It seems highly probable that a a drastic increase in the fines would have been sufficient. Absentmindedness about ten dollars does not necessarily imply absent mindedness about 100 or even 1,000 dollars. With higher fines he would have felt more pressure to train himself to remember, to avoid parking on the public streets as much as possible, and to arrange for his secretary to remind him. Thus, the fact that he was not engaging in any calculations at all when he committed these "crimes" does not indicate that he would not respond to higher penalties by ceasing to commit them.

So far, however, we have simply assumed that the objective is to enforce a particular law against parking. The question of whether this law is sensible, or how much effort should be put into enforcing it, has not been discussed. In order to deal with this problem, let us turn to a more modern technology and discuss a metered parking area. In such areas the government in essence is simply renting out space to people who want to use it. It may not be using a market-clearing price because it may have some objectives other than simply providing the service at a profit, but this does not seriously alter the problem. For simplicity, let us assume that it is charging market-clearing prices. It would then attempt to maximize total revenue, including the revenue from fines and the revenue from the coins inserted in the parking meter minus the cost of the enforcement system. We need not here produce an equation or attempt to solve this problem, but clearly it is a perfectly ordinary problem in operations research, and there is no reason why we should anticipate any great difficulty with it.

Other Motor Vehicle Laws

However, parking is clearly a very minor problem; in fact, it was chosen for discussion simply because it is so easy. In essence, there is very little here except calculation of exactly the same sort that is undertaken every day by businessmen. For a slightly more complicated problem, let us consider another traffic offense—speeding. Presumably, the number of deaths from auto accidents, the extent of personal injuries and the material damage are all functions of the speed at which cars travel.[5] By enforcing a legal maximum on such speed, we can reduce all of them. On the other hand, a legal maximum speed will surely inconvenience at least some people, and may inconvenience a great many. The strictly material cost of lowering speeds is easily approximated by computing the additional time spent in traveling and multiplying this by the hourly earning power of an average member of the population. This is, of course, only an approximation, leaving out of account such factors as the pleasure some people get out of speed and the diversion of economic activity which would result from the slowing of traffic. Nevertheless, we could use this approximation[6] and the costs of deaths, injuries and material damage from auto accidents to work out the optimal speed limit, which would be simply the limit which minimized total costs in all of these categories. The computation would be made in "social" terms because the data would be collected for the whole population. Individuals, however, could regard these figures as actuarial approximations for their personal optima.

To the best of my knowledge, no one has ever performed these calculations in a reasonably direct and precise way. Presumably the reason for the omission is an unwillingness to consciously and openly put a value on deaths and injuries which can then be compared with the strictly material costs of delay. When I point out to people that the death toll from highway accidents could be reduced by simply lowering the speed limit (and improving enforcement), they normally show great reluctance to give any consideration to the subject. They sometimes try to convince themselves that the reduction would not have the predicted effect, but more commonly they simply shift quickly to another subject. They are unwilling, for reasons of convenience, to approve a substantial lowering of the speed limit, but they do not like to consciously balance their convenience against deaths. Nevertheless, this is the real reasoning behind the speed limits. We count the costs of being forced to drive slowly and the costs of accidents, and choose the speed limit which gives us the best outcome. Since we are unwilling to do this consciously, we probably do a bad job of computing. If we were willing to look at the matter in the open, consciously to put a value on human life, we could no doubt get better results.

As an example of this reluctance to think about the valuation we are willing to put upon deaths and injury in terms of our own convenience, a colleague of mine undertook a study of the methods used by the Virginia Highway Commission in deciding how to improve the roads. He found that they were under orders to consider speed, beauty, and safety in presenting projects for future work. The beauty was taken care of by simply earmarking a fixed part of the appropriations for roadside parks, etc. For speed they engaged in elaborate research on highway use and had statistical techniques for predicting the net savings in time from various possible changes. It was the possibility of improving these techniques which led them to invite my colleague to make his study. For safety, on the other hand, they had no system at all.

It was clear that they did take safety into account in designing roads, and spent quite a bit of money on various methods of reducing the likelihood of accidents. They did not, however, have any formula or rule for deciding either how much should be spent on safety or in what specific projects it should be invested. They must have had some trade-off rule which they applied. This rule, however, remained buried in their subconscious even though they used fairly elaborate and advanced techniques for other problems. This is particularly remarkable when it is remembered that, given any exchange value, the computations of the amount to be spent on safety would be fairly easy.

If, for example, it is decided that we will count one fatal accident as "worth" $500,000 in inconvenience to drivers (measured in increased travel time), then, with statistics on accidents and volume of traffic, it would be possible to work out how much should be spent on safety, some such "price" for accidents must have taken some part of its reasoning, but rather sophisticated engineers were unwilling to admit, probably even to themselves,, that this was so. Perhaps more surprising, my colleague fully approved of their attitude. Basically, a "scientific" type, with a great interest in statistical decision theory, he felt that here was one place where careful reasoning was undesirable. He did not want to consider ratios between deaths and convenience himself, did not want the people who designed the highways on which he drove to consciously consider them, and did not want to discuss the subject with me.

But even if we do not like to critically examine our decision process, clearly the decision as to the speed limit is made by balancing the inconveniences of a low limit against the deaths and injuries to be expected from a high one. The fact that we are not willing to engage in conscious thought on the problem is doubly unfortunate, because it is difficult enough so that it is unlikely that we can reach optimal decisions by any but the most careful and scientific procedures. The problem is stochastic on both sides since driving at a given speed does not certainly cause an accident; it only creates a probability of an accident. Similarly, our convenience is not always best served by exceeding the speed limit, so we have only a stochastic probability of being inconvenienced. There will also be some problems of gathering data which we do not now have (mainly because we have not thought clearly about the problem) and making reasonable estimates of certain parameters. In order to solve the problem we need a table of probabilities rather like Table 5-I. Obviously, with this table and one more thing, a conversion factor for deaths and delay, we could readily calculate the speed limit which would minimize the "cost" of using the road.

Table 5-I. Effects of Speed Limits

Speed Limit (MPH)	Deaths per 100,000,000 Miles	Costs of Delay
10	1	$50,000,000,000.00
20	2	35,000,000,000.00
30	4	22,500,000,000.00
40	8	15,500,000,000.00
50	16	5,000,000,000.00
60	32	2,000,000,000.00
70	64	500,000,000.00

Equally obviously, no direct calculation of this sort is now undertaken, but our speed limits are set by a sort of weighing of accident prevention against inconvenience. The only difference between our present methods and the one I have outlined is that we are frightened of having to admit that we use a conversion ratio in which lives are counted as worth only some finite amount of inconvenience, and we refuse to make the computations at a conscious level and hence are denied the use of modern statistical methods.

Having set a speed limit, we now turn to its enforcement. If, for example, the limit is 50 MPH, then it does not follow that the people who drive over that speed will automatically have accidents. Nor does it follow that driving at 51 MPH is very much more likely to lead to an accident than driving a 50 MPH. The use of a simple limit law is dictated by the problems of enforcement rather than the nature of the control problem itself. If we had some way of simply charging people for the use of the streets, with the amount per mile varying with the speed,[8] this would permit a better adjustment than a simple speed limit. In practice, the police and courts do something rather like this by charging much higher fines for people who greatly exceed the speed limit. Let us, however, confine ourselves to the simple case where we have a single speed limit, with no higher fines for exceeding it by a sizable amount.

Our method of enforcing this law is in some ways most peculiar. In the first place, if a citizen sees someone violating this law and reports it, the police will refuse to do anything about it. With one specific exception, which we will footnote in a moment, you cannot be penalized for speeding unless a police officer sees you do it. Think what burglars would give for a similar police practice in their field of endeavor.

A second peculiarity is that the penalty assessed is unconnected with the attitude of mind of the person who violates the speed limit.[9] Driving at 70 MPH may get you a fine of 100 dollars or a ten-year sentence, depending upon the occurrence of events over which you have no control. Suppose, for example, two drivers each take a curve in the highway at 70. The first finds a police car on the other side, gets a ticket and pays a fine. The second encounters a tractor driving down his side of the road and a column of cars on the other side. In the resulting crash, the tractor driver is killed, and the outcome may be a ten-year sentence for the driver of the car.[10] We can assume both men exceeded the speed limit, for the same motives, but the second had bad luck. Normally we like to have penalties depend upon what the defendant did, not on external circumstances beyond his control. (The only other situation in which this kind of thing is done involves the rule which makes a death caused while committing a felony murder regardless of the intent.)

The peculiarity of this procedure is emphasized when it is remembered that the man who risks being sent up for ten years for killing someone in an accident almost certainly had no intent to do so. He was driving at a high speed in order to get somewhere in a hurry, an act which normally leads to a moderate fine when detected. The heavy sentence comes not from the wickedness of this act, but from the fact that he drew an unlucky number in a lottery. The case is even clearer in those not terribly rare cases where the accident arises not from conscious violation of the law but from incompetence or emotional stress (losing one's head). In ordinary driving we frequently encounter situations where a small error in judgment can cause deaths. A man who has no intent to drive carelessly may simply be a bad judge of distance and try to pass a truck where there is insufficient room. An excitable person may "freeze" when some emergency arises, with the result that there is an accident which could easily have been prevented. Both of these cases might well lead to prison terms in spite of the complete lack of "criminal intent" on the part of the defendant. "If a driver, in fact, adopts a manner of driving which the jury thinks dangerous to other road users . . . then on the issue of guilt, it matters not whether he was deliberately reckless, careless, momentarily inattentive, or doing his incompetent best."[11]

As anybody who has studied game theory knows, a mixed strategy may pay off better than a pure strategy. It may be, therefore, that the combination of three different treatments is better than a simpler rule providing a single and fairly heavy penalty for speeding, regardless of whether you hit anyone or happen to encounter a policeman while engaged in the criminal act. But, although we must admit this possibility, it seems more likely that a single penalty based on the intent of the individual would work better in preventing speeding. The probable reason for the rather peculiar set of rules I have outlined is simply the functioning of the court system. If someone who disliked me alleged that he had seen me speeding and I denied it, the court would have to decide who was lying without much to go on except the expressions on our faces. Since "dishonesty can lie honesty out of countenance any day of the week if there is anything to be gained by it," this is clearly an uncertain guide. Thus, under our current court system, permitting people to initiate prosecutions for speeding by stating that they had seen someone doing so would almost certainly mean that innumerable spite cases would be brought before the courts, and that the courts would make many, many mistakes in dealing with them.

Similarly, the use of two sets of penalties for speeding, depending on factors not under the defendant's control, is probably the result of judicial performance. Charging a very heavy fine or relatively brief imprisonment for every speeding conviction would very likely be resisted by judges who do not really think speeding is very serious unless it kills somebody. That this is the restriction cannot strictly be proven, but at least some evidence can be provided for it. In Virginia, as in many states, multiple convictions for traffic offenses can result in removal of the driving license. The state has encountered real difficulty in getting its judges to carry out this provision. Under the conditions of modern life the deprivation of a driver's license is a real hardship, and judges apparently do not like to impose it for a speeding offense simply because the offender has been convicted twice before. Similarly, if a license is suspended, the courts are unlikely to inflict a very heavy penalty on the man who drives anyhow, provided he avoids killing someone.[12]

It is probable that problems of judicial efficiency account for another peculiarity of the motor traffic code; i.e., it is almost impossible for an individual to defend himself against the accusation. Normally the police officer's testimony is accepted regardless of other evidence. Further, in general, the penalty exacted for the average minor violation of the code is small if the defendant pleads guilty, but high if he does not. Parking offenses, for example, may very commonly be settled for one or two dollars on a guilty plea, but cost ten to twenty if you choose to plead not guilty. This amounts to paying the defendant to plead guilty. As almost anyone who has had any experience with a traffic court is aware, most of the people who get tickets are indeed guilty, but those who are not guilty normally plead guilty anyway because of this system of enforcement.

Obviously we could apply the same line of reasoning to deal with all other parts of the traffic code. The problem is essentially a technological one. By the use of some type of exchange value and evidence obtained from statistical and other sources, we could compute a complete traffic code which would optimize some objective function. In practice we do not do this because of our reluctance to specify an exchange value for life. Nevertheless, we get much the same result, albeit with less accuracy and precision, by our present methods.

Tax Evasion

Turning now to the income tax law, we must begin by noting that apparently almost anybody can get special treatment. The present laws and regulations are a solid mass of special rules for special groups of people. There are innumerable cases where some particular wealthy man or large corporation has succeeded in obtaining special tax treatment. Nevertheless, we can consider how the existing tax code should be enforced.

Unfortunately, even the enforcement is full of loopholes. In the first place, there are a great many people (special classes that readily come to mind are doctors, waitresses, and farmers) who have special facilities for evading the income tax. It is also widely believed that certain groups (the farmers in particular) have been able to make use of their political power to see to it that the Internal Revenue Service does not pay as much attention to detecting evasion by them as by other groups. Nevertheless, we can assume that the tax code contains within it both a set of special privileges for individuals and instructions for evasion which apply only to certain classes, and hence that the true tax law is residual after we have knocked all these holes in what was originally a rather simple piece of legislation.

There are further difficulties. The individual presumably is interested in the taxes being collected from other people because he wants the government services which will be purchased by them. He would prefer to be left free of tax himself, but this is unfortunately not possible. He, in a sense, trades the tax on his own income for the benefit which he obtains from the purchase of government services by the entire community. It is by no means clear that for everyone the present amount of government services is optimal. If I felt that the total amount of government services being purchased today was excessive (i.e., that lower tax rates and lower levels of service were desirable), presumably I would feel relatively happy about systematic evasion of a tax law on the part of everyone. On the other hand, if I felt that the present level of government services was too low and the taxes should be higher, I might conceivably feel that "overenforcement" is desirable.

Even if I am happy with the present level of government expenditures, it is by no means obvious that I should be terribly much in favor of efficient enforcement of the revenue code. I might favor a revenue code which sets rates relatively high and an enforcement procedure which permits a great deal of evasion to lower rates and better enforcement procedures which brought in the same revenue. Surely I would prefer the former if I had some reason to believe that I would be particularly able to evade the taxes. But even if I assume that everyone will have about the same ability to evade, I might still prefer the higher rates and higher level of evasion. Nevertheless, it seems to me that most people would prefer the lowest possible level of tax for a given net return. I have been unable to prove that this is optimal,[13] but it does seem to me to be reasonable that this would be the appropriate social goal. In any event, that is the assumption upon which our further calculations are built. It would be relatively easy to adjust these calculations to any other assumption on this particular matter.

Table 5-II. Definitions of Symbols

C_P	=	Private cost of enforcement (includes cost of incorrect tax penalties)
C_R	=	Cost of revenue protection service
I	=	Income
I'	=	Some part of income
L_C	=	Likelihood of compliance
L_D	=	Likelihood of detection of evasion
N	=	Social return on tax (excess burden not subtracted)
P	=	Penal rate for detected noncompliance
R	=	Tax rate
T_R	=	Tax Revenue (net of direct enforcement costs)

Under these circumstances and on these assumptions, the return in taxation to the government from various levels of enforcement can be seen by Equation 1, which is fairly lengthy but really simple. (See Table 5-II for definitions of symbols.)

$$T_R = L_C \cdot R \cdot I + (1 - L_C) \cdot I' \cdot L_D \cdot P - C_R \qquad (1)$$

The first term on the right of the equal sign is the likelihood that individuals will fully comply with tax laws, multiplied by the tax rate and income. Note that this is deliberately somewhat ambiguous. It can be taken as any individual's tax payments or the payment for the economy as a whole, depending on which definition we choose for income. We add to this the probability that an individual will attempt to evade payment of taxes on all or part of his income, times the probability of detection of his evasion, times the penalty he will be compelled to pay on the evasion. This gives us the total return which the community will receive. There is, of course, the cost of maintaining the inspection and revenue collection system, which is subtracted from this output in the final term C_R.

Ignoring, for the moment, the taxpayer's propensity toward accepting risks, the conditions for a favorable decision to attempt *to evade* the tax legally payable on some particular portion of his income is

$$L_D \cdot P \cdot I' < R \cdot I' \qquad (2)$$

That is to say, if the likelihood of detection times the penalty he must pay on detection is less than the rate that he would legally pay, he would appropriately attempt to evade. It will be noted that both in this inequality and in the previous equation there is an implicit assumption that the individual will be able to pay a fine if he is found to have evaded the tax law. The reason that the individual is normally able to pay a fine is simply that in general those who get into income tax difficulties are well off.

Nevertheless, although this is a very good approximation, it is not entirely accurate. The income tax authorities do sometimes attempt to put people in prison for tax evasion. In general, the Internal Revenue Service has a dual system. If you make a "tax saving" which is relatively easy for them to detect, they will normally adjust your return and charge you a relatively modest interest payment. If, on the other hand, you do something which is quite hard to detect, which normally means a directly dishonest statement, they assess a much heavier penalty. From their standpoint no doubt this is sensible as a way of minimizing enforcement costs.

There is another peculiarity of the income tax policing process. Usually the policeman himself (i.e., the Internal Revenue man) simply assesses a deficiency on the face of the form if he does not suspect what is technically called evasion. This is usually the complete legal proceeding. In small cases the individual normally pays, although he may complain to the person making the assessment. It is highly probable that in this matter, as in other small claims litigation, there is a great deal of inaccuracy on both sides. Since these are small matters, the use of a cheap but relatively inaccurate procedure is optimal. For major matters, however, very elaborate legal proceedings may be undertaken. These proceed at first through the administrative channels of the Internal Revenue Service and turn to the regular courts only if all administrative methods are exhausted. Here one would anticipate a great deal more care and far fewer errors, and there is no doubt that this is the case.

Returning, however, to our basic equations, it will be noted that the likelihood of quiet compliance (i.e., the likelihood of the income-tax payer's making no effort to evade) is a function of the likelihood of detection of evasion as shown in Equation 3:

$$L_C = g(L_D) \tag{3}$$

The likelihood of detection of evasion is a function of two things, as shown in Equation 4:

$$L_D = h_1(C_R) + h_2(C_P) \tag{4}$$

One of these,, of course, is simply the amount of resources that we put into the revenue service. The second, however, is the resources that we force the private taxpayer to put into keeping records and filing returns and doing other things which make it easier to enforce the tax revenue code. Thus, Equation 1 was incomplete. Equation 5 shows the net social benefit, or loss from the tax, including the factor C:

$$N = L_C \cdot R \cdot I + (1 - L_C) \cdot I' \cdot L_D \cdot P - C_R - C_P \tag{5}$$

It will be noted that I have, for these computations, ignored problems of excess burden.

The term C_P is interesting and very comprehensive. It not only includes the troubles involved in filling out the income tax forms, which we all know may be considerable, but also the necessity of keeping our accounts in such form that the Internal Revenue Service may survey them. It includes the possibility that we will be audited even if we have not violated the law. It does not include any penalty which we might incur if we have violated the law, because that is included under P. It includes a number. of other things which are somewhat less obvious, however. It includes the inconvenience we might suffer occasionally when the Internal Revenue Service is investigating a potential violation of the internal revenue code by someone other than ourselves; we might, for some reason, have some evidence which the Internal Revenue Service wants and be compelled to furnish it. It also includes the possibility that the Internal Revenue Service will wrongly suspect us and will then assess an incorrect fine upon us. Lastly, of course, it includes legal expenses involved in all of the above. Thus, it is by no means a small figure.

Still, the problem is relatively easy. We should simply maximize N.[14] Examination of this equation indicates some superficially not terribly probable consequences. We could, for example, be in favor of increasing enforcement even though we know it is likely to raise our own payments. It will be noted that there is nowhere in the equation the assumption that we will obey the law and others will not. If we really believe that the government money is being spent for something worthwhile, then we make a net gain of some nature from increasing N. It is true that the N in our equation represents this net gain very crudely, since it takes a total figure rather than a marginal figure, but we need not worry about this.

As noted above, we might feel it desirable to include some kind of risk aversion factor. If the penalty for evasion of the tax code is quite large, let us say 25 times the tax that is evaded, and if we feel that there is a fair probability of the Internal Revenue Service going wrong in assessing such penalties, then our term C_P could be large. This might still maximize the value of N, but if we are risk avoiders, we might prefer a lower value of N in order to avoid the risk of being assessed such a very large penalty.

But these are refinements. Basically we could calculate an optimum tax enforcement policy from a set of equations such as those here. I think that if the reader considers his own reactions he will realize that his own attitude towards the income tax authorities is based upon something like this form of reasoning. He does, of course, hope that the income tax authorities will give him special treatment and does his best to obtain it. But insofar as this special treatment has already been taken into account, his behavior would be appropriately described by Equation 2. His behavior with respect to general social policy in this period would then be described more or less by a desire to maximize N in Equation 5. There may be some people who have strong moral feelings about their own payments under the income tax, but I have never run into them. Most of my friends will talk about the desirability of the income tax, but I also find them discussing in detail what they can get away with. In fact, I suspect that moral considerations are less important in tax enforcement than any other single part of the law.

Summary

In this article we have discussed two areas of the law with which the reader is likely to have fairly great personal experience. We have demonstrated in both cases the very simple computational tools for defining an "optimum law." Application of these computational tools would, it is true, require the development of certain empirical information we do not now have but they are nevertheless suitable guides to further work. Further, our computational tools in this respect are simply formalizations of the thought processes now used by most people in dealing with these matters.

Footnotes

[1] This article is part of a larger project in which efforts are made to apply economic reasoning to many aspects of law including more serious crimes than are discussed herein.

[2] The approach is new only in terms of the 20th century. Bentham, Mill and a number of other 19th-century scholars took a rather similar approach to crime. Unfortunately, the modern apparatus of welfare economics or cost-benefit analysis was not available to the 19th-century scholars and hence they were not able to make as strong a case for their position as can now be made. For a recent example of much the same approach see Becker (1968).

[3] We are now discussing the early development of parking regulations. The relatively recent invention of the parking meter has changed the situation drastically and will be discussed later.

[4] I am indebted to Professor Alexandre Kafka for the "price list" analogy. He insists, following his own professor, that the entire criminal code is simply a price list of various acts.

[5] Recently this relationship has been somewhat obscured by the publication of Ralph Nader's *Unsafe at Any Speed*. It is undoubtedly true that cars can be designed to reduce fatalities in accidents and, for that matter, that highways can be designed to reduce accidents. Recent discoveries of methods of reducing skidding by improved highway surfaces probably indicate that there is more potential in highway improvement than in car redesign. Nevertheless, for a given car and highway, speed kills.

[6] For those who object to approximation, more elaborate research, taking into account much more of the costs of slowing down traffic, could be undertaken.

7 Note that I am ignoring all consequences of accidents except deaths and that it is assumed that the speed limit is the only variable. These are, of course, simplifying assumptions introduced in order to make my table simple and the explanation easy. If any attempt were made to explicitly utilize the methods I suggest, much more complex data would be needed. The figures are, of course, assumed for illustrative purposes only.

8 Needless to say, the cost of driving 50 MPH in a built-up area would be higher than in the open countryside.

9 There is a partial and imperfect exception to this for certain special cases. The man who speeds to get his wife to the hospital before the birth of their child is perhaps the one who gets the most newspaper attention.

10 Note that the rule that a traffic offense is prosecuted only if seen by a police officer is not followed in the event of a serious accident. A third driver may be imagined who took the curve at the same speed and met neither the police nor the tractor. He would, of course, go off scot-free even if his offense were reported to the police.

11 Hill v. Baxter 1 QB (1958), p. 277.

12 Possibly, given the difficulties of enforcement, a restriction of the license rather than a removal might be wise. Restricting the license of a multiple offender to a limited area, including his home, a couple of shopping centers and his place of employment, together with a low speed limit, say 30 MPH, might appeal to judges who would be unwilling to remove the license totally. Judges might also be more inclined to give heavy sentences to people who violate such restrictions than to people who continue to drive to work in spite of the lack of a license.

13 I sincerely hope that some of my readers may be able to repair this admission.

14 J. Randolph Norsworthy (1965) has studied present-day Internal Revenue procedures on the assumption that they behave somewhat in

accord with the instruction of maximizing T_R. His methods are quite different from ours, but his doctoral dissertation is well worth studying.

References

Becker, Gary: "Crime and Punishment: An Economic Approach." *Journal of Political Economy*, 74:169-217, 1968.

Norsworthy, J. Randolph: *Tax Evasion*, doctoral dissertation, University of Virginia, 1965.

STANDARDS FOR DISTRIBUTING A FREE GOVERNMENT SERVICE: CRIME PROTECTION

Carl S. Shoup

A government distributing services free of direct charge must decide how much of each service each household or firm is to receive.

If, indeed, no one can be excluded from enjoyment of a service when it is rendered, and the amount received is the same for all, the decision is made when the level of service is determined.

Often, however, some degree of exclusion is practicable, or varying intensities of service may be rendered to different households or firms. Here, questions of equity and efficiency emerge, similar to those encountered in taxation. Shall a certain service, say police protection, be distributed equally among the residents of a city? What does "equally" imply? If a service is not distributed equally, what other standards, perhaps implicit, are employed?

In fact, little is known about distribution of government services by location, race, religion, income class, or other category. Usually, no record is made, no estimate attempted. The laws providing for the service are silent in this respect; the authorizing or appropriating committees of legislatures do not discuss it; budgets submitted by the executive say nothing about how a given service is to be distributed among the users. This silence reflects in part a social propensity to discriminate covertly in ways that are not tolerable in taxation, where the pattern of impact is more obvious. For example: education has been distributed unequally, by social class, race, or color, in communities that would not think of distributing the tax bill by those indicia.

Sometimes a fixed amount of free service is offered on a first-come or queuing basis; rationing is by time and patience, which are more evenly distributed than money income. More often, administrators allot a service in the light of what they infer of the legislator's or executive's aims.

The pattern of initial distribution can be evaluated only if the extent to which benefits from the service are passed forward or backward is known, or at least assumed. Again, the problem is similar to that faced in appraising taxes. The present analysis bypasses the issue of

Reprinted with permission from *Public Finance/Finances Publiques*, vol. 19 (1964) pp. 383-394.

"shifting and incidence" of benefits from government service by assuming that the benefits remain with the original recipients.

The service chosen here, for illustrative purposes, is protection of persons against crime in residential districts of a city (the analysis does not cover business districts); urban "police protection," for short, thus abstracting from all other uses of the police force, such as controlling traffic or maintaining an oppressive regime in power. To simplify the argument, all crimes are considered of equal importance. The rate of crime per capita, for a given period of time, is imagined as being computed for each residential district in the city. Equality of crime rates per capita among residential districts is taken to signify equal probability, for any person in one district compared with any person in any other district, that he will be the victim of a crime in a given time period. Such probability is taken as a measure of the product, police protection; the lower the probability, the greater the product. If every person faces the same probability, the service, police protection, is said to be distributed evenly, or equally.

It need not be assumed that equal distribution of free police protection is an optimum distribution. Even those who favor equal distribution of income need not apply this standard for any one commodity, say food, or clothing, or housing, in view of differences in consumer tastes. Still, equal distribution of police protection has enough intuitive appeal to warrant an examination of its implications, especially its implication for another intuitively attractive rule, minimization of total number of crimes in the city as a whole.

This second goal, minimization of crime, with a fixed amount of police resources available, is achieved when an increment of police input will reduce the number of crimes by the same amount no matter where it is placed within the city, or at what time of day. The marginal cost of preventing one more crime will then be the same everywhere in the city. But achievement of this goal will usually leave some of the city's districts more crime-ridden than others, that is, the rate of crime per capita will be higher in some districts than in others. Crime will have been minimized at the cost of distributing police protection unequally.

In part this inequality might be the result of differences in population of districts. Let us suppose that one of the city's districts had three times the population of another, and that initially the crime rate per capita is the same in the two districts. Let us further suppose that transfer of one policeman to the more populous district from the less populous district would prevent two more crimes in the more populous district while allowing one more crime in the less populous district. This assumption might be reasonable, because the absolute number of crimes is, of course, larger in the more populous district. The assumption becomes especially reasonable if the two districts cover about equal areas. Under these conditions, the policeman should be transferred, if number of crimes in the city as a whole is to be minimized. But after the transfer has been made, the crime rate per capita in the less populous district will be higher than before, that in the more populous district will be lower, and the crime rates per capita will therefore be unequal in the two districts. It will now be more risky to live in the less populous district than in the more populous district.

Even if the two districts are equal in population, minimization of crime will commonly result in unequal crime rates per capita among districts, because disruptive social forces, aggravated by poverty, are stronger in one than in another. It is this cause of difference in crime rates per capita that will be the subject of the following analysis, which abstracts from differences in population among districts by assuming equal population in all districts.

In this analysis, a city is divided into two residential districts, P and R. P is a district of poor households; R, of rich. P and R are equal in population and area. Initially, crime in the city as a whole is minimized, but the crime rate is higher in the poor district than in the rich.

In both districts, prevention of crime is an increasing-cost industry. As crime is reduced, it becomes more difficult to prevent one more crime. The level of difficulty is measured by the marginal cost of crime prevention. If the police force is so distributed that this level is the same in Districts P and R, so that crime is minimized, it will be only a coincidence if the rates of crime remaining in P and R are the same.

Figure 13-1 illustrates this generalization. The x-axis of the diagram measures the crime rate: the number of crimes occurring in the district in question during a given period of time.[1] The y-axis measures the marginal cost of crime prevention: this is the cost of preventing one more crime in that district during that period of time. The curve, R_0R_1, shows the cost of preventing one more crime for any given level of existing crime, in District R. Only a segment of the curve is shown. We do not know the total of crime prevented, so there is no point in trying to extend the curve out to the right where it would intersect the x-axis. The intersection would indicate the rate of crime that would be occurring if there were no police force at all. Such a question is scarcely answerable, and certainly is of no practical import. Nor is the curve extended to the left where it could cut the y-axis, indicating the marginal cost when all crime was prevented. Attainment of such a goal is quite impossible, if only because some crimes are the result of many and unforeseeable forces that happen to combine at a given time and place.

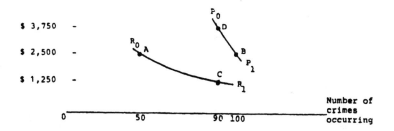

P_0P_1: Marginal cost curve for poor area.
R_0R_1: Marginal cost curve for rich area.

Figure 13-1. Differing Marginal Costs of Crime Prevention in Rich and Poor Areas of Equal Population.

In Figure 13-1, if transfer of a policeman, being paid $5,000 a year, from the rich district to the poor district would prevent two more crimes a year in the poor district and allow two more crimes a year to occur in the rich district, the marginal cost of crime prevention is the same in both districts, and is $2,500. Crime is minimized. At the same time, we assume, the number of crimes occurring is 50 a year in the rich district and 100 in the poor district. This state of affairs is reflected by Points A and B in Figure 13-1.

If, now, several policemen were transferred from the rich district to the poor district, crime would no longer be minimized. If so many policemen were transferred from District R to District P that the crime rate rose in R from 50 to 90, the crime rate in P would decline only from 100 to 90. The implied assumption of this kind of rate of transformation will be expressly stipulated in Figure 13-2. At these levels, as indicated by points C and D in Figure 13-1, the cost of preventing one more crime in R would be only $1,250; in P, $3,750. Evidently, a small reverse transfer of police service from P to R would now reduce crime in R at the rate of three per $3,750 of expenditure increase while unleashing crime in P at a rate of only one per $3,750 of expenditure reduction. There would be a net gain of two crimes prevented. Yet there is this to be said for points C and D: with this distribution of the police force, the rate of crime is equal in the two districts, at 90 per year. A resident of R now faces the same probability of being victimized by crime as does a resident of P.

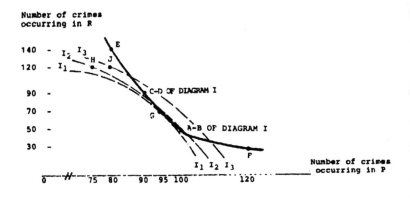

Figure 13-2. Transformation (Production-Possibility) Curve and Indifference Curves for Distribution of a Fixed Total Amount of Police Protection Between Districts P and R (of Equal Population).

One might be tempted to say that, by moving from points A and B to points C and D, equity could be achieved at the cost of economic efficiency. But this would be an incorrect assertion, for two reasons.

First, the C-D combination, equal crime rates and unequal marginal costs, is not demonstrably inefficient economically in the sense that by a reallocation of resources some individuals could be made better off without others being made worse off. Any reallocation of the police force from C-D that benefitted residents of R would harm residents of P, and vice versa.

Second, equality of crime rate in Districts R and P is not necessarily the best test of equity even on a rough, common sense basis. Perhaps the residents of P are more careless than those of R, or more interested in other goals than suppression of crime; the more law-abiding residents of R may then argue that it would be unjust to them, to aim at equalizing crime rates in the two districts. The R residents may further argue that, even if the higher crime rate (at equal marginal costs) in P is due to causes beyond control of the residents of P, more crimes in total may be being prevented in P than in R, even though the remaining crime is at a higher level in P than R. There are, say, many more policemen assigned to P than to R, even at points A-B, where marginal costs are equal but the crime rate in R is only 50 against 100 in P. This assumption that a greater total of crimes is being prevented in one district than in another is a dubious one, since we can never know what total of crimes would occur in a district if no police force at all were allocated to it. But the fact that total input is demonstrably greater—more policemen in P than in R—carries a strong, if irrational, weight in the argument. When comparison of total outputs is impossible, the desire to get an answer of some sort leads easily to a comparison of total inputs.

In the face of these conflicting interests of the different consuming groups, we can only suggest how the issue is in fact determined, by presenting the problem as one of rates of transformation and indifference patterns. Figure 13-2 serves this purpose. On the x-axis is measured the number of crimes occurring in District P; on the y-axis, the number occurring in District R. Each crime is still assumed to be equally noxious. The two districts have the same population.

The given police force may be so distributed between Districts P and R that there are 90 crimes occurring in each. This point C-D on the curve EF: it represents points C and D on Figure 13-1, the equal-protection distribution of police. Alternatively, the police force may be so distributed that 100 crimes are occurring in P but only 50 in R. This is shown by point A-B, which reflects points A and B in Figure 13-1. The line joining A-B and C-D in Figure 13-2 is the production-possibility curve for the two products, prevention of crime in P and prevention of crime in R, with a given total police force. In Figure 13-2 this line has been extended a little in both directions, to points E and F (these points are not reflected in Fig. 13-1), to emphasize the increasing cost of preventing crime in P, or in R, or in both. This production-possibility curve is convex to the origin rather than concave, as in the usual diagram, because the axes measure undesirable things, "anti-goods," rather than desirable ones. The object is to minimize the number of crimes occurring, not explicitly to maximize the number of crimes prevented (recall that we can never ascertain the latter).

When 100 crimes are occurring in P and 50 in R, a reallocation of police that reduces crime in P from 100 to 90, that is, prevents 10 crimes, leads to an increase of 40 crimes in R, where the rate rises from 50 to 90. A further transfer of policemen to P that prevents another 10 crimes, reducing the crime rate there from 90 to 80, gives rise to 50 more crimes in R, where the rate rises from 90 to 140.

On this same diagram there may be plotted a system of indifference curves. They may be community indifference curves,, or just police department curves; at any rate, whoever decides these matters has some implicit system of preferences and indifferences.

We assume that the decision maker becomes more and more concerned over an incremental crime in one district, the higher is the crime rate there compared with the other district. Consider indifference curve I_1, which passes through points J and C-D. It says, for instance, that if the crime rate were 120 in R and 80 in P (point J) an equally attractive (or unattractive!) combination would be attained by reducing crime in R by 30 and permitting an increase of crime in P by only 10, so that the rates would be 90 and 90 (point C-D).

The indifference curve is concave to the origin, rather than convex, as in the usual indifference curve diagram, since the axes measure anti-goods rather than goods. An indifference curve closer to the origin represents a preferred position. Thus, curve I_2 which passes through points H and A-B, yields a smaller total of crime in either one of the districts for a given amount of crime in the other district. If 120 crimes are occurring in R, 75 will be occurring in P on indifference curve I_2 (point H) and 80 on indifference curve I_1 (point J).

The best possible combination will be achieved at that point where the closest-in indifference curve is tangent to the crime-prevention-possibility curve. In Figure 13-2 this point is assumed to be at G, that is, neither at C-D (equal crime rates) nor at A-B (equal marginal costs). At point G, 95 crimes are occurring in P and 70 in R. Figure 13-2 has been constructed deliberately to cause the optimum point to fall at G, to illustrate the fact that there is nothing in the nature of the case that requires the optimum to be at C-D or A-B.

Equal population has been assumed up to this point for Districts P (Poor) and R (Rich). Let us suppose, instead, that although the districts cover equal areas P contains three times as many people as R, and that a distribution of police that equates crime rates per capita will not equate the number of crimes prevented by a marginal policeman. Starting from this position, i.e., equal crime rates per capita, transfer of one policeman from R to P would, let us assume, prevent three more crimes in P while allowing one more crime in R. This transfer would, of course, result in a crime rate per capita higher in R than in P. It might now appear that the goal of minimization had become an ambiguous one. Transfer of one policeman from R to P does indeed reduce the total absolute number of crimes in the city as a whole. But the service that residents of P desire is reduction of crime in P per resident of P; and R's residents desire reduction of crime in R per resident of R. The transfer of one policeman from R to P would increase the former service only by just as many percentage points as it would reduce the latter service (three less crimes in an area three times as populous, against one more crime in the other area). From this concept of product, if everyone counts for one, no gain in total product is achieved by the transfer.

In fact, however, this apparent conflict between two concepts of minimization is nothing but the conflict between "equity" and "efficiency" encountered above when population was assumed the same in the two districts, but with the roles of the districts reversed. When enough policemen have been transferred from R to P to minimize total crime, the crime rate per capita will be higher in R than in P. It will be so, because the residents of R live in a more sparsely populated area than the residents of P. This fact is analogous to the supposition made earlier (though with the reverse result) that the inhabitants of P were more crime-ridden, owing to poverty, than those of R.

Every crime has counted for one, in the analysis thus far. In fact, some types of crime are regarded as more serious than others, and some types of crime (not necessarily the same ones) are more difficult to reduce. These refinements can be incorporated into the analysis by postulating a production-possibility curve for a given police force in a given district that shows by how much one kind of crime can be reduced at the expense of allowing more of the other crime to occur, and by a system of indifference curves that show what combinations of amounts of the two crimes are regarded with equal appreciation or equal dismay, and what combinations are reviewed as preferable or inferior to other combinations.

The city may be able to afford so much police service that crime is reduced in both R and P, not quite to the point where crime is zero, but to the point where crime is so random, with respect to location, that no one can foresee whether the transfer of a policeman from one district to another would result in an increase or a decrease in total crime. The test for the existence of this state of affairs, assuming a small absolute number of crimes, would be the occurrence of crimes in the several districts of a city within, say, a year, in a series that approximated the Poisson distribution, much as did the famous series of death by horsekicks in Prussian army-corps-years. Let the city consist of, say, ten districts, and let crimes be counted in each district for each of, say, three years. If the average number of crimes per district per year is given by z, and the frequency distribution of crimes per district per year turns out to approximate the following distribution:

Number of crimes in a district in a year

	0	1	2	3	4
Frequency	$\dfrac{z^0 e^{-z}}{0!}$	$\dfrac{z^1 e^{-z}}{1!}$	$\dfrac{z^2 e^{-z}}{2!}$	$\dfrac{z^3 e^{-z}}{3!}$	$\dfrac{z^4 e^{-z}}{4!}$

$\ldots$ and so on, $= e^{-z} = z e^{-z}$

we may then conclude that causes in terms of location cannot be assigned to the crimes that do continue to exist,[2] and that the foregoing analysis in terms of equating costs and benefits at the margin cannot be applied.

Footnotes

[1] In Figures 13-1 and 13-2, absolute number of crimes in the two districts are compared, since it comes to the same as crime rate per capita under the asumption of equal population.

[2] In other words, the probability of any number of crimes in any given district-year, where y is the given number of crimes and z is the average number of crimes observed per district-year is

$$P(y) = \frac{z^y e^{-z}}{y!}$$

A crime is here an isolated event in a continuum of space-time; we count the number of time crimes did occur but cannot count (so vast is the number) the number of times it did *not* occur.

"DOES PRISON PAY?" REVISITED

Anne Morrison Piehl and John J. DiIulio, Jr.

Returning to the Crime Scene

Several years ago, in these pages, we tried to referee an acrimonious debate between criminologists who insisted that prisons "cost too much" and those who responded that they "protect too little." Our contention was that both sides of the debate were stating their positions far too strongly given the lack of available empirical evidence. By presenting new survey data, we hoped to bring a little calm into the storm. But we succeeded only in changing the storm's direction—toward us. Shorn of most of our peacekeeping illusions, we are back to revisit the question, "Does prison pay?"—again by way of new survey data.

Our original offering was a cost-benefit analysis of imprisonment based on a 1990 prisoner self-report survey we conducted in Wisconsin. The survey, based on a sample of 6 percent of the state's prison population, found that in the year before their incarceration, half of the prisoners had committed 12 crimes or more, excluding drug crimes. Using the best available estimates of prison operating costs and the social costs of crime, we calculated that imprisoning 100 convicted felons who offended at the median rate cost $2.5 million, but that leaving them on the streets cost $4.6 million. We noted that for as much as a quarter of prisoners, other correctional options, such as probation, intensive drug treatment, or some other programs, might well be even more cost effective than imprisonment, and we stressed the need for more research.

What we offer now is a new prisoner self-report survey, one that we conducted in New Jersey in 1993 of a random sample of 4 per-

Anne Morrison Piehl is assistant professor of public policy at the Kennedy School of Government, Harvard University. John J. DiIulio, Jr., is professor of politics and public affairs at Princeton University and director of the Brookings Center for Public Management. Piehl and DiIulio are among the contributors to a new Brookings Project, The New Consensus on Crime Policy, headed by DiIulio and Joan R. Petersilia, of the University of California at Irvine. This article is a follow-up on one Piehl and DiIulio wrote for the fall 1991 issue of The Brookings Review, *entitled, "Does Prison Pay?"*

Reprinted with permission from *Brookings Review Magazine*, Winter, 1995, pp. 21-25. Copyright © 1995 by Brookings Institution Press, Washington, D.C.

cent of recent male entrants to the state's prison population. Analysis of this survey reconfirms our earlier finding: prison pays for most state prisoners. Most state prisoners are either violent or repeat offenders who pose a real and present danger to the physical safety or property of any communities into which they might be released. For them, assuredly, prison pays. But prison does not pay for all prisoners. It does not pay for all convicted felons. Most emphatically, it does not pay for all convicted drug felons. The public and its purse could benefit if 10–25 percent of prisoners were under some other form of correctional supervision or released from custody altogether.

Most Prisoners Are Dangerous Repeat Criminals

According to Lawrence A. Greenfeld of the U.S. Bureau of Justice Statistics, fully 94 percent of all state prisoners have either been convicted of a violent crime or been previously sentenced to probation or incarceration (see figure 1). Greenfeld's 94 percent statistic is unassailable. But even it understates the actual number and severity of crimes committed by state prisoners.

In the first place, adult prisoner profiles do not reflect the crimes committed by prisoners before they were of age to be legally tried, convicted, and sentenced as adults. Most state prisoners have long juvenile records which are officially closed to adult authorities and are not considered by adult courts at sentencing time. According to our New Jersey survey, two out of three prisoners had served time in a juvenile institution. Other studies have shown that about 60 percent of youths aged 18 and under in long-term secure facilities have a history of violence. Many studies reveal that between a quarter and a third of juvenile criminals are high-rate offenders who commit a mix of violent and property crimes. Juveniles account for about a fifth of all weapons arrests and have set frightening new homicide records in the 1990s.

In a recent survey, 93 percent of judges in the juvenile system agreed that juvenile offenders should be fingerprinted, and 85 percent agreed that juvenile records should be open to adult authorities. As it now stands, however, juvenile crimes of assault, rape, robbery, burglary, and murder will mean nothing in adult courts and will not appear in statistical profiles of prisoners' criminality.

Figure 1. Profile of Prison Inmates, 1991

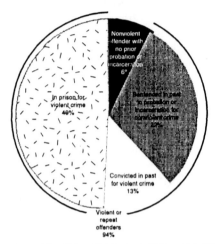

Nonviolent offender with no prior probation or incarceration 6%

In prison for violent crime 49%

Sentenced in past to probation for imprisonment for any violent crime 22%

Convicted in past for violent crime 13%

Violent or repeat offenders 94%

Source note: Lawrence A. Greenfeld, *Survey of State Prison Inmates, 1991* (Bureau of Justice Statistics). Statistics based on a sample representing 711,000 adults in state prisons.

Second, more than 90 percent of all criminal cases do not go to trial because the offender pleads guilty to a lesser charge. Even violent crimes are routinely plea-bargained—and estimated 77 percent of rape cases, 85 percent of aggravated assault cases, and 87 percent of robbery cases. Unless one believes that all charges that are plea-bargained away are for crimes that the offender did not commit, then one must admit that actual crimes are swept under the criminal-records rug by plea bargaining. As yet no systematic empirical studies have estimated the deflationary effects of plea bargaining on the length and severity of prisoners' criminal records. But many prosecutors believe that the effects are large, and evidence is growing all around the country that they are right.

Third, as our two prisoner self-report surveys plainly reveal, most prisoners commit many times more nondrug felony crimes than they are ever arrested, convicted, and imprisoned for committing.

In the late 1970s the RAND Corporation conducted prisoner self-report surveys in Texas, Michigan, and California. Among other things, RAND's surveys showed that the median number of crimes, excluding all drug crimes, committed by prisoners the year before they were incarcerated was 15. In the late 1980s amidst the first round of controversies over benefit-cost analyses of imprisonment, some asserted that the RAND numbers could not even come close to being replicated in bigger-sample, more up-to-date surveys.

Both our prisoner self-report surveys were modeled on the RAND survey, though in both the sample was much larger. The 1993 New Jersey survey found that the median number of nondrug crimes committed by prisoners the year before their imprisonment was 12—exactly what it was for Wisconsin prisoners in 1990, and three lower than it was for prisoners in RAND surveys.

Although the exact replication is striking, future surveys will no doubt show that 12 is not a magic number. But serious analysts must now concede that there is less reason to be skeptical that the typical prisoner commits many undetected crimes, excluding drug crimes, the year before his incarceration.

In sum, the Greenfeld data alone are enough to rebut the notion that most state prisoners are petty, first-time, or mere drug offenders with few prior arrests, no previous convictions, no history of violence, and no potential for doing criminal harm if released tomorrow morning. And when we acknowledge that most prisoners commit crimes as juveniles, most prisoners plea bargain away crimes they have committed as adults, and most prisoners have committed a slew of undetected crimes the year before their incarceration, that notion is not only decidedly distorted but downright dangerous. It is a myth that anti-incarceration activists and their allies should be free to peddle, but that no responsible policymaker, prosecutor, judge, journalist, academic, or average citizen can afford to buy.

Calculating Social Costs

Estimating the social costs and benefits of competing transportation or environmental policies is no analytical picnic. But esti-mating them for imprisonment and other sentencing options is a certain analytical migraine.

For starters, it is widely asserted that it costs $25,000 to keep a prisoner behind bars for a year. But the latest Bureau of Justice Statistics figures for average annual spending per prisoner are $15,586 for the states and $14,456 for the federal Bureau of Prisons (which holds about 10 percent of all prisoners). These figures are calculated by dividing the total spent on salaries, wages, supplies, utilities, transportation, contractual services, and other current operating expenses by the average daily inmate population.

But hidden and indirect costs of running prisons might bring the $25,000 figure closer to reality than the official spending averages would allow. For example, some tiny but nontrivial fraction of government workers outside of corrections (human services, central budgeting offices) spend time on matters pertaining to prisoners. And Harvard economist Richard Freeman and others suggest that incarceration decreases post-release employability and lifetime earnings potential. Thus an ideal estimate of the social costs of imprisonment would include any relevant spending by other government agencies, plus whatever public unemployment compensation, welfare, and health expenditures result from the negative short- and long-term labor market effects of imprisonment on ex-prisoners.

Also, there is wide inter-and intra-system variation not only in what it costs to operate prisons, but in how prison dollars are allocated as between security functions (uniformed custodial staff), basic services (food, heat, medical supplies), treatment programs, recreational facilities, plant maintenance, and other expenditures. Whatever the best estimate of prison operating costs, such cost differences suggest that efficiency losses are occurring in some places and that efficiency gains are possible in others.

The cost-effectiveness of prisons, however, is by no means strictly determined by correctional administrators. Over the past 25 years the courts have had a major impact on both the total costs of operating prisons and the distribution of prison dollars between security and other needs. For example, in the wake of a sweeping court order, prison operating costs in Texas grew from $91 million in 1980 to $1.84 billion in 1994, a tenfold increase in real terms, while the state's prison population barely doubled. Texas in now one of the least 20 states that spends less than half of every prison dollar on security.

Finally, it is worth remembering that barely a penny of every federal, state, and local tax dollar goes to support state prisons and local jails. State and local governments spend 15 times what the federal government spends on corrections. But state and local spending on prisons and jails amounts to only $80.20 per capita a year, or $1.54 per capita a week.

Estimating Social Benefits

Whatever the best estimate of how much it costs society to keep a convicted criminal behind bars for a year, how do we decide whether it's worth the money? Imprisonment offers at least four types of social benefits. The first is retribution: imprisoning Peter punishes him and expresses society's desire to do justice. Second is deterrence: imprisoning Peter may deter either him or Paul or both from committing crimes in the future. Third is rehabilitation: while behind bars, Peter may participate in drug treatment or other programs that reduce the chances that he will return to crime when free. Fourth is incapacitation: from his cell, Peter can't commit crimes against anyone save other prisoners, staff, or visitors.

At present, it is harder to measure the retribution, deterrence, or rehabilitation value of imprisonment to society than it is to measure its incapacitation value. The types of opinion surveys and data sets that would enable one to arrive at meaningful estimates of the first three social benefits of imprisonment simply do not yet exist.

Thus, we focus exclusively on the social benefits of imprisonment measured in terms of its incapacitation value. As columnist Ben Wattenberg so vividly put it, everyone grasps that "A thug in prison can't shoot your sister." Thus, if a given crime costs its victims and society X dollars in economic and other losses (hospital bills, days out of work, physical pain, and emotional anguish), and if we know that, when free, a convicted criminal commits Y such crimes per year, then the yearly social benefits of imprisoning him are equal to X times Y divided by $25,000. If the ratio is greater than 1, then the social benefits exceed the costs and "prison pays" for this offender; but if the ratio is lower than 1, then the social costs exceed the benefits and it does not pay to keep him locked up.

But remember: we are monetizing the social benefits solely in terms of imprisonment's incapacitation value. Because there is every reason to suppose that the retribution, deterrence, and rehabilitation values of imprisonment are each greater than zero—that is, because it is virtually certain that in addition to incapacitating criminals who would commit crimes when free, prison also succeeds in punishing, deterring, and rehabilitating at least some prisoners under some conditions—our estimate of the net social benefits of imprisonment is bound to be an *under*estimate. And if, therefore, our estimate measured only in terms of prison's incapacitation value is positive, it means that the actual social benefits of imprisonment are even higher and that prison most definitely pays.

Several recent advances have been made in measuring the costs of crime to victims and society. For example, a recent Bureau of Justice Statistics study reports a total of 33.6 million criminal victimizations in 1992. The study estimated that in 1992 crime victims lost $17.2 billion in direct costs—losses from theft or property damage, cash losses, medical expenses, and lost pay from work.

But the BJS estimate did not include direct costs (for example, medical costs) to victims incurred six months or more after the crime. Nor did it include decreased work productivity, the less tangible costs of pain and suffering, increased insurance premiums and moving costs due to victimization, and other indirect costs.

A 1993 study by Ted R. Miller and others in *Health Affairs* took a more comprehensive view of the direct costs of crime and included some indirect costs as well. The study estimated the costs and monetary value of lost quality of life in 1987 due to death and injuries, both physical and psychological, resulting from violent crime. Using various measures, the study estimated that each murder costs $2.4 million, each rape $60,000, each arson $50,000, each assault $25,000, and each robbery $19,000. The estimated total cost over the lifetime of the victims of all violent crimes committed during 1987–1990 was $178 billion per year, or many times the BJS estimate of direct economic costs.

Even these estimates, however, omit the detailed cost accounting of site-specific, crime-specific studies. For example, a recent survey of admissions to Wisconsin hospitals over a 41-month period found that 1,035 patients were admitted for gunshot wounds caused by assaults. These patients accumulated more than $16 million in hospital bills, about $6.8 million of it paid by taxes. Long-term costs rise far higher. For example, just one shotgun assault victim in the survey was likely to incur costs of more than $5 million in lost income and medical expenses over the next 35 years.

Likewise, several studies have estimated the number of crimes averted by incapacitating criminals. For example, BJS statistician Patrick J. Langan has shown that in 1989 an estimated 66,000 fewer rapes, 323,000 fewer robberies, 380,000 fewer assaults, and 3.3 million fewer burglaries were attributable to the difference between the crime rates of 1973 and those of 1989. As Langan has observed, if only one-half or one-quarter of the reductions were due to rising incarceration rates, that would still leave prisons responsible for sizable reductions in crime. Also he has estimated that tripling the prison population from 1975 to 1989 reduced reported and unreported violent crime by 10–15 percent below what it would otherwise have been, thereby preventing a conservatively estimated 390,000 murders, rapes, robberies, and aggravated assaults in 1989 alone.

Results of the New Jersey Study

What can the New Jersey prisoner self-report survey contribute to a cost-benefit analysis of imprisonment? Table 1, adapted from Mark A. Cohen's analysis of jury awards to crime victims, lists our estimates of the social costs of rape, robbery, assault, burglary, auto theft, and petty theft. For each offender in the New Jersey sample we multiplied these amounts by the annualized number of offenses reported of each type. Table 2 ranks the resulting social costs of crime for the sample. The median social cost of crime was about $70,098. In other words, half of the prisoners in the sample inflicted more costs on society and half less than $70,098. The social cost associated with the prisoner in the 25th percentile (that is, 75 percent of the sample inflicted higher social costs than he did) was about $19,509, and at the 10th percentile it was $1,650.

Table 3 converts the figures in table 2 to benefit-cost ratios by dividing the social benefits by $25,000, the cost of imprisoning one prisoner for one year. Dividing the median social cost per crime of $70,098 by $25,000 yields a benefit-cost ratio of 2.80: for every dollar it costs to keep a median-offending prisoner behind bars society saves at least $2.80 in the social costs of crimes averted.

The prisoner at the 25th percentile was essentially a high-rate property offender, reporting that he committed auto thefts at a rate of three a year, burglaries at a rate of six a year, and petty thefts at a rate of 24 a year. Dividing the total social cost of these crimes by the cost of incarceration yields a benefit-cost ratio of 0.78. And at the 10th percentile, the ratio is a clearly cost-ineffective zero.

Just Say No to No Parole

Clearly, the social benefits of incapacitating criminals, however great they may be, are nonetheless subject to the law of diminishing returns.

Make no mistake: within three years of their community-based sentences about half of all probationers either abscond or are returned to prison for a new crime, while roughly half of all parolees are convicted of a new crime. Of the 5 million people under correctional supervision in this country at any given time, 72 percent are not incarcerated. Even violent offenders serve barely 40 percent of their sentences in confinement. Each year community-based felons commit millions of crimes, many violent, that could have been prevented if they had been imprisoned for all or most of their terms.

But efforts, in Virginia and elsewhere, to abolish parole are too tough by half. For while about half of all parolees recidivate, the other half do not. Nationally, each year we spend more than 7.5 times more on prisons and jails (which house 28 percent of offenders) than we do on probation and parole (which account for the remaining 72 percent) combined. Thus we spend more than 20 times as much to hold each prisoner as we do to supervise each community-based offender. No doubt a large fraction of the parole population should be imprisoned. But a no-parole policy lowers rather than increases the chances that the system will sort offenders cost-effectively.

This is especially true where drug offenders are concerned. Between 1980 and 1992 the fraction of new state prisoners whose most serious conviction offense was a drug offense rose from 6.8 percent to 30.5 percent. Does that mean that one-third of the prison population consists of "mere drug offenders"? By no means. The vast majority of this group are recidivists with many a nondrug felony on their rap sheets, to say nothing of juvenile crimes, crimes they plea-bargained away, and crimes they got away with completely.

Then what fraction of prisoners might be accurately characterized as "drug-only offenders," meaning offenders whose only adult crimes have been drug crimes? At this point we have no way of knowing. But about 27 percent of the New Jersey sample reported that in the four months before incarceration their *only* offenses were drug sales. Nearly a quarter said they first got involved in crime to get money for drugs. And 3 percent were convicted of drug possession and reported no other crimes.

To be consistent methodologically, we must consider the incapacitation benefits of incarcerating such a substantial population. Doing so dramatically changes the results and the implication of our analysis. We believe that the best estimate of the incapacitation effect (number of drug sales prevented by incarcerating a drug dealer) is zero, and therefore value drug crimes (sales and possession) at zero social cost. Other analysts, including many whom no one can accuse of being soft on drug crime or in favor of drug legalization, have reached similar conclusions. For example, in a recent issue of *Commentary*, James Q. Wilson observed that prison terms for crack dealers "do not have the same incapacitative effect as sentences for robbery. . . . [A]drug dealer sent away is replaced by a new one because an opportunity has opened up." Many law enforcement and corrections officials have reached the same conclusion.

As table 4 shows, including drug offenders in our analysis lowers the cost-effectiveness of incarceration across the board: even at the median, imprisonment appears to be very expensive. If even half of the inmates who report that their only crime was selling drugs are telling the truth, then 15 percent of New Jersey's spending on prisons is being devoted to "sending a message" about drug dealing. We are open to convincing evidence that the public is willing to pay substantial sums for retribution against drug dealers. And we are aware that certain types of prison-based drug treatment programs can work to reduce the chances that an offender will return to drugs or crime upon release. But let no one suppose that by incarcerating most drug offenders we succeed in averting lots of drug crimes. If there is an empirically sound argument for a no-parole policy that makes no distinctions between drug-only offenders and other prisoners, we have yet to hear it.

Forging a New Consensus?

When we first ventured into the "Does prison pay?" debate, we were struck by the absence of empirical data to buttress the large claims being made on both sides. Now more than ever we are convinced that the path to a new intellectual consensus in this area, as in crime policy generally, can be paved not by disagreeing more amicably about the implications of what is already known (though that could be a pleasant change), but by agreeing more fully about the gaps in our knowledge and how best to fill them.

For example, many want drug-only offenders locked up regardless of the questionable incapacitation or general deterrence benefits of doing so. Likewise, others want to legalize drugs outright. But honest minds on both sides must admit that we do not yet have a definite estimate of the fraction of the prison population that consists of drug-only offenders.

Little by little analysts are beginning to sketch a picture of the amount and severity of crimes committed by prisoners when free and to explain the conditions under which some community-based felons succeed in staying drug- and crime-free. But we need a much fuller picture, a much clearer explanation.

In short, a new intellectual consensus on crime policy can be built not by avoiding the hardest policy-relevant empirical questions, but by attempting to identify and answer them, preferably in common with those with whom we are now most inclined to disagree strongly. Through a new Brookings research project, we hope to help foster just such a consensus.

Table 1. Estimates of Social Costs of Selected Crimes

Crime	Social Cost
Rape	$56,280
Robbery	12,060
Assault	11,518
Burglary	1,314
Auto theft	2,995
Fraud, forgery, petty theft	110

SOURCE: Mark Cohen, "Pain, Suffering, and Jury Awards: A Study of the Cost of Crime to Victims." *Law and Society Review*, vol. 22, no. 3 (1988), as adjusted for inflation and transfer of wealth by the authors.

Table 2. Social Costs of Property and Assault Crimes by New
Jersey Inmates

Offender	Social Cost
Average (mean)	$1,600,499
Median	70,098
25th percentile	19,509
10th percentile	1,650

SOURCE: Authors' calculations from the 1993 New Jersey Inmate Survey.
N=419. Drug sales, homicides, and weapons offenses are excluded.

Table 3. Benefit-Cost Ratios Implied by Table 2

Offender	Ratio
Average (mean)	64.02
Median	2.80
25th percentile	0.78
10th percentile	0.07

SOURCE: Same as table 2.

Table 4. Benefit-Cost Rations for Property, Assault, and Drug
Crimes

Offender	Ratio
Average (mean)	40.10
Median	0.36
25th percentile	0.00
10th percentile	0.00

SOURCE: Same as table 2. N=669. Homicides and weapons offenses are
excluded.

GO DIRECTLY TO JAIL AND DO NOT COLLECT? A LONG-TERM, STUDY OF RECIDIVISM, EMPLOYMENT, AND EARNINGS PATTERNS AMONG PRISON RELEASEES

Karen E. Needels

* * *

Between 1970 and 1993, the fraction of the U.S. population in prison rose by more than 260%. Because the current price tag of keeping a prisoner incarcerated is more than $20,000 per year, this dramatic increase in incarceration rates has been a significant source of growth in public-sector spending (Maguire, Pastore, and Flanagan 1995). Furthermore, Greenfeld (1985) estimated that about 60% of the individuals admitted to prison in any year have been in prison before. Why do so many prison releasees continue to rotate through the prison door repeatedly, spending only a short time out of prison before returning there?

Beckerrian economic models of crime provide one explanation for high recidivism rates (Becker 1968; Ehrlich 1973; Piehl 1994; Witte and Tauchen 1994). According to these models, when rationally acting individuals are deciding whether or not to commit a crime, they consider the expected payoffs from the crime and the expected costs from conviction (determined by the probability of conviction and the size of the punishment). Additional costs from conviction include lost legal-sector earnings during incarceration

This is a substantially revised version of the latter half of the fourth chapter, titled "We'll Be Seeing You Again: The Revolving Prison Door and the Earnings Between Rotations," of my doctoral dissertation. This research was assisted by an award from the Social Science Research Council (through funding from the Rockefeller Foundation), the National Science Foundation, and the Industrial Relations Section of Princeton University. I especially would like to thank David Card, Henry Farber, John Dilulio, the Princeton University labor lunch participants and three anonymous reviewers for constructive suggestions. Jason Brancazio and Chris Burris provided excellent research assistance. I am also grateful to the Georgia Department of Corrections, the Georgia Crime Information Center, and the Georgia Department of Labor for providing the data used. Any errors, however, are my own.

and any losses in future earnings because of incarceration. Future earnings may be lower for several reasons. Some employers are unwilling to hire prison releasees, individuals do not develop marketable skills while in prison (so the wages they can get are lower), and individuals with prior arrests or incarcerations are more likely to be incarcerated (regardless of whether they commit crimes or not). Individuals with low levels of human capital face poor labor market opportunities; consequently, illegal activities are relatively more profitable for them. Both raw data and statistical analyses confirm that those with low education levels, those with low work experience levels, and minority populations are more likely to have poor labor outcomes, high incarceration rates, and high recidivism rates (see, e.g., Chung, Schmidt, and Witte 1991; Freeman 1996; Maguire et al. 1995). One might expect individuals with low levels of human capital to make the same criminal participation decisions repeatedly, leading to high rates of recidivism.

Other explanations for the relationships between demographic and human capital characteristics, labor market outcomes, and recidivism rates exist. Theories of dual labor markets suggest that some individuals (and probably most prison releasees) are trapped in jobs offering low pay and requiring low skills and low workforce commitment (Doeringer and Piore [1971] 1985). These individuals have little incentive to invest in skills. Furthermore, employment interruptions resulting from their criminal activity or incarceration create few costs. Another interpretation is that criminals are not "rationally optimizing" at all, except in a tautological sense—criminals do not maximize their benefits from crime and legal-sector earnings because they are radically present oriented and do not think about the future (DiIulio 1996; Wilson and Abrahamse 1992). The relationship among crime, human capital, and employment arises because criminals only pursue activities that provide immediate gratification. They therefore do not invest in human capital— the legal sector earnings gains are slow to materialize, whereas gains from crime are often immediate (and punishment is slow to materialize). Some researchers, such as Sampson and Laub (1993) and Farrington (1986), consider the social support networks available to youths and adults. Family, employment, and institutional structures (such as churches and the criminal justice system) influence rates of offending. The stronger the bonds to conventional society, the lower the probability and rate of offending.

A large body of literature has used either aggregate or individual-level data to examine the relationship between labor market success and criminal activity. Witte (1976), for example, examined earnings patterns of prison releasees from North Carolina. She found that the earnings of these releasees were lower after incarceration than before but that earnings levels rose for the 2 years immediately following release. Freeman (1991) likewise provided insight into the "scarring" effects of incarceration by contrasting labor market outcomes before and after incarceration. Using several different data sets on youths, he concluded that incarceration dramatically decreases the likelihood of employment. He found that labor force participation rates for young men dropped 30% between the 6 months before incarceration and the 3 months afterward.

Short-term studies containing labor market outcomes shortly after their samples are released from prison may have only limited ability to estimate long-run employment patterns. Rauma and Berk (1987) suggested that "short term studies may capture only the effect of the first job after release and the pressures of parole agents and family to be employed" (p.4). Hence earnings observed over a very short time window after release may not be indicative of earnings behavior over a long time span. If this is the case, then labor market patterns for prison releasees may be even bleaker than Witte and Freeman have suggested.

Researchers typically have not had access to a long panel of information on both criminal activity and earnings to examine long-run employment patterns. Kitchener, Schmidt, and Glaser (1977), for example, tracked releasees from the federal prison system over an 18-year period but did not have earnings information. One of the most notable follow-up studies on criminally active individuals, the study of the Philadelphia 1945 birth cohort, barely mentions employment (Wolfgang, Thornberry, and Figlio 1987). Other data sets that allow a long-term follow-up of delinquency, criminal activity, and occupational attainment are not generalizable to most adult prison populations (see, e.g., Polk et al. 1981) or do not contain extensive information on demographic characteristics (Grogger 1991).

Sampson and Laub (1993) have conducted the most extensive long-run examination of the employment patterns of offenders. They reconstructed data originally collected and analyzed by Glueck and Glueck (1952). Using a mixture of official records and interview-based observations at 7-year intervals, Sampson and Laub found that job stability is an important predictor of criminal behavior for a maturing cohort of both delinquents and nondelinquents. Although contributing significantly to the understanding of how criminal activity and employment interact, these researchers were unable to measure year-to-year changes in earnings.

I use a unique data set containing 17 years of criminal activity and 9 years of earnings for a large sample of men released from the Georgia prison system in 1976 to examine how human capital characteristics such as race, education, age, and criminal history affect employment rates and earnings levels for prison releasees. Because a substantial portion of the sample had no recorded earnings, a model of labor supply allowing for zero earnings was used to estimate both the employment decision and the level of earnings. This research expands on other research because it contains a large, generalizable sample of prison releasees, has a long earnings follow-up (compared with earnings only shortly after release), combines earnings with recidivism, and analyzes both employment and earnings levels. I first describe the sample used; next, I describe labor market patterns and analyze the characteristics affecting employment and earnings levels. Finally, I offer some conclusions.

Data Description

Sample Background and Construction
During 1976 and 1977, researchers conducted a unique social experiment designed to test the effectiveness of an income support program for newly released prisoners in reducing recidivism rates and increasing employment outcomes. Known as the Transitional Aid Research Project (TARP), the random-assignment experiment involved several thousand prisoners released from the Georgia and Texas state prison systems (Rossi, Berk, and Lenihan 1980; Smith, Martinez and Harrison 1978; Stevens and Sanders 1978; Zeisel 1982). The results of the experiment, after a 1-year follow-up, were disappointing. Individuals in the treatment groups were no less likely than individuals in the control groups to return to prison during the year after release. A long-term evaluation of the differences

between the treatment and control groups confirmed the absence of any large or statistically significant treatment effects on either recidivism or earnings (Needels 1994). Because no long-run effects of TARP are apparent, the Georgia sample can be considered representative of prison releasees from a southern state in the mid-1970s.

The TARP experiment provided the basis for a unique data set combining criminal histories, information on subsequent arrests and incarcerations, and employment outcomes for a representative sample of prison releasees.[1] Using the universe of prisoners in the TARP experiment, I merged prison and probation spells recorded by the Georgia Department of Corrections (GDOC) with arrests histories from the Georgia Crime Information Center, earnings data from the Georgia Department of Labor (GADOL), and self-reported (interview) data from the TARP experiment.

* * *

Official records on labor market outcomes included quarterly earnings data from 1983 to 1991, by employer, as reported for unemployment insurance purposes. More than 90% of all jobs are covered by the unemployment insurance system (Blank and Card 1989). Using official earnings records does miss some earnings, biasing the measure of earnings downward, but these data avoid recall problems associated with retrospective self-reporting over a long period of time, particularly when employment spells are short and intermittent.[5] * * *

Although about one fourth of the sample was eligible for payments similar to unemployment insurance payments in the TARP experiment, Needels (1994) concluded that the experiment treatment had no long-run effect on employment or recidivism. I therefore pooled the TARP treatment and control groups. Because the TARP sample was a random sample of releasees, the findings here should be generalizable to men with similar demographic and criminogenic characteristics released from prison during the late 1970s.

Although 2,443 individuals were released from the Georgia prison system between December 1975 and September 1976, only 1,176 men were used in this analysis.[6] The 1,267 individuals who were not included in the final sample were excluded for a variety of reasons. For example, 778 individuals were not part of the original

TARP experiment (thus interview information is missing).[7] Another 536 individuals were excluded because their arrest records could not be matched to TARP information. Also excluded from the sample were 95 women, 71 individuals who were older than age 45 in 1976, 24 individuals who were recorded as deceased during the follow-up period, and 36 individuals whose prison records were inconsistent or missing.[8] The older individuals were excluded to help to eliminate biases in the results from unobserved deaths and retirement; the small group of women was excluded because the expected criminal and labor force patterns of women differ substantially from those of men. Finally, 48 men whose administrative records contained no social security number, as well as 21 individuals who were incarcerated during all 9 years for which earnings data were collected, were excluded.

Table 1 provides evidence on the ways in which the sample of prison releasees differed from the population of men in Georgia during this time period. Because the TARP panel data and the 1990 U.S. census (5% sample for Georgia) measure demographic characteristics differently, and in different time periods, comparisons are only suggestive. Blacks, accounting for more than one half of the sample of prison releasees, were overrepresented; in contrast, fewer than one fourth of all men in this age range in Georgia were Black. Furthermore, men released from the Georgia prison system in 1976 were younger and had less education than did the comparable Georgia population. The mean education level of the TARP releasees—9.7 years of schooling—was quite low, whereas the tested education level was almost 4 years below education level attained.[9] Prison releasees were disproportionately high school dropouts. The prison releasees' average age in 1991 was 40 years. In the 1990 U.S. census, mean education was 12.9 years; mean age in 1991 was 44 years.

Direct comparisons between the census data and the prison releasee data on marital status and health-related problems can only be suggestive, as these characteristics vary substantially over time. Only one third of prison releasees were married in 1976; one might expect that this fraction would have increased as the sample aged. However, even this fraction is lower than the comparable statistic for men in the same age range as the TARP sample in 1976; that is,

Table 1: Demographic Characteristics of the Prison Releasee
Sample and Georgia Men in U.S. Census
(in percentages, unless otherwise stated)

	Prison Releasee Sample	Georgia Men
Black	56.7	21.1
Education (years)[a]	9.7	12.9
High school graduate	21.6	75.0
Tested functional grade equivalent (years)[b]	5.8	—
IQ score (points)[b]	93.6	—
Age in 1991 (years)[c]	40.1	44.4
Married[d]	33.0	76.2
Divorced[d]	13.2	13.5
Medical problems[e]	17.5	11.8
Self-reported alcohol problems[f]	19.0	—
Not born in Georgia	16.7	31.0
Sample Size	1,176	56,281

SOURCE: Transitional Aid Research Project (TRAP) panel data and 1990
U.S. census of population and housing public use microdata sample (5%)
for Georgia.
NOTE: The census data were restricted to males age 32 to 59 in 1990 (who
were age 18 to 45 in 1976).
[a] Years of education are not recorded in the census data. Average values in
the educational categories were used to construct a measure of years of education.
[b] Functional grade equivalency and IQ scores are recorded from the prison
spell ending in 1976.
[c] Ages from the 1990 census data are projected 1 year to 1991.
[d] Marital status is measured as of 1976 for the prison releasee sample.
Divorced denotes "widowed, separated, or divorced."
[e] A dummy variable for medical problems equals 1 for the TARP sample if
prison officials (as of 1976) recorded health-related limitations for the individual and equals 1 if the census respondent noted that he was limited in
the kind or amount of work because of a disability.
[f] A dummy variable for self-reported alcohol problems (as of 1976) equals 1
if the man reported either that he had an alcohol problem or had ever been
treated for an alcohol problem. This measure is available for about one half
of the full sample, who were interviewed during the TARP experiment.

the percentage of men between the ages of 18 and 45 in the general population who are married is much higher than one third. Men identified in the census data as married and as divorced, separated, or widowed comprised 76% of the sample, respectively.

Table 1 compares the percentage of men aged 32 to 59 in the population who had medical problems with the comparable percentage for the TARP sample (whose health status was measured as of age 18 to 45). Because older men are more likely than younger men to have medical problems, Table 1 suggests that the sample of prison releasees was significantly more likely than the general population to have had medical problems.

Arrest and Incarceration Patterns

The raw arrest and incarceration patterns of the 1,176 men in the sample are presented in Table 2. Although arrests and incarcerations are not perfect measures of either criminal activity or time removed from the labor market, they are used here to suggest the sample's continued involvement in the criminal justice system. Statistics in Table 2 are shown for the full panel (1976 to 1993) and for the time for which earnings data were available (1983 to 1991). As a whole, the sample averaged almost six arrests, and about 14% of the time each in prison and on probation. These high levels of officially recorded criminal activity must be kept in mind as labor

Table 2: Arrest and Incarceration Patterns

	1976 to 1993	983 to 1991
Percentage ever rearrested	82.6	—
Number of arrests[a]	5.8	3.1
Percentage ever reincarcerated	61.1	—
Percentage of time in prison	14.3	13.6
Percentage of time on probation	14.1	15.9

SOURCE: Transitional Aid Research Project (TARP) panel data.
[a] Arrest records are available only through May 1992.

market patterns are examined. At some point between release from prison in 1976 and June 9, 1993, 83% and 61% of the sample were rearrested at least once and reincarcerated at least once, respectively. Twenty-five percent of the sample members were reincarcerated once, 14% were reincarcerated twice, and the remaining 22% were reincarcerated three or more times between 1976 and 1993 (not shown). The sample averaged 1.4 prison spells and 1.1 probation spells between 1976 and 1993. Nearly one third were rearrested during the first year after release, and one half were rearrested within 3 years (not shown).[10]

Figure 2 shows the time in prison, the time under probationary supervision, and the time either in prison or on probation, by year, from 1983 to 1991. Sample members were flowing in and out of prison (and on and off probation) during the entire 9-year window for which earnings data are available. Annually, these 1,176 men spent an average of 14% of their time in prison during the 9 years and 16% of their time on probation. When subgroups of the sample are compared—for example, high school dropouts and high school graduates, Blacks and Whites, or different age categories—similar patterns are found (not shown). Blacks, high school dropouts, and younger sample members spent more time under criminal justice supervision, on average, than did Whites, high school graduates, and older sample members, respectively.

The total time under supervision, shown in Figure 2, appears to decline only very slightly over time, with the increase in time on probation almost exactly canceling out the decrease in time in prison. To examine if the aggregate time under supervision was constant over time, I regressed the mean percentage of time under either form of supervision for the entire sample on a constant and a time trend, therefore fitting a line to the data points in Figure 2. The coefficient for the time trend is -0.005 (t value = -4.826), suggesting that time under supervision decreases very slightly over time.[11,12] Coefficients for time trends in similar regressions, using mean time in prison and mean time on probation as the dependent variables,

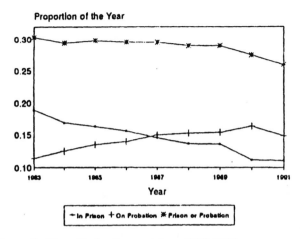

Figure 2: Time Under Supervision, 1983-1991

are -0.010 (*t* value = -15.450) and 0.005 (*t* value = 5.322), respectively. The shift from crimes that receive stiffer sentences (incarceration) to those with lighter sentences (probation) suggests that individuals may be responding to different incentives later in life compared to when they were younger. In the next section, I examine labor market outcomes to determine if legal-sector earnings may be associated with this pattern.

Labor Market Patterns

Figure 3 shows the prison releasees' employment rates from 1983 to 1991. These rates are extremely low, especially given that most of the men were in their prime working years. Employment was measured broadly—an individual was considered to be employed during a given year if he had any officially recorded earnings in any of the four quarters of the year. This standard is substantially more generous than measures of contemporaneous employment. The line denoted "unadjusted" shows that between 30% and 40% of the

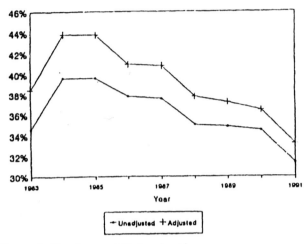

Figure 3: Employment Rates, by Year

sample had any officially recorded earnings in each year, with the highest levels of employment in 1984 and 1985. Because some men were incarcerated for full calendar years, the line denoted "adjusted" indicates the percentage of men who were not incarcerated during a full year who had officially recorded earnings. Graphs of the quarterly data would provide a similar picture, except that the quarterly data are noisier. The unadjusted percentages of the sample employed in each of the 36 quarters ranged from 26% to 34% whereas adjusted percentages ranged from 29% to 40% (not shown).

Figure 4 presents the mean unadjusted and adjusted earnings levels per year. Here, the adjustment calculated the annual earnings that sample members would have received if they had not been incarcerated for part of the year. (That is, if a sample member earned $3,000 during 6 months and was incarcerated for the other 6 months in a year, his adjusted annual earnings would be $6,000.) The patterns in the figure complement those shown in Figure 3; mean earnings levels were highest during the mid-1980s. Earnings levels for prison releasees seem to be sensitive to the business cycle, with the lowest mean earnings levels occurring during years in which the economy was relatively weak.[13]

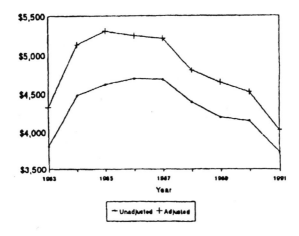

Figure 4: Mean Earnings per Year, 1991 Dollars

Employment and earnings patterns similar to those in Figures 3 and 4 are found in the raw data over time for subgroups of the prison releasee sample (not shown). Adjusted annual participation rates for Blacks, for example, were 36% in 1983; they peaked at 44% in 1985 and dropped to 32% in 1991. Adjusted participation rates for Whites were 41% in 1983; they peaked at 45% in 1985 and dropped to 35% in 1991. Adjusted annual participation rates for the youngest sample members (those age 18 to 25 in 1976) ranged from 37% to 48%, with the peak participation rates around 1984 and 1985. In contrast, rates for individuals age 26 to 45 in 1976 ranged from 26% to 36% (peaking in 1985). Earnings levels adjusted for time incarcerated had similar subgroup patterns: Whites, high school dropouts, and younger individuals had higher mean earnings levels in each of the 9 years. The raw data cannot distinguish whether these prison releasees are more likely to participate in the labor market during business booms because they can receive higher wages or if they are unable to find employment during business downturns.

Additional details on the sample's relatively poor labor market performance over all 9 years are presented in Table 3. More important, only 71% of the sample had any reported earnings (covered by unemployment insurance) during the 9-year span from 1983 to 1991. The second panel of Table 3 contains information only on men with

Table 3: Earnings Data, by Race, Education, and Age Categories

	All	Race		Years of Education		Age in 1976	
		White	Black	<12	≥12	18-25	26-45
Number of individuals	1,176	509	667	922	254	770	406
Number of social security numbers[a]	1.12	1.06**	1.16**	1.12	1.10	1.12	1.12
Proportion with any earnings	.71	.70	.72	.71	.70	.76**	.61**
For those with earnings:							
Number of individuals	832	354	478	655	177	585	247
Mean total earnings	$54,804	$70,929**	$42,862**	$49,597**	$74,073**	$54,968	$54,416
Median total earnings	$26,236	$35,609	$22,054	$23,323	$46,606	$29,082	$22,026
Average earnings per year	$6,089	$7,880**	$4,762**	$5,511	$8,230**	$6,108	$6,046
Proportion of quarters employed	.44	.47*	.41*	.44**	.50**	.45	.41
Proportion of free quarters employed	.50	.51	.49	.49	.54	.52**	.45**
Earnings per normalized year free	$6,788	$8,428**	$5,572**	$6,224**	$8,976**	$6,900	$6,524
Number of quarters on longest job	9.3	10.1**	8.7**	9.0*	10.4*	9.3	9.3
Number of employers	6.1	5.8	6.4	5.9**	6.0**	6.4**	5.4**

SOURCE: Transitional Aid Research Project (TARP) panel data.

a The variable number of social security numbers" reflects the mean number of social security numbers on an individual's prison record. An individual may have more than one social security number associated with his prison record because of either deliberate falsification by the prisoner or typographical errors in the prison records' database. Needels (1994) explained the data-cleaning process to ensure that earnings records were properly matched to sample members.

*p≤.10 (two-tailed test); ** p≤.05 (two-tailed test).

any recorded earnings. Earnings were quite low—approximately $6,100 per year. Although most jobs available to prison releasees are presumably low paying, spells of employment in the informal (untaxed) sector or nonemployment may partly explain the low earnings levels.[14] Employment rates, measured by the number of quarters with any earnings, also were low, even for the subset of the sample with any recorded earnings. An average of 44% of those with any earnings in 36 quarters reported earnings in any one quarter.

Because about 15% of TARP participants' time from 1983 to 1991 was spent in prison, Table 3 also presents measures of employment focusing on the amount of time "free." Employment rates during all 9 years, divided by the number of days not in prison during this 9-year window, measured in years. Even after controlling for the time incarcerated, normalized earnings still were less than $6,800 per year. By comparison, the poverty threshold for a single individual during this period ranged from about $4,500 to $6,200, average annual pay in Georgia was more than $16,000, and the median household income in Georgia was well over $25,000.[15]

Recall that other researchers (Sampson and Laub 1993) found job stability to be an especially important factor in criminal desistance. During the 9 years covered by these data, sample members with any official recorded earnings averaged more than six employers. Hall (1982) found that male workers eventually settle into "lifetime jobs," but this finding clearly does not hold for the sample of prison releasees. Frequent incarceration and unemployment spells regularly undermined job stability.

Bound and Freeman (1992) and Welch (1990) found that labor force participation rates for Blacks diverged from those for Whites, in part because Blacks had greater involvement in the criminal justice system. Conditional on having been incarcerated, however, the data in Table 3 show that employment rates do not differ dramatically across racial and education groups. Although Blacks and high school dropouts spent less total time than Whites and high school graduates in the unemployment-insurance-covered labor market, these differences narrow when the higher rates of incarceration of the former groups are considered. For men with earnings, the fraction of free quarters spent employed is insignificantly different across racial or education groups (where "free quarters" are defined as quarters during which an individual spends at least 1 day not incarcerated).

Patterns of success in the labor market (as measured by earnings per normalized year free) are more similar to those obtained in conventional samples: Blacks earned 34% less than Whites, and high school dropouts earned 30% less than high school graduates. Hence the raw data on the effects of race and education on earnings appear to support standard labor economic findings.

Not consistent with traditional labor market evidence, however, is the earnings difference across the two age groups. Only 61% of releasees age 26 to 45 in 1976 had any earnings over 9 years, in contrast to 76% of younger releasees.[16] Even conditional on any reported earnings, the percentage of free quarters with associated earnings was lower for the group of older releasees. Total earnings during this 9-year window, as well as earnings normalized by time free, were insignificantly lower for the older group, however. This pattern suggests that the critical decision is the choice (or opportunity) to work. Unlike the contrast across racial and education groups (in which employment rates were similar and earnings levels were different), the two age categories had similar earnings patterns conditional on any earnings—but they had very different employment rates.

Many factors may account for the seemingly low employment rates found in this sample, especially among older men. The most likely causes are employment in the underground economy or in uncovered sectors of the unemployment insurance system, mobility out of state, early retirement, and death. However, men with recorded deaths (during a prison or probation spell) and those older than age 60 in 1991 were excluded from the sample. Although the low cutoff age should help to eliminate biases resulting from unrecorded deaths and early retirement, some men might have died or moved out of state without any official record of their whereabouts. Clearly, a large fraction of the older cohort's nonincarcerated time was spent with no earnings.

The criminal records data can be exploited to explore the plausibility of some of the explanations for low observed labor market outcomes. Individuals with at lest one recorded criminal activity could not have lived outside of Georgia during the entire 9-year period or have died before 1983. To estimate how much of the difference in employment rates is accounted for by these potential explanations, in Tables 4 and 5 the sample is divided according to whether an individual had at least one officially recorded arrest, probation, or prison spell after 1982. Together, the tables show that about 30% of the sample had no post-1982 criminal activity. Overall, those who had no officially recorded criminal activity during this period had very low employment rates, at 47% (158/[158 + 176]), but very high relative earnings, conditional on having earnings.[17] For those with earnings, the mean earnings per year were nearly twice as large for criminal desisters as for recidivists ($10,137 compared with $5,141). Controlling for differences in time incarcerated narrows the earnings gap, but not completely: The mean normalized earnings per time nonincarcerated remains about 49% lower for recidivists.

Among individuals with officially recorded criminal activity, those with no earnings spent 22% of the 9 years in prison (Table 5). Among individuals who were criminally active after 1982, the average percentage of time between 1983 and 1991 spent in prison by those with no earnings was not significantly higher than the percentage for those with earnings. Hence the data suggest that men

Table 4: Earnings and Incarceration Rates, by Post-1982 Criminal Activity, for Individuals with Any Earnings

Variable	All	No Criminal Activity After 1982	Criminal Activity After 1982	Test Value
Mean age in 1976	24.3	26.5	23.8	<.01
Mean earnings per year	$6,089	$10,137	$5,141	<.01
Fraction of quarters employed	.44	.55	.41	<.01
Earnings per normalized year free	$6,788	$10,137	$6,004	<.01
Fraction of free quarters with employment	.50	.55	.48	.01
Percentage not born in Georgia	14.9	13.8	15.1	.65
Percentage of time incarcerated, 1983 to 1991	14.8	—	18.3	—
Number of individuals	832	158	674	—

SOURCE: Transitional Aid Research Project (TARP) panel data.

Table 5: Incarceration Rates, by Post-1982 Criminal Activity,
for Individuals With No Earnings

Variable	All	No Criminal Activity After 1982	Criminal Activity After 1982	Test Value
Mean age in 1976	27.1	28.4	25.8	<.01
Percentage not born in Georgia	21.1	26.9	15.0	<.01
Percentage of time incarcerated, 1983 to 1991	10.6	—	21.8	—
Number of individuals	344	176	168	—

SOURCE: Transitional Aid Research Project (TARP) panel data.
NOTE: Individuals with no social security numbers in Georgia Department of Corrections records and those who were incarcerated during all 9 years of potential earnings records were excluded from the analysis.

who do not have official earnings are not statistically significantly more involved in the criminal justice system—and that the missing earnings are probably not caused by unusually high incarceration rates.

* * *

It is impossible to determine whether the 15% of the sample with no criminal activity or legal earnings died, moved out of state or retired, or were involved extensively in the underground economy (and/or learned how to avoid arrest while conducting their criminal enterprises). Although Blank and Card (1989) indicated that the coverage provided to workers by the unemployment insurance system expanded during the 1980s, men in the sample might have had extensive involvement in the underground economy. No direct insight on underground and illegal earnings can be gained from this data set (except to note the continued high offense rate for property crimes). However, the sample members' limited success in making a transition to legal employment status (employment covered by unemployment insurance)—coupled with the high rates of continued criminal activity discussed in the previous section—is apparent. The strong correlations among the different demographic and criminal history characteristics do suggest the need for multivariate analysis of employment and earnings patterns. The following discussion presents this analysis.

Characteristics Affecting Employment and Earnings Levels

The first column of Table 6 presents an ordinary least squares (OLS) model of the log of earnings, using total reported earnings between 1983 and 1991 (for the 832 men with any reported earnings). Although the earnings data cover a long period, this aggregate measure in used because of the high degree of cyclicality in employment (and overall low employment levels) for those in the sample. Consistent with findings for the general population, the OLS model indicates that Blacks and those with less education had significantly lower earnings than did their counterparts. A more extensive prior incarceration history decreased earnings, as did a greater number of prior arrests. Other measures of criminal history, such as prior probation history, whether an individual was paroled or had the sentence commuted in 1976, and the types of prior crimes committed (drugs, property or violent offenses) did not seem to affect earnings significantly (not shown). Likewise, whether an individual had medical problems or self-reported alcohol problems did not significantly influence earnings (not shown).

* * *

When selection is taken into account, the changes in the point estimates of the human capital and criminal history variables on earnings levels are minimal. Blacks and high school dropouts earned substantially less than did their respective counterparts. Age and its square affected earnings neither separately nor jointly, however, although the two terms were jointly significant in the selection equation and overall. (Several adjusted measures of age, such as age minus years of education and incarceration, did not provide greater predictive power.) Consistent with the results in Table 4, this finding suggests age may not effectively measure human capital development for prison releasee samples. First-time offenders and men with fewer arrests earned more than did their counterparts.

Table 6: Analysis of Total Earnings, 1983–1991
(standard errors in parentheses)

Dependent Variable Equation	OLS[a] Log (Total Earnings)	Heckman's Two-Step Selection			
		Log (Total Earnings)		Log (Total)	
	Earnings)	Selection	Earnings	Selection	Earnings
Intercept	8.529**	-.090	8.677**	-.183	9.251**
	(1.19)	(.710)	(1.185)	(.719)	(1.138)
Black	-.423**	.031	-.432**	.059	-.381**
	(.125)	(.083)	(.123)	(.084)	(.120)
Education	.111**	.001	.112**	.012	.093**
	(.031)	(.020)	(.031)	(.020)	(.030)
Age	.061	.073	.054	.057	.042
	(.085)	(.049)	(.085)	(.050)	(.082)
Age^2	-.001	-.002**	-.001	-.002*	-.0008
	(.002)	(.0008)	(.002)	(.0008)	(.001)
Not born in Georgia	.038	-.268**	—	-.265**	—
	(.173)	(.108)		(.107)	
Medium-/high-security prison release	-.256*	-.289**	-.234	-.261**	-.177
	(.146)	(.092)	(.146)	(.093)	(.141)
First-offender status	.491**	.161	.479**	.139	.470**
	(.156)	(.099)	(.156)	(.101)	(.150)
Number of pre-1983 arrests	-.053**	.003	-.053**	-.006	-.037**
	(.013)	(.007)	(.013)	(.008)	(.013)
Percentage of time incarcerated from 1976 release to 1983	-.963**	.235	-.981**	.049	-.180
	(.271)	(.183)	(.271)	(.208)	(.294)
Percentage of time incarcerated during 1983-1991	—	—	—	.385*	-1.982**
				(.222)	(.315)
Percentage of time on probation during 1983-1991	—	—	—	1.378**	-.123
				(.201)	(.239)
Selection correction	—		-.158**		-.682**
			(.004)		(.016)
Number of individuals	832		1,176		1,176
R^2	0.13		—		—
Log Likelihood	—		-2,295.0		-2,249.4

[a] OLS = ordinary least squares.
*$p \le 10$ (two-tailed test); **$p \le 05$ (two-tailed test).

A higher fraction of prior time incarcerated did not significantly affect employment but dramatically decreased earnings levels.

The Heckman model with the inclusion of measures for time incarcerated and time on probation during the 9-year span for which earnings records were available is presented in columns 4 and 5 of Table 6. Not surprisingly, a greater fraction of time incarcerated from 1983 to 1991 decreased overall earnings levels, whereas time on probation was insignificantly negative. The large positive and significant coefficients for these variables estimated in the selection equation suggest that the variables may be picking up some of the effects of sample members' being in Georgia during that period.

Total earnings do not take into account time incarcerated, so Table 7 presents an analysis similar to the one in Table 6, except that the dependent variable is now the log of earnings normalized for time incarcerated. The results in both tables are similar, suggesting that the coefficient estimates on Table 6 are robust to consideration of prison time.[20] As in Table 6, age and its square do not significantly affect earnings, but they do affect whether an individual has any earnings. Blacks and those with less education earn less, but their participation in the labor market is comparable to Whites and those with more education, respectively. The only substantive difference is that the time incarcerated from 1983 to 1991 is now insignificant in determining normalized earning levels. The contemporaneous amount of time spent incarcerated does not seem to decrease the earnings capabilities significantly for this sample of prison releasees, controlling for time spent in the community. (With even more parsimonious model specifications not shown, the coefficient for the contemporaneous amount of time incarcerated is consistently negative but never achieves statistical significance.) One cannot reject the hypothesis that the coefficients in the earnings equation for the percentage of time incarcerated from 1976 to 1983, as well as the percentage of time incarcerated form 1983 to 1991, are jointly equal to zero. This suggests that both past and contemporaneous time incarcerated does not significantly affect earnings levels, conditional on employment. Therefore, time in prison may not significantly affect human capital levels for individuals who have already been incarcerated.

Table 7: Analysis of Earnings Normalized, by Time Free, 1983-1991
(standard errors in parentheses)

	Log (Earnings Normalized for Time Free)		Log (Earnings Normalized for Time Free)	
Dependent Variable Equation	Selection	Earnings	Selection	Earnings
Intercept	-.090	5.388**	-.183	5.66**
	(.711)	(1.155)	(.720)	(1.14)
Black	.031	-.384**	.059	-.390**
	(.082)	(.120)	(.084)	(.120)
Education	.001	.099**	.012	.095**
	(.020)	(.030)	(.020)	(.030)
Age	.073	.047	.057	.039
	(.049)	(.083)	(.050)	(.082)
Age^2	-.002**	-.001	-.002*	-.0008
	(.0008)	(.001)	(.0008)	(.001)
Not born in Georgia	-.268**	—	-.265**	—
	(.107)		(.107)	
Medium-/high-security prison release	-.289**	-.217	-.261**	-.185
	(.092)	(.142)	(.093)	(.141)
First-offender status	.161	.492**	.139	.476**
	(.099)	(.152)	(.100)	(.151)
Number of pre-1983 arrests	.003	-.041**	-.006	-.040**
	(.007)	(.012)	(.008)	(.013)
Percentage of time incarcerated from 1976 release to 1983	-.200 (.183)	.235 (.264)	-.272 (.209)	.049 (.294)
Percentage of time incarcerated during 1983-1991	—	—	.385* (.221)	-.207 (.316)
Percentage of time on probation during 1983-1991	—	—	1.378** (.201)	-.159 (.239)
Selection correction	-.336** (.008)		-.622** (.015)	
Number of individuals	1,176		1,176	
Log likelihood	-2,277.2		-2,249.3	

*$p \leq .10$ (two-tailed test); **$p \leq .05$ (two-tailed test).

Conclusion

I used data on arrests, incarcerations, and the officially recorded earnings of 1,176 male prison releasees from Georgia to explore the determinants of employment and earnings patterns for prison releasees. Neoclassic models of labor supply postulate that higher earnings capacity should be associated with lower levels of involvement in criminal pursuits because the opportunity costs of incarceration are greater. Heckman's selection model for estimating legal-sector employment and earnings levels was used because only 71% of the sample had any earnings during the 9 years for which data were available.

Other studies have consistently found that characteristics such as age, education, and minority status affect the labor market participation and earnings levels of prime-age men (Bound and Freeman 1992; Welch 1990). In contrast to these findings for the general population, no clear conclusions can be drawn about the applicability of the human capital model to the population of prison releasees. Race and education did not have a significant effect on the employment rates of prison releasees in this sample. Nevertheless, these two characteristics exerted a strong influence on earnings, conditional on employment. The human capital model seems supported when success in the labor market is examined; other characteristics most likely contribute, in part, to explaining the low employment rates during the 9-year window. Contrasting men who have officially recorded criminal activity to those who did not suggests that mobility across state lines may play an important role in explaining the high fraction of missing earnings records. The positive, significant coefficients in the Heckman selection equation suggest that the amount of time in prison or on probation may be picking up whether or not an individual was in the state during the period for which earnings data were available.

As Table 7 shows, contemporaneous measures of incarceration did not seem to affect earnings levels significantly, after controlling for time in the community. This pattern suggests that among the group of men studied—who already were heavily involved in the criminal justice system—time spent incarcerated did not significantly affect life-cycle earnings levels during nonincarcerated time. Public policymakers who explore optimal sentence lengths for crimes (or, more accurately, optimal lengths for sentences served) might consider placing relatively little weight on a claim that additional time incarcerated depreciates the future earnings capacity of prisoners. This conclusion has three caveats. First, prisoners clearly lose earnings while incarcerated because they are out of the community. It is their "earnings rate" when they are not incarcerated that appears to be only insignificantly lower if they are incarcerated for longer periods of time. Second, no conclusions can be made on the effects of *any* incarceration compared to alternative punishments. That is, job and family disruption—which other researchers have found to be important—may still have a significant negative effect on future earnings. Third, this analysis only pertains to changes in the length of prison spells served for men with prison histories.

The findings of the effects of age on participation and earnings support the supposition that time in the community does not affect earnings rates. As is the case with time incarcerated, being older did not influence earnings levels for this sample of prison releasees. Even measures of age, adjusted for time incarcerated, did not impact on earnings levels. Age did affect whether an individual was observed to have earnings during the 9-year time frame. Assuming that age can substitute for work experience or human capital acquisition—something often assumed for the general population—may therefore be inappropriate for individuals with extensive criminal histories. Ex-prisoners may be relegated to, or choose, employment that does not rely heavily on tenure or firm—or occupation—specific human capital. No implications from this analysis can be drawn for men who are less extensively involved with correctional supervision or for those who receive prison terms significantly out of the range of the prison terms in this data set.

Overall, men with positive earnings but no post-1982 (officially recorded) criminal activity earned substantially more than their criminally active counterparts, even after adjusting for time incarcerated (Table 4). Comprising approximately one eighth of the sample, this group of desisters made an effective transition from illegal income-generating activities to legal-sector (albeit still poorly paid) employment.

The richness of this data set will allow future research to address several important issues. First, the contemporaneous interactions between labor market involvement and crime should be explored further. Second, the effects of unrecorded mortality for middle-age prison releasees on labor market estimates, and heterogeneity in the population of prison releasees, should be examined. Examining heterogeneity, mortality rates, and mobility out of state probably will help to improve the understanding of outcomes for the substantial portion of men who have no officially recorded activity. Finally, using these 9 years of official records on both earnings levels and employers can greatly enhance our understanding of the importance of job attachment and life transitions in patterns of offending and criminal desistance.

Footnotes

[1] It is conceptually possible that there might be long-run "sleeper effects" of the Transitional Aid Research Project (TARP) treatment, regardless of the short-run effects. Throughout this analysis, I have not included covariates for TARP treatment status.

* * *

[5] The relevance and size of this bias also depend on the type of question being asked. If one is concerned that prison releasees are not able to meet basic material needs, such as food and shelter, then failing to include off-the-books income, illegal income, and public or private social assistance in the measure of earnings might generate different findings than would including all sources of income. If one is asking whether prison releasees are making effective transitions to legal-sector employment, then using official earnings probably causes a much smaller bias. I focus on the latter question.

6 The 1,176 men in the final sample were about 1 year younger on average than the men excluded from the sample; moreover, a greater percentage were Black and released to urban areas. They reported younger ages at first arrest and incarceration (by about 1 year each), served shorter prison terms (by about 3 months), and were less likely to have been released from prison for the first time (70% compared with 83%). Although these differences suggest that the sample was not fully representative of all men released from Georgia prisons during 1975 and 1976, the sample members were more nearly similar to current male prisoners than were their excluded counterparts (Maguire, Pastore, and Flanagan 1995).

7 Individuals returning to an out-of-state location on release or to certain rural settings, as well as individuals with outstanding detainers or warrants for arrest or reincarceration, were excluded from the TARP experiment. A sample size of 2,000 was targeted for the experiment, so other individuals released during 1976 were excluded after the quota for TARP subjects had been met (Rossi, Berk, and Lenihan 1980).

8 Because these categories overlap, the sum of the exclusions as listed is greater than 1,267.

9 Regardless of what a prisoner reports as highest school level completed, an examination usually is administered on admission to prison to determine whether the individual is in need of educational training and, if so, the level at which the individual should be placed.

10 When I examined the timing until the first rearrest and/or reincarceration, I used time to refer to the number of days since release. Hence, the chronological dates associated with "1 year after release" vary by released date.

11 One cannot reject the hypothesis that total time under both types of supervision was constant between 1977 and 1993 (the full panel length except for the first year), although clearly some substitution between prison and probationary supervision occurred over time.

12 Time spent reincarcerated increased dramatically during the first 2 to 3 years after release in 1976: this pattern was followed by a slight dip, a small increase, and then a fairly steady decline in time spent in prison. In contrast to the trend of decreasing incarceration rates, the fraction of time under probation steadily increased during the 17-year follow-up window.

13 Unemployment rates in Georgia for men ranged from 4.4% in 1987 to 7.3% in 1991. The year with the second highest unemployment rate, at 6.9% was 1983 (U.S. Department of Commerce, various years).

14 Because earnings are reported quarterly, no measures of wages per hour or hours per week are available.

15 Tables 701, 728, and 730 from *Statistical Abstract of the United States 1992*; Table 664 from Statistical *Abstract of the United States 1989*; and Table 698 from *Statistical Abstract of the United States 1985*.

16 In each year, employment rates for those not incarcerated for the full year ranged from 26% to 36% for the older group and from 37% to 49% for the younger group. Employment rates were significantly different from each other, with a p value of less than 1% in each year.

17 Eighty percent (674/[674 + 168]) of the releasees with any criminal activity recorded after 1982 had some positive earnings.

* * *

20 In the selection equations, the coefficients from using the different dependent variables should be, and are, almost identical.

References

Becker, Gary S. 1986. "Crime and Punishment: An Economic Approach." *Journal of Political Economy* 73: 169–217.

Blank, Rebecca and David Card. 1989. *Recent Trends in Insured and Uninsured Employment: Is There an Explanation?* National Bureau of Economic Research Working Paper No. 2871. Cambridge MA: National Bureau of Economic Research.

Bound, John and Richard ·B. Freeman. 1992. "What Went Wrong? The Erosion of Relative Earnings and Employment among Young Black Men in the 1980s." *The Quarterly Journal of Economics* 107:201-32.

Chung, Ching-Fan, Peter Schmidt, and Ann D., Witte. 1991. "Survival Analysis: A Survey." *Journal of Quantitative Criminology* 7:59–78.

DiIulio, John J., Jr. 1996. "Help Wanted: Economists, Crime, and Public Policy." *The Journal of Economic Perspectives* 10:3–24.

Doeringer, Peter and Mike Piore. [1971] 1985. *Internal Labor Markets and Manpower Analysis*. Armonk, NY: M. E. Sharpe.

Ehrlich, Isaac, 1973. "Participation in Illegitimate Activities: A Theoretical and Empirical Investigation." *Journal of Political Economy* 83:521–65.

Farrington, David P. 1986. "Stepping Stones to Adult Criminal Careers." Pp. 359-84 in *Development of Antisocial and Prosocial Behavior*, edited by Dan Olweus, Jack Block, and Marian Radke-Yarrow. New York: Academic Press.

Freeman, Richard B. 1991. "Crime and the Economic Status of Disadvantaged Young Men." Paper presented at the Conference on Urban Labor Markets and 'Labor Mobility, Airlie, VA, March 7, 1991.

_____.1996. "Why Do So Many Young Men Commit Crimes and What Might We Do about It?" *The Journal of Economic Perspectives* 10:25–42.

Glueck, Sheldon and Eleanor Glueck, 1952. *Delinquents in the Making.* New York: Harper & Row.

Greenfeld, Lawrence, 1985. *Examining Recidivism*, Bureau of Justice Statistics Special Report. Washington, DC: U.S. Department of Justice, Bureau of Justice Statistics.

Grogger, Jeff. 1991. "The Effect of Arrest on the Labor Market Outcomes of Young Men." Unpublished manuscript.

Hall, Robert. 1982. "The Importance of Lifetime Jobs in the U.S. Economy." *American Economic Review* 72:716–24.

Heckman, James J. 1974. "Shadow Prices, Market Wages, and labor Supply." *Econometrica* 42:679–94.

Kitchener, H., A. Schmidt, and D. Glaser. 1977. "How Persistent Is Post-Prison Success?" *Federal Probation* 41:9–15.

Maguire, Kathleen, Ann L. Pastore, and Timothy J. Flanagan, eds. 1995. *Sourcebook of Criminal Justice Statistics—1994.* Washington, DC: U.S. Government Printing Office.

Needels, Karen. 1994. "Go Directly to Jail and Do Not Collect? A Long-Term Study of Recidivism and Employment Patterns among Prison Releasees." Unpublished doctoral dissertation, Princeton University, Department of Economics.

Needels, Karen and Anne Morrison Piehl, 1991. "The Theory of Criminal Deterrence: A Survey." Mimeo, Princeton University, Department of Economics.

Piehl, Anne Morrison. 1994. "Economic Issues in Crime Policy." Unpublished doctoral dissertation, Princeton University, Department of Economics.

Polk, K., C. Alder, G. Bazemore, G. Blake, S. Cordray, G. Coventry, J. Galvin, and M. Temple. 1981. *Becoming Adult: An Analysis of Maturational Development from Age Sixteen to Thirty of a Cohort of Young Men.* Final Report of the Marion County Youth Study. Eugene: University of Oregon, Department of Sociology.

Rauma, D. and R. A. Berk. 1987. "Remuneration and Recidivism: The Long-Term Impact of Unemployment Compensation on Ex-Offenders." *Journal of Quantitative Criminology* 3:3-27.

Rossi, P.H., R.A. Berk, and K. J. Lenihan. 1980. *Money, Work, and Crime: Experimental Evidence.* New York: Academic Press.

Sampson, Robert J. and John Laub, 1993. *Crime in the Making: Pathways and Turning Points through Life.* Cambridge, MA: Harvard University Press.

Smith, C. L., P. Martinez, and D. Harrison. 1978. *An Assessment: The Impact of Providing Financial or Job Placement Assistance to Ex-Prisoners.* Huntsville: Texas Department of Corrections.

Stevens, J. L. and L. W. Sanders. 1978. *Transitional Aid for Ex-Offenders: An Experimental Study in Georgia.* Atlanta: Georgia Department of Offender Rehabilitation.

U.S. Department of Commerce. Various years. *Statistical Abstract of the United States.* Washington, DC: U.S. Department of Commerce.

Welch, Finis. 1990. "The Employment of Black Men." *Journal of Labor Economics* 8:S26–74.

Wilson, James Q. and Allan Abrahamse. 1992. "Does Crime Pay?" *Justice Quarterly* 9:359-77.

Witte, Ann D. 1976. "Earnings and Jobs of Ex-Offenders: A Case Study." *Monthly Labor Review* 99:31–9.

Witte, Ann Dryden, and Helen Tauchen. 1994. *Work and Crime: An Exploration Using Panel Data*. National Bureau of Economic Research Working Paper No. 4794. Cambridge, MA: National Bureau of Economic Research.

Wolfgang, Marvin E., Terence P. Thornberry, and Robert Figlio. 1987. *From Boy to Man: Delinquency to Crime*. Chicago: University of Chicago Press.

Zeisel, H. 1982. "Disagreement over the Evaluation of a Controlled Experiment." *American Journal of Sociology* 88:378–89.

CRIME AND PUNISHMENT:
AN ECONOMIC APPROACH

Gary S. Becker

V. Fines

C. The Case for Fines

Just as the probability of conviction and the severity of punishment are subject to control by society, so too is the form of punishment: legislation usually specifies whether an offense is punishable by fines, probation, institutionalization, or some combination. Is it merely an accident, or have optimality considerations determined that today, in most countries, fines are the predominant form of punishment, with institutionalization reserved for the more serious offenses? This section presents several arguments which imply that social welfare is increased if fines are used *whenever feasible*.

In the first place, probation and institutionalization use up social resources, and fines do not, since the latter are basically just transfer payments, while the former use resources in the form of guards, supervisory personnel, probation officers, and the offenders' own time.[40] . . . the cost is not minor either: in the United States in 1965, about $1 billion was spent on "correction," and this estimate excludes, of course, the value of the loss in offenders' time.[41]

Moreover, the determination of the optimal number of offenses and severity of punishments is somewhat simplified by the use of fines. A wise use of fines requires knowledge of marginal gains and harm and of marginal apprehension and conviction costs; admittedly, such knowledge is not easily acquired. A wise use of imprisonment and other punishments must know this too, however, and , in addition, must know about the elasticities of response of offenses to changes in punishments. As the bitter controversies over the abolition of. capital punishment suggest, it has been difficult to learn about these elasticities.

I suggested earlier that premeditation, sanity, and age enter into the determination of punishments as proxies for the elasticities of response. These characteristics may not have to be considered in levying fines, because the optimal fines . . . do not depend on elasticities. Perhaps this partly explains why economists discussing externalities almost never mention motivation or intent, while sociologists and lawyers discussing criminal behavior invariably do. The former assume that punishment is by a monetary tax or fine, while the latter assume that non-monetary punishments are used.

Fines provide compensation to victims, and optimal fines at the margin fully compensate victims and restore the status quo ante, so that they are no worse off than if offenses were not committed.[42] Not only do other punishments fail to compensate, but they also require "victims" to spend additional resources in carrying out the punishment. It is not surprising, therefore, that the anger and fear felt toward ex-convicts who in fact have *not* "paid their debt to society" have resulted in additional punishments,[43] including legal restrictions on their political and economic opportunities[44] and informal restrictions on their social acceptance. Moreover, the absence of compensation encourages efforts to change and otherwise "rehabilitate" offenders through psychiatric counseling, therapy, and other programs. Since fines do compensate and do not create much additional cost, anger toward and fear of appropriately fined persons do not easily develop. As a result, additional punishments are not usually levied against "ex-finees," nor are strong efforts made to "rehabilitate" them.

One argument against fines is that they are immoral because, in effect, they permit offenses to be bought for a price in the same way that bread or other goods are bought for a price.[45] A fine *can* be considered the price of an offense, but so too can any other form of punishment; for example, the "price" of stealing a car might be six months in jail. The only difference is in the units of measurement: fines are prices measured in monetary units, imprisonments are prices measured in time units, etc. If anything, monetary units are to be preferred here as they are generally preferred in pricing and accounting.

Optimal fines . . . depend only on the marginal harm and cost and not at all on the economic positions of offenders. This has been criticized as unfair, and fines proportional to the incomes of offenders have been suggested.[46] If the goal is to minimize the social loss in income from offenses, and not to take vengeance or to inflict harm on offenders, then fines should depend on the total harm done by offenders, and not directly on their income, race, sex, etc. In the same way, the monetary value of optimal prison sentences and other punishments depends on the harm, costs, and elasticities of response, but not directly on an offender's income. Indeed, if the monetary value of the punishment by, say, imprisonment were independent of income, the length of the sentence would be *inversely* related to income, because the value placed on a given sentence is positively related to income.

We might detour briefly to point out some interesting implications for the probability of conviction of the fact that the monetary value of a given fine is obviously the same for all offenders, while monetary equivalent on "value" of a given prison sentence or probation period is generally positively related to an offender's income. The discussion . . . suggested that actual probabilities of conviction are not fixed to all offenders but usually vary with their age, sex, race, and, in particular, income. Offenders with higher earnings have an incentive to spend more on planning their offenses, on good lawyers, on legal appeals, and even on bribery to reduce the probability of apprehension and conviction for offenses punishable by, say, a given prison term, because the cost to them of conviction is relatively large compared to the cost of these expenditures. Similarly, however, poorer offenders have an incentive to use more of their time in planning their offenses, in court appearances, and the like to reduce the probability of conviction for offenses punishable by a given fine, because the cost to them of conviction is relatively large compared to the value of their time.[47] The implication is that the probability of conviction would be systematically related to the earnings of offenders: negatively for offenses punishable by imprisonment and positively for those punishable by fines. Although a negative relation for felonious and other offenses punishable by imprisonment has been frequently observed and deplored (see President's Commission, 1967c, pp. 139-53), I do not know of any studies of the relation for fines or of any recognition that the observed negative relation may be more a consequence of the nature of punishment than of the influence of wealth.

Another argument made against fines is that certain crimes, like murder or rape, are so heinous that no amount of money could compensate for the harm inflicted. This argument has obvious merit and is a special case of the more general principle that fines cannot be relied on exclusively whenever the harm exceeds the resources of offenders. For then victims could not be fully compensated by offenders, and fines would have to be supplemented with prison terms or other punishments in order to discourage offenses optimally. This explains why imprisonments, probation, and parole are major punishments for the more serious felonies; considerable harm is inflicted, and felonious offenders lack sufficient resources to compensate. Since fines are preferable, it also suggests the need for a flexible system of installment fines to enable offenders to pay fines more readily and thus avoid other punishments.

This analysis implies that if some offenders could pay the fine for a given offense and others could not,[48] the former should be punished solely by fine and the latter partly by other methods. In essence, therefore, these methods become a vehicle for punishing "debtors" to society. Before the cry is raised that the system is unfair, especially to poor offenders, consider the following.

Those punished would be debtors in "transactions" that were never agreed to by their "creditors," not in voluntary transactions, such as loans,[49] for which suitable precautions could be taken in advance by creditors. Moreover, punishment in any economic system based on voluntary market transactions inevitably must distinguish between such "debtors" and others. If a rich man purchases a car and a poor man steals one, the former is congratulated, while the latter is often sent to prison when apprehended. Yet the rich man's purchase is equivalent to a "theft" subsequently compensated by a "fine" equal to the price of the car, while the poor man, in effect, goes to prison because he cannot pay this "fine."

Whether a punishment like imprisonment in lieu of a full fine for offenders lacking sufficient resources is "fair" depends, of course, on the length of the prison term compared to the fine.[50] For example, a prison term of one week in lieu of a $10,000 fine would, if anything, be "unfair" to wealthy offenders paying the fine. Since imprisonment is a more costly punishment to society than fines, the loss from offenses would be reduced by a policy of leniency toward persons who are imprisoned because they cannot pay fines.

Consequently, optimal prison terms for "debtors" would not be "unfair" to them in the sense that the monetary equivalent to them of the prison terms would be less than the value of optimal fines, which in turn would equal the harm caused or the "debt."

It appears, however, that "debtors" are often imprisoned at rates of exchange with fines that place a low value on time in prison. Although I have not seen systematic evidence on the different punishments actually offered convicted offenders, and the choices they made, many statutes in the United States do permit fines and imprisonment that place a low value on time in prison. For example, in New York State, Class A Misdemeanors can be punished by a prison term as long as one year or a fine no larger than $1,000 and Class B Misdemeanors, by a term as long as three months or a fine no larger that $500 (*Laws of New York*, 1965, chap. 1030, arts. 70 and 80).[52] According to my analysis, these statutes permit excessive prison sentences relative to the fines, which may explain why imprisonment in lieu of fines is considered unfair to poor offenders, who often must "choose" the prison alternative.

Footnotes

[40] Several early writers on criminology recognized this advantage of fines. For example, "Pecuniary punishments are highly economical, since all the evil felt by him who pays turns into an advantage for him who receives" (Bentham, 1931, chap. vi), and "Imprisonment would have been regarded in these old times [*ca.* tenth century] as a useless punishment; it does not satisfy revenge, it keeps the criminal idle, and do what we may, *it is costly*" (Pollock and Maitland, 1952, p. 516; my italics).

[41] On the other hand, some transfer payments in the form of food, clothing, and shelter are included.

[42] Bentham recognized this and said, "To furnish an indemnity to the injured party is another useful quality in a punishment. It is a means of accomplishing two objects at once—punishing an offense and repairing it: removing the evil of the first order, and putting a stop to alarm. This is a characteristic advantage of pecuniary punishments" (1931, chap. vi).

[43] In the same way, the guilt felt by society in using the draft, a forced transfer to society, has led to additional payments to veterans in the form of education benefits, bonuses, hospitalization rights, etc.

[44] See Sutherland (1960, pp. 267-68) for a list of some of these.

[45] The very early English law relied heavily on monetary fines, even for murder, and it has been said that "every kind of blow or wound given to every kind of person had its price, and much of the jurisprudence of the time must have consisted of a knowledge of these preappointed prices" (Pollock and Maitland, 1952, p. 451).
   The same idea was put amusingly in a recent *Mutt and Jeff* cartoon which showed a police car carrying a sign that read: "Speed limit 30 M per H—$5 fine every mile over speed limit—pick out speed you can afford."

[46] For example, Bentham said, "A pecuniary punishment, if the sum is fixed is in the highest degree unequal. . . . Fines have been determined without regard to the profit of the offense, to its evil, or to the wealth of the offender. . . Pecuniary punishments should always be regulated by the fortune of the offender. The relative amount of the fine should be fixed, not its absolute amount; for such an offense, such a part of the offender's fortune" (1931, chap. ix). Note that optimal fines . . . do depend on "the profit of the offense" and on "its evil."

[47] Note that the incentive to use time to reduce the probability of a given prison sentence is unrelated to earnings, because the punishment is fixed in time, not monetary, units; likewise, the incentive to use money to reduce the probability of a given fine is also unrelated to earnings, because the punishment is fixed in monetary, not time, units.

[48] In one study, about half of those convicted of misdemeanors could not pay the fines (see President's Commission, 1967c, p. 148).

[49] The "debtor prisons" of earlier centuries generally housed persons who could not repay loans.

[50] Yet without any discussion of the actual alternatives offered, the statement is made that "the money judgment assessed the punitive damages defendant hardly seems comparable in effect to the criminal sanctions of death, imprisonment, and stigmatization" ("Criminal Safeguards . . . ," 1967).

[52] "Violations," however, can only be punished by prison terms as long as fifteen days or fines no larger than $250. Since these are maximum punishments, the actual ones imposed by the courts can, and often are, considerably less. Note, too, that the courts can punish by imprisonment, by fine, or by *both* (*Laws of New York*, 1965, chap. 1030, Art. 60).

WHY DO SO MANY YOUNG AMERICAN MEN COMMIT CRIMES AND WHAT MIGHT WE DO ABOUT IT?

Richard B. Freeman

In the past two decades or so, more and more American men, particularly the young, the less educated and blacks, have been involved in crime, despite an increased risk of imprisonment. From the mid-1970s to the mid-1990s, the United States roughly tripled the number of men in prison or jail; so that by 1993 one man was incarcerated for every 50 men in the workforce. Incapacitation of so many criminals should have greatly reduced the crime rate: if the worst offenders are in prison, they can't mug, rob or otherwise commit offenses against the citizenry. But no such drastic reduction in crime occurred. The number of crimes reported to the police roughly stabilized while the rate of victimizations (which includes crimes not reported to the police) dropped far less rapidly than could reasonably be expected. Noninstitutionalized men evidently "replaced" incarcerated criminals in committing crimes.

Why? What induces young American men, particularly less educated and black men, to engage in crime in large numbers despite the risk of imprisonment? Is the rising rate of criminal involvement related to the collapse in the job market for the less skilled? Is "locking them up" the only efficacious way to fight crime?

In this essay I examine these questions. I show that participation in crime and involvement with the criminal justice system has reached such levels as to become part of normal economic life for many young men. I present evidence that labor market incentives influence the level of crime and argue that the depressed labor market for less skilled men in the 1980s and 1990s has contributed to the rise in criminal activity by less skilled men. Given the high

---

Richard B. Freeman is Professor of Economics, Harvard University, and Research Fellow, National Bureau of Economic Research, both in Cambridge, Massachusetts. This paper was written while he was a visitor at the Centre for Economic Performance, London School of Economics, London, Great Britain.

Reprinted with permission from *Journal of Economic Perspectives*, Vol. 10, No. 1, Winter 1996, pp. 25-42. Copyright © 1996 Journal of Economic Perspectives.

costs of crime and imprisonment, even marginally effective crime prevention policies can be socially desirable.

Magnitudes of Criminal Involvement

The participation of American men in crime is staggering. Consider first the number of men convicted of crime and sent to prison or jail. In 1993, 910,000 were in state or federal prison; an additional 440,500 were in jail, for a total of 1,350,500 incarcerated.[1] With a male workforce of 69.6 million or so, this is one man incarcerated for every 50 men in the workforce! This proportion is approximately the same as the share of long-term unemployed men on the dole in many western European countries. For every person incarcerated in the United States, approximately 2.1 were on probation and 0.5 were on parole—an additional 3,511,300 men with criminal involvement. All told, 7 percent as many men were "under the supervision of the criminal justice system" (incarcerated, paroled or probated) as were in the workforce.[2]

Most of those involved in crime are young. In 1993, 2.9 percent of 25-to 34-year-old American men were incarcerated.[3] Approximately 10 percent of men in this age group were under supervision of the criminal justice system.

Many of those involved in crime are black. In 1993, about 7 percent of black men over 18 were incarcerated. One black man was in prison for every 11 black men in the workforce. Combine race and age, and you find that 12 percent of black men aged 25-34 were incarcerated.

A disproportionate number of men in prisons are high school dropouts: the 1991 *Survey of State Prison Inmates* reports that two-thirds had not graduated high school, though many had obtained a general equivalency degree (U.S. Department of Justice, Bureau of Justice Statistics, 1993). Among 25- to 34-year-olds, approximately 12 percent of male dropouts were incarcerated in 1993.

Combine race, age and education: in 1993, 34 percent of high school dropout 25- to 34-year old black men were incarcerated. Since many of those noninstitutionalized will be put on probation or released on parole, a majority of the young male black dropout population—which makes up 15 percent of black men aged 25-34—is under the supervision of the criminal system.[4]

When prisoners complete their sentences, a large number do not return to society rehabilitated to enter the job market. Prisoners have high recidivism rates (Needels, 1994). Many offenders sentenced to prison eventually return to society with their labor market skills and opportunities reduced and their criminal skills and opportunities enhanced. Young men who have been incarcerated have poor employment records years into the future, controlling for many observable factors and in comparison to their own preprison employment record (Freeman, 1992). Criminality declines with age (raising questions about the extent to which incarceration of aged criminals reduces crime), but crime is not a "teenage thing." Rather, the population of offenders is a relatively permanent part of American society—an "underclass" problem group that will not disappear naturally.

The numbers incarcerated or under supervision of the criminal justice system in the United States are a decimal place beyond comparable statistics in other advanced countries. In the United Kingdom, which has the highest rate of incarceration in western Europe, approximately 50,000 men were in prison in 1993, 0.3 percent of the number of the workforce. The 1992 incarceration rate for the entire population in the United States was five to 10 times that for western European countries (Central Statistical Office, 1995, p. 167).

What is comparable in western Europe to the U.S. prison population are men who have been unemployed and on the dole for a long time. In 1992, approximately 2 percent of the male workforce was unemployed for over one year in Europe's largest economy, Germany. In the United Kingdom, the figure was 5.1 percent. In France, it was 23.6 percent.[5] Europe's long-term jobless are also removed from the normal job market on a relatively permanent basis. Many leave unemployment to obtain disability insurance or early retirement, rather than to return to the normal job market.

The numbers incarcerated or under supervision do not measure the current rate of criminal participation. Not every criminal is caught and arrested, much less locked up. Persons under probation or parole may commit some crimes, but those not yet under supervision of the criminal justice system commit many as well.

One way to determine participation in crime is through household surveys, which ask respondents whether or not they committed crimes over some time period. A surprisingly large number of young men self-report criminal involvement, especially in samples that cover poor inner-city neighborhoods or that oversample the disadvantaged. In one widely used survey, the National Longitudinal Survey of Youth (which oversamples youths from poorer family backgrounds), 41 percent of young men admitted in 1980 that they had committed crimes in the previous year. In the 1989 Boston Youth Survey, 23 percent said that they had committed crimes (Freeman, 1992, Table 6.3) Studies that seek to verify self-reported criminal behavior (say, by checking police records on arrests) find that white youths give reasonably accurate reports, but that black youths understate their criminal involvement (Hindelang, Hirschi and Weiss, 1981).

Another way to estimate the number of persons in the noninstitutional population involved in crime is to divide numbers of crimes by crimes committed per criminal (called lambda by criminologists). Because estimates of the number of crimes per criminal differ greatly, there is a wide band of uncertainty around this calculation. Studies of prisoners suggest an average number of crimes of approximately 60 to 180 per year (Marvell and Moody, 1994, Table 1), though one may be suspicious of self-reported numbers on the order of 180. But because a small number of criminals report committing a large number of crimes, the median number of offenses per prisoner is just 12-15 per year. Since prisoners are a high-offending group, moreover, their crime rates should exceed those of the nonincarcerated population. Criminologists also estimate crimes per criminal by asking persons arrested how many times they were arrested and dividing the number of arrests by police data on the arrests per crime. These estimates suggest a rate around 11 (Marvell and Moody, 1994, p. 112). Finally, we have numbers of crimes reported by youths on household surveys. In the NLSY, nonincarcerated youths who admit having committed crimes report seven crimes over the year.

Given 15 million crimes reported to the police, 60-180 crimes per criminal implies that there are just 83,000 to 250,000 criminals: 12 crimes per criminal implies one million persons in the non-institutional population committing crimes in a year; 7 crimes per criminal implies 2.1 million persons committing crimes. Since 2.3 million arrests are made for "serious crimes" each year and some 8.5

million arrests are made for "nonserious crimes," I regard as reasonable the estimate that about 2 million noninstitutionalized persons commit crimes each year. The bottom line is clear: crime is a substantial activity among men in the United States. Given the age, race and education background of those incarcerated or arrested, it is a major activity among important subgroups.

Trends in Criminal Participation

As noted at the outset, mass incarceration of criminals should have reduced crime substantially. That it did not implies that there was a major increase in criminal activity among the noninstitutionalized population. How big was this increase? For the period from 1977 to 1992, I estimated the trend in criminal activity by the noninstitutional population through a three step procedure.

First, I calculated the reduction in crime due to the increased incapacitation of criminals under conservative assumptions about the number of crimes the newly incarcerated would have committed had they been on the street. As a simple example, assume a population of 100, in which there are 40 crimes committed a year, so that the crime/person ratio is .40. If each criminal commits 10 crimes, there are four criminals in the population. When the government apprehends and imprisons two criminals, the crime/person ratio should, by the incapacitation effect, fall roughly in half, to .204 (20/98).

Second, I compared this expected number of crimes to the actual number of crimes as reported by the Uniform Crime Report of the FBI or National Crime Survey on victimization.[6] In the illustration given a moment ago, any crime rate beyond .204 implies that those not previously committing crimes are now doing so or that those committing crimes now commit more.

Third, I divided crimes committed to the predicted number to obtain an index of the "Propensity to Commit Crime." This propensity reflects both the rate of participation of noninstitutionalized men in crime and the intensity of criminal activity. In the illustrative example, if 30 crimes were committed instead of the predicted 20, then the propensity would have risen 50 percent; if 40 crimes were committed, the propensity would have risen 100 percent. If the number of crimes committed per criminal remains constant, then

Figure 1

The Rising Propensity to Commit Crime, 1977–1992
(1977=100)

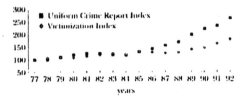

Source: Author's calculations as described in the text

changes in the calculated propensity must reflect a greater amount of criminal participation.

Figure 1 shows the trends resulting from these calculations, with the propensity to commit crime in 1977 being normalized at 100. Using 1977 as a base year is designed to choose a year not too far in the past, but prior to the large increase in the jail and prison population. One line in Figure 1 shows the results of basing this calculation on 10 crimes committed per person incarcerated, a figure based on the Uniform Crime Report statistics. The calculations indicate that if the propensity to commit crime had not increased, then the increase in the prison/jail population should have more than halved the number of crimes committed per male. But between 1977 and 1992, the crimes committed per male rose modestly. Thus, the propensity for criminal activity by noninstitutionalized men increased by 163 percent.

The second line on Figure 1 reports similar calculations using the victimization data. In this calculation, based on the National Crime Survey, I assume the number of victimization's per criminal to be 30. The result is an estimate that criminal propensity increased by 80 percent from 1977 to 1992. Alternative estimates of crimes per incarcerated person give different magnitudes to the rise in propensity without altering the message: the rate of criminal activity among noninstitutionalized men rose sharply in this period.

Labor Market Causes of Crime

The correlates and causes of crime are complex and varied: among the factors considered by criminologists are age, sex, family background, intelligence, biomedical factors, community conditions, race, crime control strategies and economic factors (Wilson and Petersilia, 1995). Without downplaying this complexity, I want to direct attention to the proposition, dear to the heart of economists, that labor market incentives influence the supply of men to crime, and, in particular, that collapse of the job market for less skilled men during the 1980s and 1990s may have contributed to their increased rate of criminal activity.

For the change in the labor market to help explain the high and rising rate of criminal participation among American men, it is necessary that a) the economic rewards from crime rose relative to those from legal work; and b) young men respond significantly to relative rewards.

The Relative Rewards of Crime

The pecuniary returns to crime depend on legitimate earnings opportunities, criminal earnings opportunities, the likelihood that crime will succeed, and the penalty that a criminal will pay if caught.

It is well established that the legitimate earnings opportunities of low skill men deteriorated substantially from the mid-1970s through the 1990s. Real earnings fell sharply for the least educated and for those in the bottom rungs of the earnings distribution. The exact magnitude of the decline in earnings depends on the specific measure of earnings chosen, the deflator, years picked, the age and skill group chosen and so on, but drops on the order of 20-30 percent that accelerated in the 1990s are a reasonable estimate (Mishel and Bernstein, 1994). Despite the putative job-creating effects of reduced pay, there was no offsetting improvement in hours worked or employment/population rates for the less skilled. To the contrary, hours worked over the year fell among those in the bottom rungs of the wage distribution (Juhn, Murphy and Topel, 1991); and employment-population rates for this group worsened in the 1970s, though not in the 1980s (Blackburn, Bloom and Freeman, 1990).

The implication is that demand for less skilled male labor plummeted.

On the other side of the incentive equation are criminal earnings. Because criminals are not forthcoming about their incomes, we do not have good estimates of how much crime pays, much less of how criminal earnings have changed over time.[7] However, responses to survey questions of *perceived* criminal opportunities suggest that criminal rewards have increased, at least among youth. In 1980, the NBER Inner City Youth Survey asked youths in Boston, Chicago and Philadelphia whether they thought they could make more "on the street" than in a legitimate job. It also asked them about their perceptions of the availability of criminal opportunities. The 1989 Boston Youth Survey, conducted at the peak of the booming "Massachusetts Miracle" job market, asked the same questions. Between these dates, the proportion of youths who reported that they could earn more on the street went up, from 31 percent in the three cities and 41 percent in Boston in 1980 to 63 percent in Boston in 1989. Similarly, the proportion who said they had "chances to make illegal income several times a day" roughly doubled over the period, to reach nearly 50 percent in 1989 (Freeman, 1992).

Youths who made money from crime in the 1980 NBER Survey of Inner City reported average annual criminal earnings of $1,807 per year, whereas in the 1989 Boston Youth Survey annual youths reported average criminal earnings of $3,008—which, deflated, implies a real increase of some 5 percent.[8] Annual criminal earnings are, the reader will note, not large. Even young men who said they committed crimes weekly in 1989 reported earnings just $5400 over the year. But transformed into "hourly rates," these figures imply hourly earnings from crime of around $10.00 for criminal activity in Boston in 1989. This exceeds the $7.50 youths reported from legitimate work and the $5.00 or $6.00 or so in take-home pay they would get from that work after Social Security and tax deductions.[9]

Estimates of the earnings for adult criminals tell a similar story. Reuter, MacCoun and Murphy (1990) surveyed drug dealers in Washington, D.C., and found that they earned $2000 per month net of expenses, which translated into $30 per hour, making drug selling "much more profitable on an hourly basis than are legitimate jobs available to the same person" (Reuter, MacCoun and Murphy,

1990, p. viii). They further estimated that the illegitimate earnings of drug dealers exceeded their legitimate earnings by enough to make it financially worth their while to spend one year in jail for every two years they sold drugs. Using the 1986 Survey of Prison Inmates, I found that criminals who said all of their earnings came from crime made $24,775 per year (Freeman, 1992), a figure comparable to Reuter's $2000 a month, but so few criminals reported that all their earnings were from crime to make this an unrepresentative statistic. On the other hand, Wilson and Abrahamse (1992) stress that criminal earnings from burglary/theft, robbery and swindling are not that high and may fall short of the legitimate earnings available to those criminals (though not necessarily on an hourly basis).

A potentially important factor contributing to criminal earnings and crime is the demand for drugs, which may have increased in the period due in part to the development of new products and sources of drugs. A huge proportion of persons arrested for nondrug crimes—from 50 to 80 percent—tested positive for drugs in 1992 (U.S. Bureau of the Census, 1993, Table 315). A substantial proportion of prisoners have been incarcerated for drugs offenses. Some persons commit crimes to make money to buy drugs: Boyum and Kleiman (1995) note that 39 percent of cocaine and crack users claim to have committed crime to get money to buy drugs. Others commit the crime of trying to meet the market demand. While we lack any valid time series measure of the shift in demand for drugs, most analysts believe that this has raised criminal earnings opportunities.

The pecuniary returns to crime depend on an additional factor: the probability that the individual succeeds with the crime. If a youth is caught, he is likely to gain little from the crime. If he in incarcerated, he obtains no legitimate earnings during this sentence and, likely as not, will have fewer legitimate earnings opportunities upon release. Since the probability of incarceration increased in the 1980s, it is possible that the relative rewards to crime actually fell, despite the sharp drop in legitimate earnings. To assess this possibility, I have examined Langan's (1991, Table 4) estimates of the increase in the chance of imprisonment for various crimes from 1974 to 1986. The largest increase is 9.1 percentage points for robbery. Langan (Table 1) finds that the median time served before release in prison in 1986 was 15 months. Thus, the increase in incarceration would cut a criminal's legitimate earnings by 11 percent (1.25 x .091) if he were fully employed during the period. This falls far short of the 30 percent drop in real earnings from legitimate work.

A more detailed analysis would contrast the effects of the fall in legal earnings and of the increased risk of incarceration on lifetime incomes. This might involve various long-term factors: how imprisonment raises the likelihood of more severe sentences in the future; the reduction in future legal employment opportunities; a possible increase in future illegal opportunities(!); and so on. But given the magnitude of decline in legitimate earnings, and probable increase in criminal earnings, I doubt that the increased chance of incarceration would tip the balance of the income calculation toward steering young men away from criminal activity.

If incarceration carries with it substantial nonpecuniary costs (prisons are not pleasant places unless you are a high-earner, white-collar criminal), the increased chance of incarceration might still have deterred crime. But as more and more young men from low-income neighborhoods are incarcerated, many observers believe that one traditional nonpecuniary cost of imprisonment—the stigma attached to having a criminal record by friends and neighbors—has weakened greatly. If the stigma of incarceration falls with the proportion incarcerated, the effect of prison as a deterrent to crime is weakened.

My bottom-line assessment of the pecuniary side of the calculus is that earnings from crime increased relative to earnings from legal work in the 1980s, and that the hourly rewards to crime exceeded the hourly rewards from legal work. The next question is whether the magnitude of supply response to the change in returns is large enough to have contributed significantly to the rise in criminal propensity.

Responses to the Return to Crime

There is diverse evidence that young men respond to economic incentives for crime and that their response may be sufficiently large to play a role in the rise in criminal propensity.

First, the demographics of the criminal population show that those who commit crimes consist disproportionately of persons with low legitimate earnings prospects—the young, the less educated, persons with low test scores, and so on. It is at least plausible that these characteristics are a greater limitation on earning in legal activities than in illegal activities. In fact, some evidence from the NLSY suggests that schooling, age and test scores pay off more in the normal job market than in crime.[10]

Second, joblessness seems associated with greater crime (Chiricos, 1987; Freeman, 1983, 1995). For example, areas with high unemployment tend to have high crime rates, though coefficients of response are not large. Time series studies also generally find that unemployment or related measures of aggregate labor market activity are associated with rises in crime, though this cyclical relation has little to do with secular changes in crime. Comparisons of individuals show that those who commit crimes are more likely to do so when they are unemployed. Longitudinal evidence shows, moreover, that persons engaged in "serious violent behavior" are more likely to terminate this if they are employed than if they are unemployed (Elliot, 1994, Table 1).

Third, greater inequality is associated with higher rates of crime (Chiricos, 1987; Freeman, 1983, 1995). Even homicide rates are correlated with measures of inequality across cities (Land, McCall and Cohen, 1990). In the most comprehensive study, Lee (1993) found a substantive positive relation between levels of earnings inequality and crime rates across metropolitan areas in 1970 and 1980. His estimates suggest that the increased inequality in the 1980s induced a 10 percent increase in crime, as measured by the FBI's Uniform Crime Report index. However, when Lee compared *changes* in inequality with *changes* in crime among metropolitan areas, he found no relation. Perhaps this is because measures of changes in inequality reflect noise in the data, or perhaps it is a clue that the cross-area relation reflects an omitted area variable rather than a true link from inequality to crime.

Fourth, individuals who commit crime have lower perceptions of the riskiness of crime, higher assessments of the relative earnings of criminal behavior and lower legitimate hourly pay. Using the NBER Inner City Youth Survey, Viscusi (1986) found that perceptions of risk and earnings opportunities influenced the supply of young blacks to crime. Using the same survey, I found a significant positive relation between criminal participation and whether individuals thought they could earn more on the street than in the job market (Freeman, 1987). Using the NLSY, Grogger (1994) estimated a supply elasticity to crime with respect to wages near unity for young men, which, applied to the observed drop in real earnings of less skilled young men, predicted a 23 percent increase in crimes committed by these youths from the mid-1970s to the late 1980s, which he points out is of comparable magnitude to the 18 percent increase in the index arrest rate for young men over the period.

Table 1 shows that one does not need complicated calculations to find a relation between the relative rewards to crime and future criminal behavior. In 1980, the NLSY asked respondents the proportions of their income that come from illegal activity. Those who had a high proportion of income from crime presumably had relatively high criminal pay compared to legitimate pay (controlling for time worked at legitimate jobs and the number of crimes committed) and thus should be more involved in crime than others and more likely to end up incarcerated in the future.[11] As the table shows, the proportion of income from illegal sources in 1980 does in fact help explain incarceration years into the future (more refined calculations correcting for time worked at legitimate jobs, crimes committed and so on, confirm this finding).

Fifth, time worked by men in the lower deciles of the earnings distribution fell in the 1980s as their real earnings fell (Topel, 1993; Juhn, Murphy and Topel, 1991; Freeman, 1995), with a magnitude that suggests a nonnegligible supply elasticity. Juhn, Murphy and Topel (Table 9), estimate that the elasticity of labor supply with respect to wages of young men in the lower deciles of the earnings distribution is on the order of 0.20 to 0.30. The finding that low-paid men worked less as their real wages fell is consistent with an increased allocation of time to crime, though it does not imply that they did in fact allocate their increased nonwork time to crime.

Sixth, many youths combine crime and work or shift between them readily. Because most criminals are self-employed, and because the U.S. job market has considerable flux, crime and legitimate work are not dichotomous choices for most young men. Joe holds a job, robs someone he meets on a dark empty street and sells drugs on the weekend. Harry sells drugs for a while, decides the street is too dangerous, gets a legitimate job for a while, loses that

Table 1: Criminal Earnings in 1979 and Future Incarceration

Proportion of Income from Crime, 1979	Percentage Incarcerated Post-1980	Sample Size
None	3.8	4,385
Very Little	7.7	984
About 1/4	6.2	128
About 1/2	17.3	98
About 3/4	29.5	44
Almost All	23.1	52

SOURCE: Tablulated from National Longitudinal Survey of Youth, question: "sometimes people can make money from the types of activities you have just read [a detailed list of crimes]. Still thinking about the last year, how much of your total income or support during the last year came from illegal activities?"

job and goes back to selling drugs. Ethnographic research shows that legal and illegal work often overlap among young drug sellers: for example, Fagan (1992) and Reuter, MacCoun and Murphy (1990) point out the phenomenon of "doubling up" of legal work and cocaine sales. This and other evidence (Hageborn, 1994) indicates that for many young men, illegal work may be temporary or transitional work that supplements difficult low-wage or otherwise unsatisfactory work. For others, legal work provides options to riskier illegal work or perhaps broadens markets for sellers of illegal goods or services.

Table 2 records the unemployment status of young men in the NLSY according to four measures of criminal activity: committing a crime; earning illegal income; being charged with a crime; and being incarcerated in the following year. The sample is limited to out-of-school youths not involved in military service. The crimes are limited to a subset of economic crimes, including shoplifting, stealing, using force to obtain things, selling drugs, conning someone, stealing an automobile, breaking into a building or aiding a gambling operation.[12] The data show that those involved in crime have lower rates of employment than those not involved in crime. But the magnitude of the employment gap is modest for those with low

Table 2:   Percentage Employed in Survey Week in 1980 by Criminal Behavior of Out of School Nonmilitary Youth

	Responses to Criminal Question		Sample Size	
	Yes[a]	No	Yes	No
Admitted Committing Property Crime	70.3	73.3	2,369	1,847
Reported Positive Illegal Income	66.0	73.2	951	3,265
Charged for Crime	58.6	71.5	744	3,279
Jail in Following Year	30.4	65.5	46	4,223

[a]Percentage of observations.
SOURCE: Tabulated from NLSY, with youths in school coded as missing. In these tabulations I have also excluded those in the military. Inclusion of youths in the military reduces the employment difference between those who reported crime and those who did not (strengthening the argument in the test) but does not noticeably affect the difference in employment rates for those in jail the following year.

levels of criminal involvement: a three-point difference between those who committed and those who did not commit crime; a seven-point difference between those with positive incomes from crime and those without such income; a 13-point difference between those charged with crime and those not charged. Only among youths who end up incarcerated a year later are crime and work roughly mutually exclusive: here the difference in employment rates is 35 points.

The ethnographic reports and NLSY data show that for many youths the line between legal and illegal work is not a sharp one: both are ways to make money. This pattern could readily make the supply of youths to crime highly elastic. Assume that young men have reservation wages for legitimate and for criminal work. Opportunities for both types of earnings activities arise intermittently, and youths act on them when the expected rewards exceed their reservation wages. In the NBER Inner City and Boston Youth surveys, many young men in inner-city poverty areas reported frequent illegal and legal earnings opportunities. Someone may need help selling stolen goods; a car with a stereo may be parked on a deserted street; the local fast-food franchise or supermarket may be hiring. If the opportunity is there, and if the likely gain exceeds the reservation wage, someone will act on it.

In sum, while we do not have a well-determined elasticity of the supply of youth to crime (any more than we have well-determined elasticities of demand or supply of many consumer goods), a collage of evidence supports the notion that young men respond substantially to the economic returns to crime. If the supply is reasonably elastic, moreover, it is easy to see why the standard incapacitation model—lock them up, they can't commit crime, so crime falls—failed to fit U.S. experience in the 1980s and 1990s. An infinitely elastic supply of crime implies a zero incapacitation effect, since each criminal locked up is replaced by another.[13] The incapacitation model may also fail to work well because legal earnings fell (as has happened since the 1970s), and/or criminal opportunities increased (perhaps because of a growth in the market for illegal drugs) and offset incapacitation effects. By focusing on the individual rather than the market, standard incapacitation models overstate the effect of increased imprisonment on crime. But even a zero incapacitation effect does not mean that society fails to gain from locking up criminals: there may still be a substantial deterrence effect from incarceration that would reduce the supply curve of young men to crime.

To identify the "true" effects of higher rates of imprisonment on crime, it is necessary to examine the relation between crime and changes in the prison population. Using a comparison across states, Marvell and Moody (1994) estimate that a 10 percent increase in the prison population reduces crime by 1.6 percent; Spelman (1994) gives comparable estimates. Levitt (1995) uses state litigation suits about prison conditions as an instrumental variable—more suits exogenously reduce the prison population—and finds that a 10 percent increase in the prison population reduces crime by 4 to 6 percent. These estimates of the reduction in crime due to increased imprisonment include labor supply responses (deterrence of crime due to greater risk; replacement of criminals due to greater opportunities), in addition to the traditional incapacitation effect.[14]

Crime, Incarceration and Economic Life

There are two indicators of the aggregate cost of crime to society. At one extreme, imagine a society that spent nothing on crime control. The aggregate cost of crime to legitimate society would then be the loss of property, lives and misery due to crime.[15] At the other extreme, imagine a society that spends so much for crime control that no crimes are committed. The cost of crime would then be the opportunity cost of crime control resources—prison, police, private spending—that could be spent on other activities. As an example of this second cost of crime to society, consider this description in the *New York Times* (April 12, 1995, p. A21) of the fiscal situation in California: "In 1995 California spent more on prisons than on higher education. Spending on prisons rose from 2 percent of the state budget in 1980 to 9.9 percent in 1995 whereas spending on higher education shrunk from 12.6 percent in 1980 to 9.5 percent. The number of inmates increased from 23,500 to 126,100 over the period and 17 new prisons were built. This was *before* the state's 'three strikes and you're out' law."

All societies are somewhere between these two extremes. The potential losses from crime lead to some spending on crime control. The costs of crime control lead to some "acceptable" level of crime. At the social optimum, society would spend just enough on crime control so that the marginal dollar spent (adjusted for deadweight loss of raising the dollar) equals the marginal reduction in social costs of crime. This requires knowledge of how social costs vary with the number of crimes and of the effectiveness of different crime control programs.

Estimates of the average cost of crime, much less of the marginal cost, are difficult to make. The National Crime Survey estimates the direct monetary losses of crimes by asking victims to estimate losses from theft or damage, medical expenses and any pay losses due to injury. The 1992 estimate was that the average burglary cost $834, the average auto theft, $3990, the average robbery $555, and so on (Klaus, 1994). The average crime was estimated to cost victims working time, as well. The total economic loss to victims of crime, including medical costs and lost work time, was estimated to be $532 per crime, or $17.6 billion for all reported crimes in that year. This is 0.3 percent of GDP.

Some criminologists have expanded these estimates to find a more inclusive cost of crime, based on jury evaluation of nonpecuniary costs (Cohen, 1988), and offer a more extensive medical evaluation of injuries, including psychological problems (Miller, Cohen and Rossman, 1993). These estimates are rough ones. Jury cases may involve greater misery than other victimizations. Some estimates include the lost legitimate earnings of incarcerated criminals, which may affect the wellbeing of spouses or children—56 percent of male prisoners have children under the age of 18 (U.S. Department of Justice, 1991, p. 10)—and which may lead to social transfers to their families. Others exclude lost earnings of the criminal, on the argument that the criminal consumes most of those earnings (Levitt, 1995). None include the suffering of the families of criminals. For all their problems, these estimates are undoubtedly closer to the truth than figures limited to the money stolen, and they exceed reported monetary losses by massive amounts. For example, the estimated average pain and suffering and cost of risk of death created by a robbery is approximately 11 times the direct monetary loss (Cohen, 1988, Table 3). Estimates of the cost of pain, suffering, and economic loss for the average crime are on the order of $2,300 (DiIulio and Piehl, 1991) to $3,000 (Levitt, 1995).[16] With 14.1 million crimes committed in 1993, according to the Uniform Crime Report, this cumulates to $32 billion to $42 billion, or 0.5 to 0.7 percent of GDP.

Of course, the crimes actually reported to police and recorded in the Uniform Crime Report are far less than the number of victimizations. It's not clear whether the average victimization would cause a loss higher or lower than the average crime. Some victimizations—such as the robbery of bicycles—cost less; others like rape, child abuse or domestic violence not reported to police may cost more. If the cost of an average crime is kept at the same rate, but multiplied by the number of victimizations reported, the social cost reaches 1.2 to 1.6 percent of GDP.

Finally, there is the additional loss of production by the incarcerated (which accrues largely to them). Prisoners are low skill, and many would be jobless if they were free, but not committing crimes. Still, 2 percent of even low-skill male workers would add perhaps 0.5 to 0.7 percent to GDP, giving a total cost of around 2 percent of GDP due to crime. These costs underlie the case for allocating considerable resources to crime control activities, including prison or alternative sentencing, and for any social programs that can prevent crime.

The resources that the state and individuals spend to control crime are more directly measurable. Most resources to control crime are public. Total expenditures on the criminal justice system in 1990 was $74 billion, or 1.3 percent of GDP. Total employment in the system was around 2 percent of U.S. employment. Within the criminal justice system, corrections (which includes prisons) are a major cost item. In 1990, $25 billion were spent on corrections. With 1.14 million persons in prison or jail in that year, the average cost is $22,000 per person.[17] Of course, the public cost must also be multiplied by the deadweight loss created by distortions of taxation or deficit financing.

Another big ticket item is private crime prevention resources. Private security guards are one of the fastest growing occupations in the United States, accounting for 0.6 percent of employment in 1992. Both households and offices undertake many crime prevention measures. Individuals allot additional resources through such diverse decisions as taking a taxi instead of walking home from the movies; locating a business in the suburbs instead of a central city, and so on. My guesstimate is that on the order of 0.6 percent of GDP is spent on private crime prevention, ranging from guards to various protective devices.

All told, approximately 2 percent of GDP is allotted to crime control activities. From one perspective, this is simply part of the overhead of running a modern society and trying to enforce rules of conduct and protect citizens. From another perspective, it is pure waste. Measured in terms of spending, if we could make contracts with potential criminals to forego crime or devise policies to train them or to subsidize their employment so that they would forego crime, one might think that we could spend up to 4 percent of GDP—that is, the 2 percent presently lost to crime and the 2 percent spent on controlling crime—and still improve social well-being. This would amount to an average of about $54,000 for each of the 5 million or so men incarcerated, put on probation or paroled. In fact, the favorable benefit-cost assessment of the Job Corps and of the highly publicized Perry Pre-School program depend in part on large estimated savings in criminal justice expenses due to reduced crime by participants. These assessments should be adjusted downward to allow for the probable replacement of one youth with another in the criminal market: they overestimate the gains from preventive activity focused on *current* criminals. Still, the magnitude of the numbers does suggest the potential value of programs to assure that potential criminals have better access to legitimate employment opportunities.

Criminologists have argued in recent years about whether prison pays on the margin. In a much-disputed study published by the National Institute of Justice, Zedlewski (1987) reported the benefits of imprisonment exceeded the costs of imprisonment by 17 to 1. But this estimate was based on each criminal otherwise committing 180 crimes; at more moderate estimates, the benefit-cost ratio of imprisonment exceeds one for the median number of crimes per criminal (12-15), but falls below one for those in the lower quartile or so of the distribution of crimes (DiIulio and Piehl, 1991). Consideration of the labor supply responses to criminal opportunities, which suggest sizable replacement of incarcerated criminals by others, supports the lower estimates.

The debate on whether prison pays indicates that crime costs are high enough to justify incarceration of offenders at current U.S. levels, though perhaps not at much higher levels, and that alternative sentencing procedures would be cost-effective for some current prisoners (Piehl and DiIulio, 1995). Clear and Braga (1995) offer a useful overview of these alternatives: house confinement, electronic surveillance, parole, and so on. The high costs of crime also suggest, however, that even a marginally effective and relatively costly jobs/crime prevention program for crime-prone groups would also pass a benefits-cost test. While I know of no "magic bullet" jobs or crime prevention program, it is a myth that all such programs invariably fail. Some have marginal positive effects. For instance, meta-analyses show that the average juvenile delinquency program has some deterrent effect, albeit modest (Lipsey, 1990). At least some anticrime early intervention programs also succeed, again on a small scale (Mendel, 1995).

In any case, if I am correct that the collapse of the job market for less skilled men contributed to their increased involvement in crime, and if the supply of youth to crime is sufficiently elastic that the criminal justice system can at best cap the crime rate at rising costs, it is difficult to see any long-term solution to crime that does not include some improvement in the labor market opportunities for less skilled youth. To make legitimate work more attractive to youths than crime requires, to be sure, increasing the likely penalty for crime, as has been the focus of recent U.S. policy, but it also could benefit from enhancing the rewards for legitimate work. A combined carrot and stick policy—increased resources for police to prevent crime; incarceration of criminals during their most crime-intensive years (not at ages 40-60, as "three strikes and you're out" may do); and increased legitimate opportunities for the less skilled—would seem to offer a way to deter at least some young men from committing crimes. The problematic part of any such policy, however, is the carrot part: finding legitimate opportunities for these young men. How to improve the job market for less skilled young American men, and reverse the huge decline in their earnings and employment opportunities, is *the problem* of our times, with implications both for crime and many other social ills.

• *Research for this paper was partially funded by the Rockefeller Foundation*

Footnotes

[1] The number of men in prison is from U.S. Bureau of Justice Statistics, Bulletin *Prisoners in 1993*; the number of persons in jail is from U.S. Bureau of Justice Statistics, Bulletin *Jail Inmates 1991*—updated by assuming a rate of growth similar to that for those in prison.

[2] For those on probation or parole, I extrapolated 1990 or 1991 figures (Freeman, 1995) to get 2,690,400 probated after conviction for crime; 600,700 on parole, for a total of 3,291,100 probated or paroled.

[3] The percentages I report are obtained by dividing the number of prisoners in a group by the noninstitutionalized population plus the number of prisoners.

[4] I have made these estimates by multiplying the number of dropouts in prison by the ratio of probatees or parolees or prisoners for the overall male population. These numbers may be biased upward, since judges may be less likely to sentence dropouts to probation than they would men with high school educations or more.

[5] These estimates are obtained by multiplying the percentage of unemployed who are unemployed for over a year form OECD, *Employment Outlook*, July 1994, Table Q with estimates of male unemployment for OECD. *Quarterly Labour Force Statistics*, Number 4, 1994. The estimated male unemployment rate is from register data.

[6] These are the two major sources of data on the volume of crime. Each year the FBI gathers the number of crimes reported by police, which is used to create the Uniform Crime Rate index. Each year the National Crime Survey asks households about victimizations for crimes. The two data sets differ in levels—the UCR gives fewer crimes than the victimization survey, because people do not report all victimizations to the police, and in trend. For efforts to reconcile the two series, see Boggess and Bound (1993).

[7] One difficulty is that most criminals are self-employed, and thus do not face a market wage but rather an earnings opportunity schedule in which hourly pay depends on the hours of work they choose. In the Boston Youth Survey, those who committed a single crime in the past year earned $752, whereas those who reported committing crimes once a week or more earned $5376, or $100 or so per week—considerably less per crime. A second reason in determining the income level of criminals is that self-reported criminal earnings may be inaccurately reported: Wilson and Abrahamse (1992) suggest that the incomes that inmates claim to have earned from various crimes are far higher than those crimes could plausibly yield.

[8] Here, I take an average of the 1979 and 1980 deflators for the earnings in the Inner City Survey, since the survey covered both years. Using the 1979 deflator gives an estimated 3 percent drop in earnings which is far short of the drop in legitimate earnings.

[9] The Earned Income Tax Credit would raise the pay of those with family responsibilities modestly. But few young men in the crime-prone groups have families and are potential recipients of this support.

[10] Since criminal earnings are poorly measured, it is not easy to document this claim. In the NLSY, I regressed the share of income from illegal sources on number of crimes reported, weeks worked in the year and three human capital measures: years of schooling, age and AFQT score. The coefficients on all three human capital measures were negative and significant, implying that schooling, age, and AFQT lowered illegal income relative to legal income.

[11] Because the NLSY has never repeated the crime module that was included in 1980, evidence on future crime behavior is limited to whether or not the respondent was interviewed in jail or prison.

[12] This leaves out some violent nonproperty crimes. Their inclusion increases the numbers committing crime without changing the results.

[13] If the supply of crime is upward-sloping, the replacement will be less than one-for-one, dependent on the magnitude of the elasticities of supply and demand. Let $S = aW + S'$ be the supply of youths to crime, where W is the relative reward to crime. Assume that when more persons commit crimes, the rewards to crime fall according to a "demand" relation: $D = -bW + D'$ measure criminal opportunities. Market equilibrium is $S = D = (aD' + bS')/(a+b)$. When incarceration reduces the supply of criminals by dS', the change in the number of criminals is $b\,dS'/(a+b)$ rather than dS'. The replacement effect is $a/(a+b)$.

[14] It's worth noting that the resultant estimates of the reduction in reported crimes or victimizations due to incapacitation are in the ballpark of the lower estimated range crimes per criminal reviewed earlier; that is, the median number of 5-15 crimes per criminal, not the 60-180 crimes per criminal reported in prisoner surveys.

[15] I use the word "legitimate" to justify including property losses as part of the cost of crime. From one perspective (mine), my picking your pocket is not a social loss; it is simply a transfer of income. Some calculations of the cost of crime exclude the property loss. Others include it. For certain purposes, we may want to distinguish between "Robin Hood" crimes that redistribute money from one person to another (picking pockets, for instance) and crimes that are purely destructive (arson, assault). The question in part hinges on the definition of society.

[16] Levitt (1995) reports $45,000 as the estimated cost per criminal and estimates that criminals commit 15 crimes per year, for the $3,000 per crime estimate that I use.

[17] Annual current operating expenditures for prisoners are on the order of $15,000 (Piehl and DiIulio, 1995). Estimates of the amortized value of prisons are on the order of $4,000 to $5,000 (Cavenaugh and Kleiman, 1990, Table 2).

References

Blackburn, Kim, David Bloom, and Richard Freeman, "The Declining Economic Position of Less Skilled American Men." In Burtless, Gary, ed., *A Future of Lousy Jobs? The Changing Structure of U.S. Wages*. Washington, D.C.: Brookings Institution, 1990, pp. 31-76.

Boggess, Scott, and John Bound, "Did Criminal Activity Increase During the 1980s? Comparisons across Data Sources." National Bureau of Economic Research Working Paper NO. 4431, Cambridge, Mass., August 1993.

Boyum, David, and Mark A. R. Kleiman, "Alcohol and Other Drugs." In Wilson, J. Q. and Joan Petersilia, eds., *Crime*. San Francisco: Institute for Contemporary Studies, 1995, pp. 295-326.

Cavanagh, David P., and Mark A. R. Kleiman, *A Cost Benefit Analysis of Prison Cell Construction and Alternative Sanctions*. Cambridge, Mass.: BOTEC Analysis Corp., prepared for the National Institute of Justice, June 1990.

Chiricos, Theodore, "Rates of Crime and Unemployment: An Analysis of Aggregate Research Evidence," *Social Problems*, April 1987, *342*, 187-211.

Clear, Todd, and Anthony Braga, "Community Corrections." In Wilson, J. Q. and Joan Petersilia, eds. *Crime*. San Francisco: Institute for Contemporary Studies, 1995, pp. 421-44.

Cohen, Mark A., "Pain, Suffering, and Jury Awards: A Study of the Cost of Crime to Victims." *Law and Society Review*, 1988, 22:3, 537-55.

DiIulio, John, and Anne Piehl, "Does Prison Pay?," *Brookings Review*, Fall 1994, 4, 29-35.

Elliot, Delbert, "Longitudinal Research in Criminology: Promise and Practice." In Westekamp, G. W., and H. J. Kerner, eds., *Cross National Longitudinal Research on Human Development and Criminal Behavior*. Netherlands: Kluwer Academic Publishers, 1994, pp. 189-201.

Fagan, Jeff, "Drug Selling and Licit Income in Distressed Neighborhoods: The Economic Lives of Street-Level Drug Users and Dealers." In Harrell, Adele, and George Peterson, eds., *Drugs, Crime and Social Isolation*. Washington, D.C.: Urban Institute Press, 1992, pp. 99-146.

Freeman, Richard, "Crime and the Labor Market." In Wilson, J. Q., *Crime and Public Policy*. San Francisco: Institute for Contemporary Studies, 1983, pp. 89-106.

Freeman, Richard, "The Relation of Criminal Activity to Black Youth Employment," *Review of Black Political Economy*, Summer/Fall 1987, 16, 99-107.

Freeman, Richard, "Crime and the Employment of Disadvantaged Youth," In Peterson, George, and Wayne Vroman, eds., *Urban Labor markets and Job Opportunity*. Washington D.C.: Urban Institute, 1992, pp. 201-37.

Freeman, Richard, "The Labor Market," In Wilson, J. Q., and Joan Petersilia, eds., *Crime*. San Francisco: Institute for Contemporary Studies, 1995, pp. 171-92.

Grogger, J., "Criminal Opportunities, Youth Crime, and Young Men's Labor Supply," mimeo, Department of Economics, University of California, Santa Barbara, February 1994.

Hageborn, J., "Homeboys, Dope Fiends, Legits, and New Jacks," *Criminology*, May 1994, 32:2, 197-219.

Hindelang, M. J., T. Hirschi, and J. Weis, *Measuring Delinquency*. Beverly Hills, Calif.: Sage, 1981.

Juhn, Chinui, Kevin Murphy, and Robert Topel, "Why Has the Natural Rate of Unemployment Increased over Time?," *Brookings Papers on Economic Activity*. 1991, 2, 75-142.

ARBITRARINESS AND DISCRIMINATION
UNDER POST-*FURMAN* CAPITAL STATUTES

William J. Bowers
Glenn L. Pierce

In the *Furman v. Georgia* decision on June 29, 1972,[1] the United States Supreme Court held by a five to four margin that capital punishment, as administered under then-existing statutes, was unconstitutional. In separate opinions, the concurring majority variously characterized the imposition of the death penalty as "freakishly rare," "irregular," "random," "capricious," "uneven," "wanton," "excessive," "disproportionate," and "discriminatory." The majority were united in the finding that the death penalty was being used in an "arbitrary" manner. The Court ruled that because death is a supremely harsh and an irrevocable form of punishment, "different in kind from lesser criminal sanctions," such arbitrariness in capital punishment was a violation of Eighth Amendment prohibitions against "cruel and unusual" punishment.[2]

The *Furman* decision did not, however, put an end to capital punishment in the United States. To be sure, two of the concurring majority—Justices Brennan and Marshall—found death as a form of punishment constitutionally unacceptable, but the other three—Justices Douglas, Stewart, and White—limited their objections to existing statutes "as applied." Justice Douglas contended that the Court's intervention was warranted because the existing statutes gave "uncontrolled discretion" to sentencers and provided "no standards [to] govern the selection of the penalty." Justice Stewart's opinion also reflected concern with discretion in the sentencing process. In his dissenting opinion, Chief Justice Burger suggested that states could restore capital punishment by drafting new statutes that would narrow and restrict the exercise of discretion in sentencing.

Reacting to the *Furman* decision, state legislatures adopted remedies varying in the restrictions they placed on sentencing discretion. These post-*Furman* capital statutes took two basic approaches: the "mandatory" death sentence, designed to eliminate sentencing control altogether, and "guided discretion" statutes,

W. Bowers and G. Pierce, "Arbitrariness and Discrimination under Post-*Furman* Capital Statutes," *Crime and Delinquency*, vol. 26, #4, October 1980, pp. 563-635. © 1980 by the National Council on Crime. Reprinted by permission of Sage Publications, Inc.

designed to limit or control the exercise of discretion by means of explicit standards to be followed in the sentencing process. Mandatory statutes were narrowly drawn to avoid ambiguity in classifying crimes as capital offenses, and the death sentence was made mandatory upon conviction for such offenses. Guided discretion statutes provide standards, typically in the form of specific aggravating and mitigating circumstances, that must be taken into account before the death sentence can be handed down. These new guided discretion statutes also provide for separate phases of the trial to determine guilt and punishment, and for automatic appellate review of all death sentences.

* * *

The Court accepted several different forms of guided discretion which vary in the limits they place on sentencing authorities.[4] Least restrictive are "aggravating only" statutes, which enumerate aggravating circumstances and permit the jury to recommend death if it finds at least one such circumstance to be present. Intermediate in restrictions are "aggravating versus mitigating" statutes, which list both aggravating and mitigating circumstances and give the jury discretion to recommend death, providing it finds that the aggravating "outweigh" the mitigating circumstances. Most restrictive are "structured discretion" statutes, which make the death sentence strictly contingent upon the jury's findings with respect to aggravation.

* * *

Each type of guided discretion statute upheld in the *Gregg* decision also provided for automatic appellate review of all death sentences. Most elaborate is Georgia's review process, which was explicitly formulated to determine

"1) whether the sentence of death was imposed under the influence of passion, prejudice, or any other arbitrary factor, and 2) whether . . . the evidence supports the jury's or judge's finding of a statutory aggravating circumstance . . . and 3) whether the sentence of death is excessive or disproportionate to the penalty imposed in similar cases considering the crime and the defendant. . . . ."[10]

* * *

The present study examines whether the new post-*Furman* capital statutes affirmed by the Supreme Court in the *Gregg* decision have, in fact, eliminated the arbitrariness and discrimination which rendered pre-*Furman* capital statutes unconstitutional. . . . We . . . consider the nature of arbitrariness, the forms it takes, and its sources in the extralegal functions of capital punishment. We then turn to the existing evidence of arbitrariness and discrimination under pre-*Furman* statutes that can serve as a baseline against which the operation of the post-*Furman* statutes may be judged. These steps will set the stage for our report of findings to date from an ongoing research project designed to evaluate the application of post-*Furman* capital statutes in terms of arbitrariness and discrimination.

* * *

The Forms and Sources of Arbitrariness

In the *Gregg* decision, the Court articulated a model of retributive justice, made most explicit in its discussion of the proportionality review. Under this model the severity of the punishment must be proportional to the seriousness of the crime and independent of legally irrelevant considerations. The death sentence must be strictly a function of legally relevant characteristics of the crime and of the defendant. The statutes themselves provide legally relevant standards for imposing the death penalty in the form of explicit, enumerated aggravating and mitigating circumstances; these establish the retributive appropriateness of death as punishment under law. The similarity standard applied upon review further requires that sentencing decisions be consistent with legally acceptable criteria evolving in practice throughout the state; it rules out legally acceptable considerations that have typically not figured in the decision to impose the death sentence.

Within this framework arbitrariness can be made quite explicit. Simply stated, it is any departure from the retributive model requiring death as punishment to be strictly a function of statutory guidelines and evolving standards of practice. That is, arbitrariness exists to the extent that legally relevant factors enumerated in statutes and emerging in practice *do not* distinguish between those who are sentenced to death and those who are not.

We can identify forms of arbitrariness in terms of "what else" accounts for the imposition of the death sentence.[20] If the extralegal influences are different in every case or occur randomly without rhyme or reason, the arbitrariness is unsystematic. We may call it "caprice." On the other hand, if the extralegal influences are systematic or consistent, they may be legally irrelevant characteristics of the defendant or of the crime. When they are characteristics of the defendant (e.g., race of offender), the form of arbitrariness is what we traditionally know as "discrimination" (against the category of defendants whose legally irrelevant characteristics make them more apt to receive the death penalty). When the legally irrelevant factors are characteristics of the crime (e.g., size of community in which it occurred) or of the victim (e.g., race of victim), the arbitrariness is a form of discrimination, but not in the traditional sense of the term. That is, offenders will be treated differently depending on where and whom they kill rather than who they are. We may call this kind of arbitrariness "disparity" or "partiality" of treatment. Of course, discrimination and disparity of treatment can have the same source. For example, deeply rooted racism might result in more severe punishment for black than for white killers, and in less severe punishment for the killers of blacks than of whites.

Arbitrariness in its various forms—caprice, discrimination, and disparity—may be linked to the extralegal functions of capital punishment. An examination of the availability and use of the death penalty historically and cross-nationally has suggested three distinct extralegal functions of capital punishment—minority group oppression, majority group protection, and repressive response—presumed to play a role in determining who, among capital offenders, will receive the death penalty.[21]

Minority group oppression refers to the selective or disproportionate use of capital punishment against offenders from groups in which members are subjugated, impoverished, or dehumanized by the political, economic, or social conditions they face. Majority group protection refers to the disproportionate use of the death penalty against those whose crimes victimize members, interests, or institutions of the powerful or dominant groups in society. Repressive response refers to the selective use of the death penalty against those whose crimes occur at times and places of tension, turmoil, conflict, or crisis, when fear of crime or other forms of social disorder is heightened.

The presumed link between these extralegal functions of capital punishment and the forms of arbitrariness defined above should be clear. Minority group oppression will tend to create arbitrariness in the form of discrimination by offender characteristics. Majority group protection will tend to produce arbitrariness in the form of victim-based disparity of treatment. Repressive response will tend to generate arbitrariness in terms of differential treatment by time and place of offense that reflects conditions apart from the crime. What may seem capricious or freakish—like being struck by lightning (to paraphrase Justice Stewart)—in a particular case may in the aggregate and over a period of time be revealed as part of a systematic pattern of differences in treatment depending on legally irrelevant characteristics of the offender, victim or crime.

Has the Court correctly evaluated the power of these statutory reforms to control and to correct the arbitrariness and discrimination prevailing under pre-*Furman* capital statutes? . . . Post-*Furman* statutory reforms are evaluated for their success in altering the prevailing patterns of arbitrariness and discrimination or overcoming the extralegal functions of capital punishment.

* * *

Hypotheses and Research Questions

The evidence from historical and cross-national research and from the studies of the administration of capital punishment in the United States during the pre-*Furman* era suggests several hypotheses about the operation of post-*Furman* capital statutes, particularly about the presence of arbitrariness and discrimination under those statutes. In this section, we present four general hypotheses, each with more specific subhypotheses. . . .

The historical and cross-national evidence that capital punishment has consistently served extralegal functions suggests that arbitrariness and discrimination are inherent in the use of death as punishment, and not contingent upon the nature or form of capital statutes. . . . [E]vidence from studies of capital punishment during the pre-*Furman* era in the United States showing that differences by race and social class of offender and victim were consistent and cumulative over successive stages of the criminal justice process, and could not be attributed to legally relevant crime or offender characteristics, further suggests that the extralegal functions of capital punishment are deeply rooted in our society, and are not likely to be eliminated by the reform of capital statutes. To be sure, such reforms might produce some measure of "process displacement," or transfer of discrimination, from the sentencing phase to other stages of the criminal justice process. But, to the extent that the arbitrary and discriminatory imposition of the death penalty is tied to deep-seated patterns of racism and classism in our society, any reduction of arbitrariness or discrimination in the sentencing process may be offset by a compensatory increase in differential treatment before sentencing. Thus, under post-*Furman* capital statutes, the extent of arbitrariness and discrimination, if not their distribution over stages of the criminal justice process, might be expected to remain essentially unchanged. These considerations are incorporated in the following set of hypotheses:

1.   The death sentence will be imposed in an arbitrary and discriminatory manner under post-*Furman* capital statutes.

1.1   It will be imposed disproportionately by race and/or social class of offender (minority group oppression).

1.2   It will be imposed disproportionately by race and/or social class of victim (dominant group protection).

1.3   It will be imposed disproportionately by offender/victim combinations in terms of race and/or social class (social boundary maintenance).

1.4   It will be imposed disproportionately by time and/or place within a given capital jurisdiction (repressive response).

2.   The disproportionate imposition of the death sentence under post-*Furman* capital statutes will not be attributable to legally relevant aggravating or mitigating circumstances.

2.1   It will be independent of legally relevant crime characteristics (e.g., contemporaneous felony, murder weapon, number slain).

2.2   It will be independent of legally relevant offender characteristics (e.g., motive, alcohol involvement, prior criminal record).
2.3   It will be independent of legally relevant victim characteristics (e.g., relation to offender, vulnerability, provocation).

* * *

3.   The restrictiveness of post-*Furman* capital statutes in how they guide or limit sentencing discretion will not eliminate a substantial risk of arbitrariness and discrimination.
3.1   Differential treatment will not be removed under "aggravating only" statutes (e.g., Georgia).
3.2   Differential treatment will not be removed under "aggravating versus mitigating" statutes (e.g., Florida).
3.3   Differential treatment will not be removed under "structure discretion" statutes (e.g., Texas).

* * * In the analysis that follows, we examine arbitrariness and discrimination over the criminal justice process from the point of the crime itself to the point at which the death sentence is handed down. In particular, we consider disparities in the likelihood of a death sentence by race of both offender and victim.

* * *

What follows is the first interpretive report of the findings.

* * *

Data for the Analysis

In the fall of 1977, the Center for Applied Social Research at Northeastern University began collecting data on capital punishment under post-*Furman* statutes, following a national conference on capital punishment attended by lawyers and social scientists.[67]
* * * We have obtained systematic data on (1) criminal homicides in all states since the 1972 *Furman* decision, (2) death sentences handed down and appellate review in selected states since *Furman*, and (3) the criminal justice processing of potentially capi-

tal cases from charge through sentencing in one state under the post-*Furman* capital statute.

Criminal Homicide Data

In 1976 the FBI began to include in the Supplementary Homicide Reports . . . information on arrested and/or suspected offenders. . . . Thus, since 1976 both offender and victim characteristics have been available for most killings that could be prosecuted as capital offenses. . . . We have obtained from the FBI the data on all states for the period 1973-76, and, from the state-level crime-reporting agencies of Florida, Georgia, Texas, and Ohio, the data for the year 1977.[69]

* * *

Death Sentence and Appellate Review Data

In the fall of 1977, we began to compile detailed information on all persons sentenced to death in the states whose capital statutes were specifically upheld in the *Gregg* and companion decisions—Florida, Georgia, and Texas. These three states were responsible for approximately half of all death sentences handed down under post-*Furman* capital statutes in effect at that time. In the spring of 1978, we also began to compile such data for Ohio, which brought the representation of post-*Furman* death sentences to approximately 70 percent.[71] * * *

The data collection effort has involved trial attorneys and others, who have helped in compiling and validating the information in the respective statutes; with their assistance, we have acquired extensive information on offense, defendant, victim, and processing of the case from indictment through appellate review. In particular, the instruments used to compile these data have provided comparable information on felony circumstances of the crime; race of offender and victim; the statutory, aggravating, and mitigating circumstances found by sentencing authorities; and the current status of the case in the appellate review process.

* * *

Scope of the Analysis

The upcoming analysis deals with the first five years following the *Furman* decision. For Florida, Georgia, Texas, and Ohio, we examine criminal homicides committed between the effective dates (if occurring on the first of the month; if not, tabulations begin with the first of the following month) of their respective states (i.e., Florida: December 8, 1972; Georgia: March 28, 1973; Texas: January 1, 1974; Ohio: November 1, 1974) and the end of 1977, and the death sentences imposed under the post-*Furman* statutes for homicides occurring before 1978. The analysis of judicial processing in Florida is restricted to offenses that occurred before 1978 and reached the trial court dockets before the collection of data. Thus, December 31, 1977, is our cutoff date in the sense that offenses occurring after 1977, regardless of sentencing date, are excluded from this analysis.

* * *

Analysis

The stage is now set for the analysis. The questions are clear. Have the new post-*Furman* capital statutes removed the substantial risk of arbitrariness and discrimination present under pre-*Furman* statutes? Have they eliminated differential treatment of offender and victim[?] * * *

Arbitrariness by Race

By far the most substantial and consistent extralegal basis of differential treatment under pre-*Furman* was race. All but a few studies found gross racial differences in the likelihood of a death sentence; race of both offender and victim was associated with differential treatment, and race of victim was a more prominent basis of differential treatment than race of offender. If the post-*Furman* statutes have remedied the previous ills, we should find no substantial or consistent differences by race in the likelihood of a death sentence for criminal homicide under the new statutes.

The likelihood of a death sentence by offender/victim racial categories in Florida, Georgia, Texas, and Ohio is shown in Table 2. It presents the estimated number of criminal offenders,[73] the number of persons sentenced to death, and the probability of likelihood of a death sentence given a homicide for each offender/victim racial combination in each state from the effective date of the post-*Furman* statute through 1977. The likelihood of a death sentence given a criminal homicide spans the criminal justice process from the initial investigation of the crime by the police through the sentencing of a convicted offender. That is, unlike studies that begin with a sample of indictments, these data will reflect the effects of differential law enforcement as well as differential court processing of criminal homicide cases. They incorporate the effects of discretion at arrest, charging, indictment, conviction, and sentencing in the handling of potentially capital crimes.

And what do these data show? Stark differences by race of both offender and victim in all four states are apparent in Table 2. The racial pattern is consistent across states and similar to the experience under pre-*Furman* statutes. Thus, black killers and the killers of whites are substantially more likely than others to receive a death sentence in all four states. And, as in the pre-*Furman* era, race of victim tends to overshadow race of offender as a basis for differential treatment (in fact, differences by race of offender would be altogether obscured if the data were tabulated without race of victim).[74] In Florida, the difference by race of victim is great. Among black offenders, those who kill whites are nearly forty times more likely to be sentenced to death than those who kill blacks. The difference by race of offender, although not as great, is also marked. Among the killers of whites, blacks are five times more likely than whites to be sentenced to death. To appreciate the magnitude of these differences, consider the following implications of these data: If all offenders in Florida were sentenced to death at the same rate as blacks who killed whites, there would be a total of 887 persons sentenced to death; 53 blacks who killed whites, 391 whites who killed whites, 425 blacks who killed blacks, and 18 whites who killed blacks—instead of the 147 death sentences actually imposed by the end of 1977.

Table 2.   Probability of Receiving the Death Sentence in Florida,
Georgia, Texas, and Ohio for Criminal Homicide, by Race of
Offender and Victim (from effective dates of respective post-
Furman capital statutes through 1977)

Offender/Victim Racial Combinations	(1) Estimated Number of Offenders	(2) Persons Sentenced to Death	(3) Overall Probability of Death Sentence
Florida			
Black kills white	240	53	.221
White kills white	1768	82	.046
Black kills black	1922	12	.006
White kills black	80	0	.000
Georgia			
Black kills white	258	43	.167
White kills white	1006	42	.042
Black kills black	2458	12	.005
White kills black	71	2	.028
Texas			
Black kills white	344	30	.087
White kills white	3616	56	.015
Black kills black	2597	2	.001
White kills black	143	1	.007
Ohio			
Black kills white	173	44	.254
White kills white	803	37	.046
Black kills black	1170	20	.017
White kills black	47	0	.000

In Georgia, the chances of a death sentence are slightly less in magnitude but remarkably similar in pattern to those in Florida. Overall, the likelihood of a death sentence is 30 percent lower in Georgia than in Florida (.026 for Georgia, .037 for Florida), but much of this difference is due to the greater proportion of black/black killings in Georgia. For the respective offender/victim racial categories, the differences are less: 24 percent lower for black offender/white victim killings, 9 percent lower for white/white killings, and 17 percent lower for black/black killings. Only the category of white offenders/black victims is noticeably different, as a result of two death sentences in Georgia and none in Florida. Hence, the difference in statutory form in these two states—" aggravating only" in Georgia and "aggravating versus mitigating" in Florida—appears to have only a slight and not an altogether consistent effect on the chances of a death sentence, and virtually no effect in controlling or correcting racial disparities.

In Texas, the chances that a murder will result in a death sentence are considerably less; indeed, the likelihood is only about one-third the chances in Florida and one-half the chances in Georgia.[75] But the pattern of racial differences is still very much the same. In fact, despite the reduced chances of a death sentence in Texas, the racial differences, in relative terms, are generally greater.[76] Among black offenders, those with white victims are eighty-seven times more likely than those with black victims to receive the death penalty; and among the killers of whites, black offenders are six times more likely than white offenders to be sentenced to death. Perhaps the lower likelihood of a death sentence in Texas than in Florida and Georgia is a result of the more restrictive procedures of the "structured discretion" statute in Texas or of the more limited kinds of offenses which qualify for the death sentence in Texas. But it is clear that the Texas statute, despite its restrictiveness, has not eliminated differential treatment by race of offender and victim. On the contrary, race of offender and race of victim are responsible for more variation in the chances of a death sentence in Texas than in Florida or Georgia.

In Ohio, the pattern is the same; black killers and the killers of whites are more likely to receive the death sentence. Here the chances of a death sentence are greater overall than in the other three states. The relative differences by race of offender and victim are generally somewhat less than in Florida, Georgia, and Texas. Perhaps the greater likelihood of a death sentence in Ohio reflects the "quasi-mandatory" character of the Ohio statute,[77] which was overturned in the *Lockett* decision for its failure to provide individualized treatment for convicted offenders.[78] Since Ohio's statute has been invalidated by the Supreme Court, we have given the Ohio data less priority in our analysis and will not examine the operation of this statute further here.

In these four states, which accounted for approximately 70 percent of the nation's death sentences in the first five years after *Furman*, race of both offender and victim had a tremendous impact on the chances that a death sentence would be handed down. To understand to some extent the size of the effect of these racial differences, consider the following: The probability that a difference of this magnitude in the four states combined could have occurred by chance is so remote that it cannot be computed with available statistical programs. . . . And this is a conservative estimate, since the overall pattern is not a composite of widely different patterns from state to state, but rather is a reflection of the same essential pattern in states with differing mechanisms and procedures for guiding discretion.

The presence of differential treatment by race is unmistakable. But does it reflect the direct influence of race on the decisions made in the criminal justice process or could it be the result of legally relevant differences in the kinds of crimes committed by and against blacks and whites? A recent statement of this latter possibility can be found in the Fifth Circuit Court of Appeals opinion in *Spenkelink v. Wainwright*.[79] As recounted by the court, the Florida Attorney General argued

> that murders involving black victims have, in the past, generally been qualitatively different from murders involving white victims; as a general rule, . . . murders involving black victims have not presented facts and circumstances appropriate for the imposition of the death penalty.[80]

In a footnote, the court went on to quote Attorney General Shevin's enumeration of these alleged differences: "Murders involving black victims have in the past fallen into the categories of 'family quarrels, lovers' quarrels, liquor quarrels, [and] barroom quarrels'."[81]

In response to this argument, it would obviously be desirable to examine the chances of a death sentence by race of offender and victim separately for two categories of murder: those which by definition qualify for the death penalty and those which may or may not so qualify. In this connection, the statutes of Florida and Georgia make a felony circumstance—the fact that a homicide is committed in the course of another felony (e.g., rape or robbery)—an aggravating factor that qualifies the homicide for the death penalty.[82] The Texas statute explicitly defines felony killing as one of the five categories of homicide that may lead to a death sentence.[83] In effect, the distinction between felony and nonfelony homicides corresponds to the difference between crimes that definitely qualify for capital punishment and those that may or may not so qualify.

* * *

The likelihood of a death sentence by offender/victim racial category is presented separately in Table 3 for felony and nonfelony-type murders in Florida, Georgia, and Texas. The importance of a felony circumstance as a determinant of the death sentence is immediately evident. For nearly every offender/victim racial category in each state, the death sentence is more likely for felony than for nonfelony murder—five to ten times more likely on the average within offender/victim racial categories.

But the table makes it equally clear that type of murder does not account for the racial differences in treatment observed in Table 2. For felony and for nonfelony homicides alike, the differences by race of both offender and victim shown in Table 2 are again evident. To be sure, as the Florida Attorney General argued in the *Spenkelink* case, black homicide victims are less likely than their white counterparts to be killed under the potentially capital, felony circumstances (evident from the base figures in the first and fourth columns of Table 3). But it is not true, as he alleged, that this difference in the kinds of murder perpetrated against blacks as compared with whites explains or accounts for the racial differences in treatment shown in Table 2.[84]

A closer examination of Table 3 reveals a slight but consistent specification of the pattern of racial differences in treatment by type of killing. For felony homicides, race of victim becomes more clearly the dominant factor. In each of the three states, by far the

Table 3. Probability of Receiving the Death Sentence in Florida, Georgia, and Texas for Felony and Nonfelony Murder, by Race of Offender and Victim (from effective dates of respective post-*Furman* capital statutes through 1977)

Offender/Victim Racial Combinations	Felony-Type Murder			Nonfelony-Type Murder		
	(1) Estimated Number of Offenders	(2) Persons Sentenced to Death	(3) Probability of Death Sentence	(4) Estimated Number of Offenders	(5) Persons Sentenced to Death	(6) Overall Probability of Death Sentence
Florida						
Black kills white	143	46	.323	97	7	.072
White kills white	303	65	.215	1465	17	.012
Black kills black	160	7	.044	1762	5	.003
White kills black	11	0	.000	69	0	.000
Georgia						
Black kills white	134	39	.291	124	3	.024
White kills white	183	37	.202	823	6	.007
Black kills black	205	8	.039	2253	4	.002
White kills black	13	2	.154	58	0	.000
Texas						
Black kills white	173	28	.162	171	2	.012
White kills white	378	48	.127	3238	8	.001
Black kills black	121	2	.017	2476	0	.000
White kills black	30	1	.033	113	0	.000

most substantial differences in the chance of a death sentence occur between those offenders who kill whites and those who kill blacks. In the case of nonfelony homicides, the overall pattern of differential treatment by race of offender and victim persists, but the greatest difference in both absolute and relative terms tends to be between the killings by blacks of white victims and all other racial combinations.

It appears, then, that among kinds of killings least likely to be punished by death (i.e., nonfelony killings), the death sentence is used primarily in response to the most socially condemned form of boundary crossing—a crime against a majority group member by a minority group member. Among those offenders more commonly (but not usually or typically) punished by death (i.e., those committing a felony homicide), there is some suggestion that cases of boundary crossing in the opposite direction—with majority group offenders and minority group victims—are selected occasionally against the prevailing race of offender and victim influences for more severe treatment.[85] But this latter pattern is a minor variation on a major theme. The primary point is this: among felony killings, for which the death penalty is more apt to be used, race of victim is the chief basis of differential treatment.

* * *

The data in this section point to more than arbitrariness and discrimination in isolation. They reflect a twofold departure from even-handed justice which is consistent with a single underlying racist tenet: that white lives are worth more than black lives. From this tenet it follows that death as punishment is more appropriate for the killers of whites than for the killers of blacks and more appropriate for black than for white killers. Either discrimination by race of offender or disparities of treatment by race of victim of the magnitudes we have seen here are a direct challenge to the constitutionality of the post-*Furman* capital statutes. Together, these elements of arbitrariness and discrimination may represent a two-edged sword of racism in capital punishment which is beyond statutory control.

* * *

Conclusion

In the first five years after the *Furman* decision, racial differences in the administration of capital statutes have been extreme in magnitude, similar across states and under different statutory forms, pervasive over successive stages of the judicial process, and uncorrected by appellate review. Moreover, these differentials have been fully consistent with the pattern of racial disparity occurring under capital statutes invalidated by the *Furman* decision. That is, differential treatment by race of offender and victim has been shown to persist post-*Furman* to a degree comparable in magnitude and pattern to the pre-*Furman* period. It is not that the new statutes have failed to eliminate all or most of these racial differences; it is, rather, that they have failed to alter in any substantial way the cumulative·pattern of differential treatment by race that was present under the now unconstitutional pre-*Furman* capital statutes.

Is it possible that the patterns of differential treatment we have documented here do not actually reflect arbitrariness and discrimination in the administration of capital punishment? The answer turns on whether these apparent departures from even-handed justice can be explained in terms of legally relevant factors or are the result of legally irrelevant influences.

A critical limitation on the available legally relevant explanations for such treatment differentials is that they must come from a strictly defined set of legally relevant factors which are enumerated as aggravating and mitigating circumstances in the statutes that provide for the death penalty. In other words, a plausible explanation of these racial . . . disparities of treatment would have to be found among these statutory provisions.

A further limitation is set by the empirical fact that only a subset of these legally possible explanations are found sufficiently often to account for racial . . . differences in the likelihood of a death sentence. That is, aside from the heinous and vile, and felony-related aggravating circumstances, the others are not found often enough to constitute a sufficient explanation, statistically, for the observed racial and regional differences in treatment.

With respect to racial differences, we have noted the argument that the kinds of killings with whites as victims and committed by blacks differ from other homicides in legally relevant ways—that is, the allegation that killings of whites are more often committed under felony circumstances and killings by blacks are more often heinous and vile. The evidence presented here has taken felony circumstance, specifically, into account as it is determined by police who investigate the crime and by prosecutors who prepare cases for trial. The data show that whether police or prosecutors'classifications are used, there are clear differences in treatment by both victim's and offender's race among felony-type murders and among killings classified as nonfelony homicides. In other words, felony circumstances do not account for the racial differences.

* * *

This is not to say that killings of whites and killings by blacks will not seem more vile and heinous to most people. Where there is animosity, prejudice, and stereotyping along racial lines—resulting, perhaps, from long-standing patterns of discrimination and deeply rooted racial attitudes and fears—people will be more shocked and outraged by members of the subjugated or subordinated racial group, and especially by killings in which a minority group offender crosses racial boundaries to murder a majority group victim.[98]

Moreover, the people who have these attitudes and fears are also the ones who serve as jurors and who elect prosecutors and judges to execute their laws. In effect, the stereotype and similarity of racial difference in treatment under different laws in different states and over different stages of the criminal justice process, and particularly at points of discretion for prosecutors and sentencing authorities within steps of the process, are consistent with this explanation in terms of extralegal influences.

* * *

More can and is being done to show how the differentials by race . . . and other sources come about. But we have come far enough to see that the system of capital punishment under post-*Furman* statutes has done little, if anything, to remedy the ills of the pre-*Furman* era. The burden of proof should now be shouldered by those who argue that the death penalty can be imposed without arbitrariness and discrimination. Those charged with judicial and executive responsibility for the present system of capital punishment should now take the initiatives needed for bringing the present system of injustice to a halt.

Footnotes

1 *Furman v. Georgia*, 408 U.S., 238 (1972).

2 The Court had previously held in *McGoutha v. California*, 402 U.S. 183 (1971) that discretion in capital sentencing that might result in arbitrary or discriminatory imposition of the death penalty was not a violation of the Fourteenth Amendment "due process" clause. The finding of arbitrariness in *Furman v. Georgia* served, however, to sustain an Eighth Amendment challenge which explicitly incorporated the unique severity and finality of capital punishment.

* * *

4 For an analysis of the distinctions among guided discretion statutes in terms of the limits they place upon sentencing authorities, see "Discretion and the Constitutionality of the New Death Penalty Statutes," *Harvard Law Review*, vol. 87, no. 8 (1974), pp. 1690-719, esp. pp. 1699ff. The distinctions introduced here draw on this analysis.

* * *

10 Georgia Code Ann. sec. 27-2537.

* * *

12 [*Gregg v. Georgia* at 2938.]

* * *

[20] In this connection, Black has written, " . . . where the technical materials (precedents, statutes, constitution) do not produce a clear answer—a condition often evidenced by disagreement as to the answer among equally competent and disinterested people—then obviously, since an answer is given *something else* produces it. This something else may be the judge's sense of policy, justice, fairness. This is undoubtedly the usual case, in overwhelming preponderance. The judge may, in obedience to the style of our law, conceal the operation of these factors from the public or, quite often, from himself, but they must be there, or disagreement on questions of law among equally learned and honest judges could not occur." Charles L. Black, Jr., *Capital Punishment: The Inevitability of Caprice and Mistake* (New York: W.W. Norton, 1974), pp. 78-79.

[21] William Bowers, *Executions in America* (Lexington, Mass.: D.C. Heath, 1974), pp. 165ff.

* * *

[67] 1977 Death Penalty Conference, Howard University, Washington, D.C. The meeting was jointly sponsored by the NAACP Legal Defense Fund and the Center for Studies in Criminology and Criminal Justice, University of Pennsylvania.

* * *

[69] We subsequently obtained the Supplementary Homicide Reports data on all states for 1977 and 1978 from the FBI, but not in time for the information to be incorporated into this report of findings.

* * *

[71] These estimates are based on a state-by-state count of death sentences compiled by the National Criminal Justice Information and Statistics Service, *Capital Punishment* (Washington, D.C.: Dept. of Justice, November, 1978). This is part of the National Prisoner Statistics series.

* * *

[73] The method of estimating the number of criminal homicides by offender/victim category is described in Appendix A, and the specific adjustment factors employed for each state are given in a note below Table 2.

[74] When race of victim is ignored, white offenders are more likely to receive a death sentence in three of these four states: Florida (white = .044, black = .030), Georgia (white = .040, black = .020), Texas (white = .015, black = .011). Without considering race of victim, black offenders exceed whites in the chances of a death sentence only in Ohio (white = .044, black = .048).

[75] The latest statewide listing of death sentences available from the Texas Judicial Council was current as of May 1978, so it may not include some death sentences that were eventually imposed for murders committed in 1977 or earlier. Given a pace of about twelve death sentences per year in Texas, with an average elapsed time between offense and sentence of six to eight months, we estimate that roughly six to eight death sentences might have been missed. Our figures for Texas, therefore, may underrepresent death sentences by six to eight cases, not more than 10 percent of the total.

[76] Furthermore, the Texas figures probably underestimate the extent to which blacks and whites, or members of minority groups versus the majority group, are treated differently. We know from the Texas Judicial Council reports that persons with Spanish surnames were overrepresented among those sentenced to death; eleven death sentences of such persons were imposed. But, because it was not possible to distinguish Hispanics from whites in the Supplementary Homicide Reports data, we could not tabulate the figures for blacks and whites excluding Hispanics or differentiate between blacks and Hispanics on the one hand and whites on the other.

[77] See *Harvard Law Review*, vol. 87, no. 8 (1974), p. 1709, note 133, for discussion of the definition of "quasi-mandatory."

[78] Under the Ohio statute, the jury considered only aggravating circumstances. If the jury found an aggravating circumstance, death was automatically the recommended punishment. The judge was then required to take evidence on mitigating circumstances. If the judge found no mitigating circumstances, the death sentence was imposed; otherwise, it was not.

[79] *Spenkelink v. Wainwright*, 578 F.2d 582 (CA5, 1978). (The spelling of the petitioner's name in the media reports and in the court briefs is often "Spinkellink" or "Spinkelink.")

[80] Ibid., at 617.

[81] Ibid., at 617, note 37.

[82] See notes 5 and 6, edited from this presentation but may be found in source from which taken.

[83] See note 8, edited from this presentation but may be found in source from which taken.

[84] Ironically, the evidence of gross differences in the likelihood of a death sentence by race of victim presented in the *Spenkelink* appeal was restricted to cases of murder committed under felony circumstances (essentially the data for Florida in the first three columns of Table 3). With respect to these data, the argument that blacks were typically or disproportionately the victims of killings provoked by quarrels was essentially irrelevant. The data explicitly excluded the overwhelming majority of killings attributed to quarrels or similar passion-filled conflict. The failure to appreciate this point would appear to have been a fatal mistake even at the appellate level.

[85] In each state, the fewest homicides are reported for the white offender/black victim category. Hence, the likelihood estimates for this category are least stable and comparisons between this category and the others are least reliable.

* * *

98 Walter Berns has advanced anger, outrage, and the need for vengeance as the rationale for capital punishment (see Walter Berns, *For Capital Punishment: Crime and the Morality of the Death Penalty* [New York: Basic Books, 1979]); but what he ignores is that these are often sources of injustice. They serve, for example, as the lynch mob's justification. This argument confuses the desire for vengeance with the principle of retribution. Vengeance is a human sentiment; retribution is a standard of justice. Vengeance rooted in anger ignores the distinction between legal and extralegal considerations in the act of vindictive punishment; retribution requires only that the punishment be proportional to the legally relevant characteristics of the crime and the offender—not that the punishment replicate the crime. Punishment that imitates the crime is not imposed for rape, assault, or arson—and surely, such punishment would be regarded as cruel and unusual for its obviously vengeful nature. The imposition of death as punishment for murder has the same primitive, vengeful nature. To be sure, motives of anger and the desire for revenge are implicit in the willingness to punish, and more so the more serious and shocking the crime. The irony is that the crimes for which capital punishment is advocated most strenuously are those in which extralegal influences are most powerful. When the punishment is death, the sensitivity of the motives of anger and revenge to extralegal influences makes arbitrariness and discrimination irrevocable.

The argument that society needs the death penalty for its deterrent or educative function is ignorant of the empirical facts. If anything, the effect of executions, according to the overwhelming bulk of credible empirical evidence, has been to increase rather than to decrease the incidence of homicides (see "Deterrence or Brutalization: What is the Effect of Executions?" by the present authors, . . . especially the review of previous research). If capital punishment teaches anything, it appears to be the lesson of lethal vengeance. Once the extralegal influences of capital punishment become clear, as they are in these data, it is not difficult to see how and why the death penalty has a brutalizing effect on society. Simply stated, the death penalty encourages the exercise of lethal vengeance in the name of justice, rather than just retribution under law.

DETERRENCE OR BRUTALIZATION:
WHAT IS THE EFFECT OF EXECUTIONS?

William J. Bowers
Glenn L. Pierce

A critical feature of the continuing debate over capital punishment has been the impact of executions on society. Advocates of the death penalty say that it protects society by dramatically demonstrating to would-be murders that such a crime does not pay. Opponents argue that capital punishment brutalizes society because executions show that lethal violence is an appropriate response to those who offend.

Historically, these arguments came into bold relief in the debate over public executions in America in the 1830s and 1840s. Advocates argued that removing executions from public view would deprive them of their unique power as a deterrent. Opponents said that public executions stimulate the kinds of violence for which they are imposed. These opposing arguments also figured in the controversy over press coverage of executions in the 1890s and later. Indeed, they surfaced again recently in response to a proposal to televise executions in Texas. Some, including once presidential hopeful John Connally, see this as the best way to "harness the deterrent power" of the death penalty. Others are afraid that televising executions would incite imitative execution-like behavior in society. They cite Gary Gilmore's execution as a case in point, saying it was followed by a rash of bizarre acts of violence by mentally unstable persons apparently seeking public attention. What are the assumptions and implications of these two opposing positions?

Deterrence

The deterrence argument assumes a rationalistic perspective in which human behavior is seen as a function of individually perceived costs and benefits of alternative choices or actions. The individually perceived costs and benefits are further assumed to reflect directly, if imperfectly, objectively ascertainable variations in these costs and benefits to the individual. Thus, in the case of mur-

W. Bowers and G. Pierce, "Deterrence or Brutalization: What is the Effect of Executions?," *Crime and Delinquency*, vol. 26, #4, October 1980, pp. 453-484. © 1980 by the National Council on Crime. Reprinted by permission of Sage Publications, Inc.

der, not unlike other less violent and more instrumental crimes, deterrence theory assumes that potential offenders exercise rational judgment in deciding whether or not to kill and that they are predictably sensitive to the actual range of variation in certainty and severity of legal punishment for murder at the time of the decision to act. This rationalistic view is familiar in economics, and has served as the basis for a theory of legal punishment, at least since Jeremy Bentham.

From what we know about murder, however, there is reason to doubt these assumptions. Most murders are acts of passion between angry or frustrated people who know one another.[1] Indeed, many murders are the result of assaults occurring under the influence of alcohol,[2] and many of the murderers are persons who have previously and repeatedly assaulted the victim.[3] Encounters that result in murder typically involve "face saving"[4] or the maintenance of favorable "situational identities"[5] in the presence of threats, insults, and demands for compliance. In a recent study, having intoxicated and unarmed victims is what best distinguished imprisoned killers from those incarcerated for aggravated assault.[6] We know further that extreme brutality or cruelty toward the victim or killing in the act of another crime is the circumstance most likely to bring down a death sentence.[7] In effect, most murderers, and particularly those who reach death row, do not fit the model of the calculating killer.

Moreover, it is doubtful that the calculating potential offender, even if he wanted to do so, could make a rational decision that takes execution risk into account. Police statistics reported to the Federal Bureau of Investigation and execution records from the National Bureau of Prisons indicate that only a small fraction of criminal homicides have resulted in executions—no more than 2 percent per year since 1930.[8] It has been virtually impossible for the public to know the proportion of first degree or capital murders for which executions were carried out in a given jurisdiction over a given period of time. Even experts[9] have found it difficult to estimate the number of capital murders.[10] About the only way potential offenders can develop some vague impression that committing murder has become more or less risky is from the number and pacing of executions as reported in the press.

Beyond these misgivings about the rational model of the murder decision, there is further reason to doubt that potential offenders actually get the deterrence message executions are presumed to convey. An execution can be viewed from various vantage points. If one could put himself in the shoes of the offender who gets executed, he might see that the same could be in store· for him were he to follow in that offender's footsteps. That is, the person who identifies with an executed offender may get the deterrence message. But the psychology of identification tells us that people identify personally with those they admire or envy. What we know about those murderers who are eventually executed makes it seem quite unlikely that any sane or rational person will identify with them. They are characteristically uneducated, impoverished misfits who have committed cruel or cowardly acts without provocation or remorse. They may have strangled small children, killed whole families, dismembered their victims, and the like. Will calculating potential murders identify with them, or will they not, instead, contrast themselves with these wretches? Might they not infer that the death penalty is reserved as punishment only for people unlike themselves?

Brutalization

The argument that executions have a brutalizing effect draws on different assumptions about the message that executions convey.
* * *

The lesson of the execution . . . may be to devalue life by the example of human sacrifice. Executions demonstrate that it is correct and appropriate to kill those who have gravely offended us. The fact that such killings are to be performed only by duly appointed officials on duly convicted offenders is a detail that may get obscured by the message that such offenders deserve to die. If the typical murderer is someone who feels that he has been betrayed, dishonored, or disgraced by another person—and we suggest that such feelings are far more characteristic of those who commit murder than a rational evaluation of costs and benefits—then it is not hard to imagine that the example executions provide may inspire a potential murderer to kill the person who has greatly offended him. In effect, the message of the execution may be lethal vengeance, not deterrence.

Implicit in the brutalization argument is an alternative identification process, different from the one implied by deterrence theory The potential murderer will not identify personally with the criminal who is executed, but will instead identify someone who had greatly offended him—someone he hates, fears, or both—with the executed criminal. We might call this the psychology of "villain identification." By associating the person who has wronged him with the victim of an execution, he sees that death is what his despised offender deserves. Indeed, he himself may identify with the state as executioner and thus justify and reinforce his desire for lethal vengeance.

Granted, it is uncommon to think of potential murders as self-righteous avengers who identify with the executioner; but the more common view that they will think of themselves as criminals and identify with those who are executed may be wishful thinking. We have already observed that those who get executed are a wretched lot with whom few would identify—the kinds with whom one might identify his worst enemies. Perhaps the reason people are inclined to believe that potential murderers will recognize their criminal tendencies and be deterred by the executions of other murderers is that this distinguishes "them" from the rest of "us" and provides a justification for executions that masks the desire for lethal vengeance. Also, by imagining that potential murderers will get the deterrence message, the "law-abiding" have the satisfaction of believing that they are taking effective steps to combat society's most heinous and feared crimes.[13]

Executions might stimulate homicides in other ways. For some people the psychology of suggestion or imitation may be activated by an execution. In this connection, research on the aftermath of the John F. Kennedy assassination and two highly publicized mass murders has shown that they were succeeded by significantly increased rates of violent crime in the months immediately following.[14] The investigators offer the following three-point interpretation of imitative violence:

One, aggressive ideas and images arise. Most of these thoughts are probably quite similar to the observed event, but generalization processes also lead to other kinds of violent ideas and images as well. Two, if inhibitions against aggression are not evoked by the witnessed violence or by the observers' anticipation of negative consequences of aggressive behavior, and if the observers are ready to act violently, the event can also evoke open aggression. And again, these aggressive responses need not resemble the instigating violence too closely. Three, these aggressive reactions probably subside fairly quickly but may reappear if the observers encounter other environmental stimuli associated with aggression—and especially stimuli associated with the depicted violence.[15]

Furthermore, there is evidence that such a process of suggestion or stimulation may also include an element of identification with the victim. Thus, research on highly publicized suicides has shown that they are followed in the succeeding month by a significantly higher than expected number of suicides in the population.[16] It is estimated, for example, that Marilyn Monroe's suicide provoked some 363 suicides in the United States and Britain.[17]

As an escape from life, execution may be preferable to suicide to some troubled individuals. Although most people find it hard to imagine, there are many cases of persons who have killed others for self-destructive motives.[18] In these cases, the individuals typically have a deep-seated antipathy toward themselves and others, a need to express and act on their feelings, and a guilt-inspired desire to be punished for their feelings and actions. For those burdened with self-hatred, death by execution is punishment as well as escape. With the crime that leads to execution, the offender also strikes back at society or particular individuals. The execution itself may provide an opportunity to be seen and heard, to express resentment, alienation, and defiance. Thus, even for the troubled few who may find it possible to identify with the executed criminal, or at least with his situation, the message of an execution may be imitation rather than deterrence.

* * *

Indeed, death-risking behavior is sometimes a way of affirming one's commitments and winning favor in society. It is a sign of courage and bravery in wartime, a source of recognition and admiration among sportsmen and adventurers, an affirmation of honor in the face of insults, and a demonstration of allegiance with others who share a common cause or fear. The very existence of the death penalty may provide some fanatical or troubled people with an unparalleled opportunity to "prove a point" or draw attention to themselves. Of the last three to be executed, Gilmore sought death and publicity, Jesse Bishop accepted death and did not refuse publicity, and only John Spenkelink preferred not to die.

Existing Evidence

Most studies have examined variations in the availability or use of executions over extended periods of time with officially recorded statistics on murder or homicide for evidence of whether death as punishment prevented or provoked the kinds of crimes for which it was imposed. A few studies have focused on the more immediate impact of executions by examining homicides in the days, weeks, and months surrounding executions. In our review of this empirical literature, it will be convenient to distinguish between studies of the longer-term effects of executions conducted with data on homicides for years or longer periods of time and studies of their more immediate impact done with data on homicides nearer to the time of execution.

Long-Term Effects

Well over a century ago, when capital punishment was under attack and public executions in the United States were coming to an end, the impact of executions on homicides was being studied with statistics from various countries covering extended periods of time. Perhaps America's most prominent compiler and interpreter of these data was Massachusetts legislator and man of letters, Robert Rantoul, Jr.[24] * * *

* * *

At the critical juncture in the history of capital punishment in the United States, after executions had ceased and the Supreme Court had declared previous capital statutes unconstitutional, a new brand of research on the effects of executions appeared using annual execution and homicide data—as Rantoul had done well over a century earlier. Instead of comparing matched abolition and retention jurisdictions as Sellin and others had done, this econometric modeling approach attempted to adjust statistically, by multiple regression techniques, for differences across states or over time which could be expected to produce differences in homicide rates that otherwise might mistakenly be attributed to the imposition of executions.

In 1975, Isaac Ehrlich published the first econometric study of execution risk and homicide rates, based on data for the nation as a whole over the period 1933-69.[34] This study purported to show—contrary to all previous investigations—that each execution saved seven or eight innocent lives by deterring murders that would otherwise occur.[35] This work is noteworthy not for the validity of its claims, which have now been discredited by a number of reanalyses of these data,[36] but for its impact in promoting the cause of capital punishment[37] and for the series of further studies it provoked. These latter studies have, on balance, yielded more empirical support for the brutalizing than for the deterrent effect of executions.[38]

What did careful reanalyses of these data show? First, execution risk tended to be positively associated with homicide rates from the mid-1930s through the early 1960s, using Ehrlich's data and analytic approach.[39] Second, the relationship also tended to be positive in the 1960s when this period was examined independently of the earlier years.[40] Third, the relationship tended to be even more positive, approaching statistical significance, when less flawed homicide data were used in the analyses.[41]

In this connection, the National Academy of Sciences' critique of Ehrlich's work on capital punishment noted that errors in the measurement of homicides would tend to introduce a negative bias[42] or "illusion of deterrence" into Ehrlich's findings[.]

* * *

Studies have gone on to show with Ehrlich's data and with other time series and cross-sectional data sets that positive execution effects occur with the addition of explanatory variables omitted from Ehrlich's analysis. Thus, positive execution effects have emerged in time series analyses with measures of handgun ownership[44] and noncapital violent crime rates[45] and in cross-sectional analyses with variables reflecting certainty and severity of imprisonment for criminal homicides[46]—despite the negative bias that error in measuring homicides may introduce.[47] In the only analysis we know of that is not subject to the negative bias introduced by the common term problem (execution risk is a conditional measure computed by dividing the number of persons executed in 1960 by the number of murderers imprisoned in that year), William Bailey[48] found statistically significant positive effects of execution risk on homicide rates consistent with a brutalizing effect of executions.

Short-Term Impact

At the high point of executions in America in the mid-1930s, research began to deal with the more immediate impact of executions. . . . In 1935, Robert Dann examined five executions in Philadelphia (occurring in 1927, 1929, 1930, 1931, and 1932) which had in common the fact that no other execution had been imposed within sixty days.[49] Dann then tallied the homicides occurring in sixty-day periods before and after each of these executions and reported a total of 91 homicides before and 113 homicides after each of these five executions—an average increase of 4.4 homicides in the sixty days after each execution. * * *

Dann's work inspired a parallel study of the impact of death sentences on homicides in Philadelphia. In 1958, Leonard Savitz examined the eight weeks before and after death sentences were handed down in four well-publicized cases.[51] . . . When the Savitz data are adjusted for monthly variations in homicides in Philadelphia, they yield an expected number of 36 capital murders in the eight-week periods after these four death sentences,[52] indicating that there were 5 more murders than would be expected—an average of 1.25 more murders per death sentence—in the eight weeks after these death sentences were handed down.* * *

Dann's work also stimulated a study of the more immediate impact of executions in California. In 1956, William Graves tabulated homicides from the records of San Francisco, Los Angeles, and Alameda counties over the period 1946-55 for each day of the week in which an execution was imposed and for each day of execution-free weeks immediately before and after the week of an execution (excluding execution-free weeks between two execution weeks). . . . Graves found that on Thursdays and Fridays during execution weeks (the day before and the day of execution) homicides were slightly higher, and on Saturdays and Sundays of execution weeks (the first and second days after execution) homicides were slightly lower than the corresponding days of the execution-free weeks immediately before and after. Graves observed that the slight depression in homicides in the two days immediately after an execution "is almost exactly canceled out by its earlier 'brutalizing' effect."[53] * * *

* * *

Quite recently, another study of this sort appeared which quite specifically addressed itself to the brutalizing effect of executions. In 1979, David King examined the monthly incidence of homicides in South Carolina for the effect of newspaper publicity about executions. Over the period of 1951-62 he identified twenty months in which stories on executions appeared in the state's daily paper with the largest circulation.[56] . . . He reported that the delayed brutalizing effect in the month after an execution story was statistically significant in his relatively small sample of twenty cases at the .10 probability level.

In summary, studies of the long-term effect and short-term impact of executions give ample indication that executions may have—contrary to prevailing belief—not a deterrent but a brutalizing effect on society by promoting rather than preventing homicides. The earliest research in the period of public executions was fully and strongly consistent with such a brutalizing effect. Later studies comparing periods of abolition and retention between and within jurisdictions consistently show lower homicide rates at times and places of abolition, suggesting that the availability, and by implication the use, of the death penalty stimulates homicide. And, recent studies using econometric modeling and regression estimation techniques have begun to reveal more positive than negative estimates of the effects of execution risk on homicide rates—notwithstanding analytic problems which have tended to bias results in favor of deterrence.

Among the smaller number of studies which have examined homicides in the days, weeks, and months following executions, the evidence of a slight brutalizing effect is again consistent. In three

California counties, there was a slight but discernible increase in homicides (.25 per execution) within ten days of an execution. In the relatively large city of Philadelphia, there was a slightly larger increase in homicides after executions (1.6 per execution) and after death sentences (1.2 per death sentence) within roughly two months after these events. And statewide in South Carolina there was a comparable increase in homicides after execution stories (1.2 per execution story) within roughly two months of publication, the increase concentrated in the month after an execution story appeared.

Given the size of the brutalizing effect as reflected in the short-term impact studies, it is not surprising that most investigators working with aggregate annual homicide data failed to detect brutalizing effects. For perspective on this point, take the study of execution stories in South Carolina as an example. South Carolina had an estimated 24 additional homicides over the period 1951-62 as a result of executions (20 execution stories x 1.2 homicides per story). This is an average of 2 more homicides per year—less than 1 percent of the annual average of 222 homicides, and less than 10 percent of the average year-to-year fluctuation of 20.4 homicides over this periods. The stronger effect of other factors on homicide rates and the fact that such variables are imperfectly controlled by contiguous matching procedures and not all included or accurately measured in regression adjustments would further obscure such a brutalizing effect. The impact of an execution story is less apt to be lost in the monthly average of 18.5 homicides or the average monthly fluctuation of 5.3 homicides. And other factors affecting homicide rates, but inadequately controlled by matching procedures or regression adjustments, are likely to change less from month to month than from year to year.

For research to evaluate an effect of this sort, then, there will be premiums in the data used for analysis on (1) *temporal refinement*, enabling one to isolate effects which may be relatively immediate and short-lived for the duration of their impact, and at the same time to restrict the period over which potentially confounding effects of other influences may operate, and (2) *larger sample size*, so that relatively slight effects which are nevertheless consistent and recurrent can be detected with statistical reliability and estimated with accuracy and precision. The study described below was designed with these considerations in mind.

Data and Analysis

With the publication of the Teeters-Zibulka inventory of *Executions under State Authority: 1864-1967*,[57] systematic information has become available on some 5,706 executions imposed over the past century. For most states this represents a complete listing of executions since they were moved from local jurisdictions to the central authority of the state. The inventory includes information on type of offense, county of prosecution, race and age of offender, appeals before execution, and, for present purposes, date of execution.

* * *

Of all states, New York has imposed the most executions under state authority, some 695 since 1890 when it became the first state to use the electric chair. New York has also had more homicides than any other state for most of this period. . . . The comparatively high incidence of homicides and executions in New York and the relatively long period of time over which data are available on a monthly basis make New York the state best suited to the purposes of our analysis.

The analysis to be presented here is a simple one. It asks how the number of homicides in a given month is affected by the occurrence of executions occurring monthly.[61] The monthly homicide figures run from their starting point in January, 1907 through August, 1964, a year after the last execution in New York State. The monthly execution data for this analysis cover the period from January, 1906 through the date of New York's last execution, in August 1963. For purposes of statistical analysis, this is a time series of 57 years and 8 months, or some 692 monthly observations.

Our concern is with the impact of executions on homicides. We estimate by multiple regression techniques how homicides in a given month, HO_t, are affected by executions occurring in each of the twelve preceding months, EX_{t-i} (where $i = 1, 2..., 12$). Thus, we have chosen to examine the effects of executions on the incidence of homicides for up to a year. The fundamental form of the regression model is

$$HO_t = EX_{t-i}.$$

We know there are seasonal variations in homicides. Homicides are generally more numerous in the summer months. December, however, is an exception; apparently the holiday season creates conditions conducive to homicide.

It also happens that in New York State, executions have been consistently more numerous in some months than in others. January has been the leading month for executions, with an average of 2.0 over the period of the study. July and August rank second and third, with averages of 1.5 and 1.2, respectively. October and November are conspicuously low execution months, with averages of 0.1 and 0.2—perhaps authorities are reluctant to schedule executions as Christmas approaches.

* * *

Furthermore, we know that both homicides and executions display disparate long-term trends. In parallel fashion, they both rise to a peak in the mid-1930s. After that, homicides drop off to a plateau in the 1940s and 1950s, and then begin a precipitous rise as our time series comes to an end. By contrast, executions show a consistent downward trend after the mid-1930s.

* * *

In the sections that follow we first show the estimated effects of the presence of executions in one month on homicides in subsequent months with controls for seasonality and time trend. We then introduce further controls for temporal fluctuations in the data and adjustments for autocorrelated errors of prediction.[62]

Findings

The figures reported in the upcoming tables are the unstandardized regression coefficients or "b's" that reflect the estimated change in number of homicides produced by the occurrence of executions in earlier months. Each row reports the effect of executions a designated number of months earlier (viz., 1, 2, ..., 12). Each column presents effects as estimated in equations with a time trend polynomial of designated order (viz., 1, 2 ..., 10). . . . The estimated effects are calculated in all instances with month dummy variables,

MO_i s, as controls for seasonality and for variations in the length of the months, although their effects are not shown. For each estimated equation the table shows the adjusted R^2 as a measure of goodness of fit and the Durbin-Watson statistic as an indication of correlated errors of prediction.

Estimated Effects of Executions Controlling for Seasonality and Time Trend

The most substantial, the most consistent, and the only statistically significant coefficients in Table 1 represent a brutalizing effect of executions on homicides in the following month. In the first row of the table, the estimated effects range from 1.00 in the equation without control for chronological time, to 1.92 in the equation with the seventh-order time trend polynomial. Moreover, in all equations with polynomial time trends of fourth order and higher, these estimated effects, ranging from 1.70 to 1.92, are statistically significant at the .05 level. These figures say that, on the average, the presence of one or more executions in a given month adds two homicides to the number committed in the next month.

A similar but weaker effect appears for the presence of executions two months earlier. Equations estimated with time trend controls (excluding *no TM*) show effects ranging from 1.01 to 1.41. This suggests that, on the average, executions imposed in a given month add one homicide to the number committed two months later. We say "suggest" here because the observed pattern in the data is not sufficiently strong under any of the time trend controls in this sample of 692 observations to be statistically significant at the .05 probability level.

The estimated effects of executions three to six months earlier are weaker than those in months t - 1 and t - 2 and alternate between positive and negative values. Thus, on the balance, the coefficients are negative at t - 3, positive at t - 4, negative at t - 5, and again positive at t - 6. The estimated effects of executions seven or more months earlier are still weaker, on the average, and tend to run slightly positive or negative depending on the order of the time trend control.

Table 1.   Estimated Effects of Execution on Homicides, Controlling for Seasonality with Increasing Time Trend Polynomials (January 1907 through August 1964)

Executions Lagged 1-12 Months	Estimated with Successively Higher-Order Time Trend Polynomials (time in months)										
	No TM	TM^1	TM^2	TM^3	TM^4	TM^5	TM^6	TM^7	TM^8	TM^9	TM^{10}
EX_{t-1}	1.00	1.68	1.47	1.73	1.85*	1.90*	1.70*	1.92*	1.81*	1.76*	1.75*
EX_{t-2}	.55	1.22	1.01	1.18	1.30	1.39	1.18	1.41	1.27	1.22	1.22
EX_{t-3}	-1.62	-.98	-1.18	-1.01	-.93	-.84	-1.03	-.83	-.94	-1.00	-1.01
EX_{t-4}	.32	.93	.74	.86	.97	1.06	.87	1.08	.95	.91	.90
EX_{t-5}	-.86	-.29	-.48	-.47	-.32	-.20	-.39	-.18	-.34	-.37	-.37
EX_{t-6}	-.06	.46	.27	.19	.37	.52	.33	.54	.33	.31	.33
EX_{t-7}	-.20	.27	.07	-.18	.05	.27	.06	.29	.25	.01	.04
EX_{t-8}	-.15	.32	.12	-.22	.00	.24	.04	.26	-.02	-.04	-.01
EX_{t-9}	-.33	.13	-.07	-.50	-.23	.03	-.17	.62	-.24	-.26	-.23
EX_{t-10}	-.41	.06	-.16	-.63	-.31	-.02	-.24	.00	-.30	-.31	-.27
EX_{t-11}	-.39	.09	-.14	-.61	-.23	.05	-.18	.08	-.21	-.21	-.17
EX_{t-12}	-.14	.31	.05	-.52	-.09	.23	-.01	.26	-.06	-.05	-.01
Adj. R^2	.03	.04	.05	.35	.45	.48	.48	.48	.55	.54	.53
D/W statistic	.62	.62	.62	.91	1.09	1.14	1.15	1.15	1.34	1.32	1.28

* $p < .05$, t test.
** $p < .01$, t test.

By statistical standards, the equation with eighth-order time trend controls fits the data best. It shows a higher adjusted R^2 and a more favorable D/W statistic than any of the other equations. To be sure, the strongest positive coefficients for EX_{t-1} and EX_{t-2} appear in equations with fourth-, fifth-, and seventh-order time trend polynomials. Indeed, the coefficients in the equation with fifth-order controls are all higher (more positive or less negative) than their counterparts in the best-fitting equation. Yet, the best-fitting eighth-order time trend equation provides statistically significant evidence of a brutalizing effect in the month following an execution and suggests that this effect may extend into the next month as well.

Can we do better in estimating the effects of executions on homicides? The adjusted R^2 tells us that roughly 30 percent of the variance in homicides is accounted for by our best equation. If we can improve the fit in terms of the adjusted R^2, our parameter estimates will be more reliable. The D/W statistic tells us that the errors of prediction from this equation are serially correlated. A better-fitting equation may remove this correlated error[.] * * *

Further Controls for Temporal Variation

The time trend polynomials will trace the broad contours of the movement in homicides, but they will not follow relatively abrupt and temporary departures from these steadier trends, departures that may, for example, be the product of discrete historical events. To the extent that such shifts in the level of homicides are not traced by the time trend controls, they will add to the errors of prediction and to the correlation among these errors. Furthermore, to the extent that executions are affected by such a historical event, perhaps increased or diminished in number, biases will be introduced into our estimates of execution effects. It is important, therefore, that our temporal controls incorporate the effects of such events.

War is one of the most disruptive events societies experience. Those who go to war are disproportionately from the groups in society that contribute most to the homicide rate. It is reported, for example, that New York City shrank by three-quarters of a million persons, mostly young males, during World War II.[63] Studies have shown that domestic homicide rates tend to drop off during wartime[64] and that they tend to climb precipitously immediately after war.[65] * * *

* * *

The values reflecting each year's departure from the secular time trend as estimated in our best-fitting equation with the eighth-order time trend polynomial are as follows:

Year	Departure
1941	-5.48
1942	-4.50
1943	-6.47
1944	-6.48
1945	+3.95
1946	+10.63
1947	+8.63

The war years obviously dropped well below the trend line; from 1941-44 there were on the average six fewer homicides per month than would otherwise be expected. In the year the war ended and the troops returned home in massive numbers, homicides increased substantially, to a monthly average four homicides above the trend line. In the two years after the war, homicides rose further, to ten per month above the trend line. Perhaps those who went to war came back more violent, maybe they returned to a more violent society, or possibly problems of reintegration and adjustment were the cause. In any case, the war evidently had a brutalizing effect on postwar society.

Notably, we also examined the values during the two years after World War I, introducing dummy variables for the years 1917 through 1920. None of these variables was statistically significant or displayed effects comparable in magnitude to the World War II dummies. We have therefore omitted them from our analysis.

The evidence of brutalization is even stronger in Table 2 than it was in Table 1. First, estimated parameters for executions at $t - 1$ and $t - 2$ are now larger (more positive) in nine of the eleven corresponding equations. * * *

Table 2. Estimated Effects of Execution on Homicides, Controlling for Seasonality and World War II with Increasing Time Trend Polynomials (January 1907 through August 1964)

Executions Lagged 1-12 Months	Estimated with Successively Higher-Order Time Trend Polynomials (time in months)										
	No TM	TM^1	TM^2	TM^3	TM^4	TM^5	TM^6	TM^7	TM^8	TM^9	TM^{10}
EX_{t-1}	.77	1.87	1.41	1.79*	1.94*	2.01*	1.82*	1.99*	1.95**	1.91**	1.90**
EX_{t-2}	.33	1.41	.95	1.23	1.38	1.47	1.28	1.45	1.40*	1.36	1.35
EX_{t-3}	-1.65	-.60	-1.03	-.80	-.66	-.57	-.75	-.59	-.60	-.65	-.66
EX_{t-4}	.12	1.12	.71	.91	1.03	1.11	.92	1.09	1.00	.95	.95
EX_{t-5}	-.77	.15	-.25	-.18	.53	.15	-.24	.13	.35	.99	.64
EX_{t-6}	.09	.99	.56	.57	.88	.99	.82	.98	.83	.81	.81
EX_{t-7}	-.01	.78	.34	.17	.53	.68	.50	.67	.47	.46	.47
EX_{t-8}	-.23	.50	.08	-.10	.19	.36	.18	.35	.12	.11	.11
EX_{t-9}	-.20	.56	.10	-.17	.23	.42	.23	.41	.18	.17	.18
EX_{t-10}	-.35	.39	-.11	-.36	.95	.30	.11	.30	.11	.12	.12
EX_{t-11}	-.33	.44	-.08	-.36	.15	.35	.13	.34	.12	.13	.14
EX_{t-12}	.10	.84	.30	-.15	.42	.63	.40	.62	.36	.37	.37
Adj. R^2	.13	.17	.20	.40	.53	.54	.54	.54	.59	.59	.59
D/W statistic	.65	.69	.72	.95	1.23	1.25	1.26	1.26	1.43	1.41	1.40

* $p < .05$, t test.
** $p < .01$, t test.

Again, as in Table 1, the best-fitting equation is the one estimated with the eighth-order time trend polynomial. Compared with its counterpart in Table 1, in this equation the brutalizing effect of executions at t - 1 has increased slightly (from 1.81 to 1.95) and become statistically more significant (from the .05 to the .01 probability level). The suggested brutalizing effect of executions at t - 2 also shows a slight increase (from 1.27 to 1.40), with an estimated probability level of exactly .05.[66] In fact, with controls for World War II, every coefficient in this equation has increased (become more positive or less negative); six have changed from negative to positive values, leaving only one negative estimate for executions at t - 3. The increase in adjusted R^2 (from .0.55 to 0.59), is highly significant, and the D/W statistic has improved (from 1.34 to 1.43) although it remains problematic.

* * *

Conclusions

There is room to quarrel about whether these data show a brutalizing effect of two or three homicides, on the average, occurring after a month in which an execution is carried out. It is certainly consistent with the notion of a brutalizing effect of two homicides in the first month immediately after an execution to have some "temporal spillover" into the second month after an execution. Indeed, if, on the average, executions tend to fall in the middle of a month, then the fact of two homicides in the following month suggests a six-week brutalizing effect. For executions imposed at the end of the month, this would naturally extend the duration of effect into the second month after the execution. The point is that such a distributive effect—two homicides one month later and one homicide two months later—is thoroughly consistent with a commonly observed pattern of dissipating effects over time.

The fact that we see a consistently negative (though statistically nonsignificant) coefficient for the effect of executions at t - 4 at least suggests that some of those who were stimulated to kill by the occurrence of an execution would have done so anyway, but did so sooner because of the execution. That is, just as these data suggest a third additional homicide in the second month after an execution, they also suggest (though less strongly) that one of the three might have occurred a month or so later anyway. In any case, the data definitely show an addition of at least two to the incidence of homicides, not simply a change in the timing of homicides.

Furthermore, the largely positive (but nonsignificant) coefficients for EX_{t-4} through EX_{t-12} may reflect a longer-term brutalizing effect of executions over a period from four to twelve months after an execution. Although these coefficients are slight and somewhat erratic, together they sum up to a positive value of roughly 3.00, or three additional homicides. That is to say, the presence of executions at a given point in time adds very little to the monthly number of homicides after three months have elapsed, but the data at least suggest that such an execution adds roughly three more to the number of homicides in the next nine months of the year after the execution.

It should be noted that in this analysis we have probably underestimated the brutalizing effect of executions. We have ignored those instances in which a brutalizing effect may have occurred in the same month as an execution. The analysis of this issue is complicated, however, by the possibility of a "repressive response" effect.[71] That is, whether or not an execution occurs may, in some measure, be affected by the incidence of homicides in that month (and/or the preceding one). Thus, for example, the decision to grant a stay of execution may be more difficult to make in the presence of an exceptionally high level of homicides in the days and weeks immediately preceding the scheduled date.[72] Hence, a greater than expected number of homicides in a month with an execution might reflect the impact of homicides on the occurrence of executions instead of executions on the occurrence of homicides. This matter, to be addressed in subsequent research, requires the use of a more complicated analytic model than we have dealt with here.

Of course, in states with smaller populations and/or fewer executions, the brutalizing effect will yield fewer homicides (unless it extends beyond jurisdictional boundaries). Parenthetically, this may, in part, account for the failure of previous studies based on state-level aggregate annual homicide data to detect brutalizing effects. Notably, the studies that have suggested a brutalizing effect of executions have worked with data on homicides occurring days,[73] weeks,[74] and months[75] before and after executions. Indeed, the only other study to examine monthly homicide data found borderline statistical support for a brutalizing effect in the month after the occurrence of an execution story in South Carolina.[76] In fact, the magnitude of the brutalization effect relative to the incidence of homicides was roughly similar in South Carolina and New York; South Carolina had about half the homicides in an average month (20.4 versus 40.4) and about half the brutalizing effect (1 as opposed to 2 additional homicides), despite the fact that its population was approximately one-sixth that of New York for the respective periods of analysis.

This suggests that the brutalization occurs among the pool of potential killers (as this may be reflected in the actual number of homicides) and not the population at large. This tends to confirm the notion that the brutalizing effect is specific to the person who has reached a state of "readiness to kill," in which the potential killer has a justification, a plan, a weapon, and above all a specific intended victim in mind.[77] It is precisely for such people with a victim in mind that an execution may convey the message of lethal vengeance. They need only place the intended victim in the shoes of the executed criminal, the process we have called "villain identification." Of course, some guilt-laden, self-destructive persons in a state of readiness of kill might be prompted by the execution to imitate the crime for which it was imposed.

The implications of this research, given the present status of capital punishment in the United States, are ominous. At this writing there are some 642 persons under sentence of death. If the execution of each one produced two or three homicides, the cost in innocent lives would be outstanding. Moreover, the audience for executions in this era may not be jurisdictionally specific—it may be nationwide, suggesting that the increase in homicides experienced by New York State represents only a fraction of what might be expected for the nation as a whole.

To be sure, many questions remain about the nature and magnitude of such a brutalizing effect. Strictly speaking, our findings pertain only to the impact of months with one or more executions, not to the effect of each execution in a given month. As noted above, the impact on homicides of executions in the same month has yet to be examined, as does the role of the publicity executions receive. And there are questions about the social and psychological dynamics of brutalization. Is a message of lethal vengeance an essential ingredient? Must the brutalized person associate the executed offender with persons he has come to fear or hate? Do some people, in fact, identify with the executed offender and seek to imitate his crime through some obsessive desire to gain attention, as a way of expressing abject alienation, or to act out a sublimated death wish? Is there also a deterrent effect which is simply outweighed by the brutalizing effect?

Although these questions deserve answers, they do not alter the conclusion that executions as they have been imposed historically in New York State have contributed to homicides in the month immediately following. It might be argued that this is not a necessary result, that changes in the conduct of executions could offset or neutralize the brutalizing effect we have observed. Indeed, to anticipate the argument that the fewest innocent lives would be sacrificed if all pending executions were imposed in a massive, one-month blood bath, we hasten to add that execution months in New York State had, on the average, two and seldom more than six electrocutions. Hence, these data cannot be generalized to support the argument that concentrating a great many executions into a brief time period would minimize the sacrifice of innocent lives.

The point is that the way we have carried out executions historically in the United States appears to have contributed slightly but significantly to the increase in homicides. Any argument that packaging, pacing, or publicizing executions differently would do otherwise finds no support in these data. In view of these findings, the burden of proof that a brutalizing effect can be avoided lies with those who advance this argument. Without evidence on how the observed brutalizing effect could be converted into the desired deterrent effect, these findings represent a direct challenge to the constitutionality of the death penalty for its impact on those who have not been convicted of any crime.

Footnotes

[1] Marvin Wolfgang, *Patterns in Criminal Homicide* (Philadelphia: University of Pennsylvania, 1958).

[2] *Ibid.*

[3] George Kelling et al, *The Kansas City Preventive Patrol Experiment* (Washington, D.C.: Police Foundation, 1974).

[4] David Luckenbill, "Criminal Homicide as a Situated Transaction," *Social Problems*, December, 1977, pp. 176-86.

[5] Richard B. Felson and Henry J. Steadman, "Situations and Processes Leading to Criminal Violence" (Albany, N.Y.: New York State Department of Mental Hygiene, 1979).

[6] *Ibid.*

[7] After the United States Supreme Court's 1972 *Furman v. Georgia* decision invalidating existing capital statutes, Florida and Georgia were the first states to enact new death penalty statutes that listed aggravating circumstances, at least one of which must be found by the jury before a death sentence can be imposed. The only two aggravating circumstances found in more than 10 percent of the cases receiving the death sentence in either state are those identifying murders as occurring in the course of another felony and those identifying murders as particularly heinous or as committed in a vile or wanton manner.

[8] William J. Bowers, *Executions in America* (Lexington, Mass.: D.C. Heath, 1974), pp. 22-23.

[9] William C. Bailey, "Murder and Capital Punishment," *American Journal of Orthopsychiatry*, July 1975, pp. 669-88.

[10] Notably, first degree murder of the deliberate, calculated and premeditated kind, which executions supposedly have the unique power to deter, is no longer sufficient grounds for the imposition of the death penalty. Under post-*Furman* capital statutes for an offender to qualify for the death sentence, the murder must be found to have occurred under aggravating circumstances that suggest an irrational or spontaneous response to fear or anger on the part of the offender. It would appear, therefore, that the deterrence argument has become a relatively empty justification for capital punishment.

* * *

[13] The absence of any consistent or reliable empirical evidence that the death penalty has a unique deterrent effect is amply documented in recent reviews of this body of literature. See Hans Zeisel, "The Deterrent Effect of the Death Penalty: Facts v. Faith," in *The Supreme Court Review*, 1976, Philip Kurland, ed. (Chicago: University of Chicago Press, 1977), pp. 317-43; Richard McGahey, "Dr. Ehrlich's Magic Bullet: Economic Theory, Econometrics, and the Death Penalty," *Crime & Delinquency*, October, 1980, pp. 485-502; and Richard Lempert, "Desert and Deterrence: An Evaluation of the Moral Bases for Capital Punishment" (Paper presented at the Annual Chief Justice Earl Warren Conference on Advocacy, Roscoe Pound—American Trial Lawyers Foundation, Cambridge, Mass., June, 1980).

[14] Leonard Berkowitz and Jacqueline McCauley, "The Contagion of Criminal Violence," *Sociometry*, vol. 34, no. 2 (1971), pp. 238-60.

[15] *Ibid.*

[16] David P. Phillips, "The Influence of Suggestion on Suicide: Substantive and Theoretical Implications of the Werther Effect," *American Sociological Review*, June 1974, pp. 340-54.

[17] *Ibid.*

[18] For discussion and elaboration of this point, see J. Thorsten Sellin, *The Death Penalty* (Philadelphia: American Law Institute, 1959), pp. 65-69; L.J. West, "Psychiatric Reflections on the Death Penalty," *American Journal of Orthopsychiatry*, July 1975, pp. 689-700; George Solomon, "Capital Punishment as Suicide and as Murder," *American Journal of Orthopsychiatry*, July 1975, pp. 701-11; and Bernard L. Diamond, "Murder and the Death Penalty: A Case Report," *American Journal of Orthopsychiatry*, July 1975, pp. 712-22.

* * *

[24] We are grateful to Russ Immarigeon of the National Council on Crime and Delinquency for bringing Rantouls' work to our attention.

* * *

[34] Isaac Ehrlich, "The Deterrent Effect of Capital Punishment: A Question of Life or Death," *American Economic Review*, June 1975 pp. 397-417.

[35] *Ibid.*, p. 414.

[36] The flaws in Ehrlich's data and analysis have been amply reviewed elsewhere. See William Bowers and Glenn Pierce, "Deterrence, Brutalization or Nonsense: A Critique of Isaac Ehrlich's Research on Capital Punishment," unpub. (Boston: Northeastern University, Center for Applied Social Research, 1975); William J. Bowers and Glenn L. Pierce, "The Illusion of Deterrence in Isaac Ehrlich's Research on Capital Punishment," *Yale Law Journal*, December 1975, pp. 187-208; Peter Passell and John Taylor, "The Deterrence Controversy: A Reconsideration of the Time Series Evidence," in *Capital Punishment in the United States*, Hugo A. Bedau and Chester Pierce, eds. (New York, AMS Press, 1976), pp. 359-71; Zeisel, "Deterrent Effect of the Death Penalty"; Lawrence R. Klein, Brian Forst, and Victor Filatov, "The Deterrent Effect of Capital Punishment: An Assessment of the Estimates," in *Deterrence and Incapacitation: Estimating the Effects of Criminal Sanctions on Crime Rates*, Alfred Blumstein, Jacqueline Cohen, and

Daniel Nagin, eds. (Washington, D.C.: National Academy of Sciences, 1978), pp. 336-60; and McGahey, "Dr. Ehrlich's Magic Bullet."

[37] Ehrlich's research figured prominently in the Supreme Court's decision in *Gregg v. Georgia*, as justification for the majority opinion that social science evidence concerning the deterrent effect of capital punishment was "inconclusive." Only Justice Marshall's dissenting opinion reflected an appreciation of the flaws in Ehrlich's work and the judgment that it could not legitimately be regarded as inconsistent with the overwhelming body of previous evidence indicating that the death penalty has no deterrent effect.

[38] The terms *counterdeterrent effect* and *stimulation effect* have been used by other investigators to describe a positive association between execution risk and homicide rates which we have referred to here as a "brutalizing effect of executions."

[39] Strictly following Ehrlich's analytic procedures with data virtually identical to his, the estimates for all six of his alternative measures of execution risk are positive for the period 1935-63 (Bowers and Pierce, "Deterrence, Brutalization or Nonsense," p. 198, Tab. IV).

[40] In a crude analysis of year-to-year changes in executions and homicides in states that performed executions after 1962, there was, overall, a positive association between changes in executions and changes in homicide rates (*Ibid.*, pp. 203-04, esp. Tab. VII); and a more sophisticated analysis of changes in execution risk and homicide rates over the period 1960-70 found positive "counterdeterrent" effects of execution risk on homicide rates (Brian E. Forst, "The Deterrent Effect of Capital Punishment: A Cross-State Analysis of the 1960s," *Minnesota Law Review*, May 1977, pp. 743-67).

[41] The substitution of census-based homicide figures which are more nationally representative than the FBI-based homicide estimates, especially for the early years of Ehrlich's time series, yields more positive estimates of the effects of execution risk on homicide rates (Bowers and Pierce, "Illusion of Deterrence in Isaac Ehrlich's Research on Capital Punishment," pp. 32ff, esp. Tab. II).

[42] The problem arises when the same measured variable (in this case the number of homicides occurring annually) appears in the numerator of one variable (the homicide rate) and in the denominator of another (the arrest or execution rate). Either random or systematic errors in measuring homicides will tend to produce an artifactual negative correlation between the two rates.

*   *   *

[44] Gary Kleck, "Capital Punishment, Gun Ownership, and Homicide," *American Journal of Sociology*, vol. 84, no. 4 (1979), pp. 882-910.

[45] Klein, Forst, and Filatov, "Deterrent Effect of Capital Punishment."

[46] Peter Passell, "The Deterrent Effect of the Death Penalty: A Statistical Test," *Stanford Law Review*, vol. 28 (1975), p. 61; Forst, "Deterrent Effect of Capital Punishment"; William C. Bailey, "Imprisonment v. the Death Penalty as a Deterrent to Murder," *Law and Human Behavior*, vol. 1, no. 3 (1977), pp. 239-60.

[47] In a series of studies also subject to the negative bias introduced by the common term problem, Bailey nevertheless found more positive than negative estimates of the effect of execution risk on homicide rates with annual time series data for each of five states. Positive outnumbered negative estimates in California, Oregon, and North Carolina, while the converse was true for Ohio and Utah. See the following works by William Bailey: "The Deterrent Effect of the Death Penalty for Murder in California," *Southern California Law Review*, March 1979, pp. 743-64; "Deterrence and the Death Penalty for Murder in Oregon," *Willamette Law Review*, Winter

1979, pp. 67-85; "An Analysis of the Deterrent Effect of the Death Penalty in North Carolina," *North Carolina Central Law Journal*, Fall 1978, pp. 29-49; "The Deterrent Effect of the Death Penalty for Murder in Ohio: A Time Series Analysis," *Cleveland State Law Review*, vol. 28 (1979), pp. 51-70; and "Deterrence and the Death Penalty for Murder in Utah: A Time Series Analysis," *Journal of Contemporary Law*, vol. 5 (1978), pp. 1-20.

[48] William C. Bailey, "Deterrence and the Celerity of the Death Penalty: A Neglected Question in Deterrence Research," *Social Forces*, June 1980, pp. 1308-33.

[49] Robert H. Dann, "The Deterrent Effect of Capital Punishment," *Friends Social Science Review*, vol. 29 (1935), p. 1.

* * *

[51] Leonard Savitz, "A Study in Capital Punishment," *Journal of Criminal Law, Criminology and Police Science*, November-December 1958, p. 338.

[52] [Using Wolfgang's (*Patterns in Criminal Homicide*, Tab. 8) data on homicides in Philadelphia by month for the period 1948-52, we have calculated an expected before-after ratio of homicides for each execution date in Dann's study. To obtain the expected before-after ratio for a given execution, each of the 120 days in the before-after period is weighted by the proportion of homicides occurring in the month in which it falls (according to Wolfgang's Table 8). Multiplying the observed number of homicides in the 60 days before each execution by its estimated before-after ratio and summing over the five executions yields an expected number of 105 post-execution homicides.]

[53] William F. Graves, "A Doctor Looks ar Capital Punishment," *Journal of the Loma Linda University School of Medicine*, vol. 10 (1956), p. 137. Reprinted in Bedau, ed., *Death Penalty in America*, p. 329.

* * *

[56] David R. King, "The Brutalizing Effect: Execution Publicity and the Incidence of Homicide in South Carolina," *Social Forces*, December 1978, pp. 683-87. It is noteworthy that there were twenty-four different months in which executions occurred over this period (Bowers, *Executions in America*, app. A). Hence, the vast majority of executions that occurred were covered in this newspaper.

[57] Bowers, *Executions in America*, pp. 200-401.

* * *

[61] In 1949 with the sixth revision of reclassification of the International Classification of Diseases, Injuries, and Causes of Death, death by legal execution was included in the category of willful homicides. We have, therefore, corrected the number of homicides in each month from 1949 through 1964 by subtracting from it the number of executions in that month.

[62] A dummy variable for the month September 1920 was also included in the estimation equations. Inspection of the homicide distribution revealed that the number of homicides recorded for September 1920 (81) was far above the monthly figures for this period. *The New York Times* of September 17, 1920, reported that 30 people were killed and 300 people injured in a bomb blast on Wall Street attributed to a "red plot." The death toll undoubtedly rose further by the end of the month, and we presume that the cause of death in those cases was recorded in the mortality statistics as willful homicides.

[63] H. von Hentig, *Crime: Causes and Conditions* (New York: McGraw-Hill, 1947).

[64] *Ibid.*

[65] Dane Archer and Rosemary Gartner, "Violent Acts and Violent Times: A Comparative Approach to Postwar Homicide Rates," *American Sociological Review*, December 1976, pp. 937-63.

[66] It is conventional to speak of an effect as statistically significant with a probability of less than a given level; hence, we have not supplied an asterisk in this case.

* * *

[71] William J. Bowers and Richard G. Salem, "Severity of Formal Sanctions as a Repressive Response to Deviant Behavior," *Law and Society Review*, February 1972, pp. 427-41.

[72] In this connection, Savitz's ("Study in Capital Punishment") data show an increased level of capital murders in the four weeks immediately after death sentences as compared with the preceding four weeks (26 v. 17) and Dann's ("Deterrent Effect of Capital Punishment") data show an increased level of homicides in the thirty days immediately after executions as compared with the preceding thirty days (54 v. 37). In some measure, these death sentences and executions may have been a repressive response to relatively high or rising offense levels.

[73] Graves, "Doctor Looks at Capital Punishment."

[74] Dann, "Deterrent Effect of Capital Punishment."

[75] King, "Brutalizing Effect."

[76] *Ibid.*

[77] In an analysis of psychiatric case records of persons who have committed homicide, Shervert Frazier has explicitly identified a state of readiness of kill: "A second phase—not always present—is the buildup state or state of readiness—often of hours' to weeks' duration and in rare instances of 1 or 2 years' duration. This state of readiness, by no means uniform, was universal in this series of preplanned and prearranged murders—both for murders of single individuals as well as multiple individuals. The buildup state consists of biological, cyclic, intrapsychic, and social factors" (p. 306). In this state of readiness, the killer frequently identifies one or more victims by name or status group: "Delusional ideas of the need to murder a named individual or individuals with characteristic detailed

planning and processing of the act was present in eight murderers, five of whom were multiple—a physician with a list of persons, an ex-convict with a list of guards, an adolescent with a family list, a parent with a family list, a young adult with a family list, and a neighbor with a list of members of another family. Three murderers of one individual had named a spouse, a famous person, and an employee. In each instance reasons were stated and the buildup was accompanied by a planned progression of organized behavior, detailed and carefully executed goal-oriented purposive behavior despite delusional reasons and active delusional thinking sustained from three days to over one year in duration" (p. 307). Shervert H. Frazier, "Murder—Single and Multiple," in *Aggression*, vol. 52 (res. pub.; Association for Research in Nervous and Mental Disease, 1974), ch. 16.

THE BARTLEY-FOX GUN LAW'S SHORT-TERM IMPACT ON CRIME IN BOSTON

Glenn L. Pierce
William J. Bowers

A comprehensive gun control strategy designed to reduce the incidence of gun-related crime would need to address the successive decision points leading to the use of a gun in crime: the decision to acquire a gun, the decision to carry it, and the decision to use it for criminal purposes. Existing gun control efforts have typically focused on one of these decision points at the exclusion of the other two.[1]

The approach that casts the broadest net is the one that attempts to restrict the acquisition of guns. This includes laws that regulate or limit the importation, manufacture, sale, transfer, ownership, and/or possession of firearms. Such laws will, in principle, reduce the pool of potential gun offenders; fewer people will be in a position to carry a gun or to use it for criminal purposes.

Opponents of acquisition control laws argue that, in practice, such laws will not stop serious criminals—presumed to be responsible for most gun crime—from acquiring, carrying, and using guns. Instead, they say, such laws will deprive law-abiding citizens of the guns they want and need for sport and self-protection. A testimony to the perceived need for guns is the estimated 85 to 125 million firearms in the hands of the American public—easily one gun for every two adult citizens and more than one for each household.[2]

At the other end of the spectrum are approaches aimed narrowly at the decision to use a gun for criminal purposes. Gun-use laws, commonly referred to as "weapon enhancement" statutes, typically impose an additional term of imprisonment for crimes committed with a gun. Michigan's "felony firearms statute" which adds a mandatory two years to the sentence imposed for offenses such as aggravated assault, armed robbery, forcible rape, and criminal homicide when they are committed with a gun, is an example of this approach.[3]

W. Bowers and G. Pierce, "The Bartley-Fox Gun Law's Short-Term Impact on Crime in Boston" is reprinted with permission of the authors and publisher from *The Annals of the American Academy*, vol. 455, May 1981. © 1981 by The American Academy of Political and Social Science.

A law of this kind is more attractive politically; it specifically targets the "criminal element," those who have been convicted of violent felony offenses. Consequently, organized gun interests have not strenuously opposed such statutes in states like California, Florida, and Michigan. But the effects of these weapons enhancement laws are doubtful. The most thoroughly studied of these statutes—the Michigan felony firearms law—shows no solid evidence of having reduced gun-related crime.[4] The problem with this approach may be that it targets too narrow a group of potential offenders who are too committed to criminal activity and too dependent on guns in such activity.

Perhaps the optimal approach from the standpoint of both deterrent effectiveness and political feasibility is the one that targets the decision to carry a gun outside of the home or place of business. It may be that a substantial proportion of those who become involved in gun-related crimes carry guns but do not anticipate the specific situations that will precipitate their use and do not have the time or presence of mind when confronted with these situations to weigh the punishment if caught against the immediate advantage of using a gun.

The Massachusetts legislature took this approach when it enacted the Bartley-Fox gun law, which mandated a one-year minimum prison term for the unlicensed carrying of firearms. The law was explicitly intended to reduce the incidence of gun-related crime as well as the illicit carrying of firearms. Thus when David Bartley, one of the law's framers, first submitted the bill to the Massachusetts House of Representatives, he stated that the purpose of the law was to halt "all unlicensed carrying of guns . . . and to end the temptation to use the gun when it should not even be available."

The law is unlikely to be effective against those who decide to carry a gun for a specific, short-term purpose, such as robbing a bank. The target group is rather those who carry guns on their persons or in their cars without specific criminal purpose in mind, but as a matter of life-style—those Beha has called the "casual carriers."[5] The cumulative risk of apprehension for such people may be substantial over an extended period of time, especially if police employ proactive search-and -seizure tactics.

The law confronted this group with a dramatic apparent increase in the legal risk associated with carrying a gun without a license. A concerted campaign for two months prior to the law's effective date characterized the impending consequences in the following terms: "If you are caught with a gun, you will go to prison for a year and nobody can get you out." Carrying without a license had previously been punished with a fine or suspended sentence, and only occasionally with a brief incarceration.

For its intended impact on gun-related crime, this kind of law may be said to rely upon a derivative deterrent effect. That is, by increasing the punishment imposed for one offense—carrying a gun without a license—the law is intended to reduce the incidence of other crimes: gun assaults, gun robberies, and gun homicides.

The Massachusetts gun law could, conceivably, have still further deterrent effects on gun assault, gun robbery, and gun homicide if offenders were charged for carrying without a license and had a year added to the sentence imposed for assault, robbery, or homicide.[6] Such an application of the law follows the model of a weapons enhancement statute. The available evidence suggests, however, that the approach will have little or no impact on gun-related crime.[7] Moreover, the publicity surrounding the implementation of the law gave no indication that it would be applied in this way, nor has this approach been adopted in subsequent practice to any noticeable degree.[8]

The Bartley-Fox Amendment became effective on 1 April 1975. Gun-related violent crime rates fell dramatically in Massachusetts between 1974 and 1976, suggesting that Bartley-Fox had an extraordinarily large deterrent effect. But before we accept this conclusion, it is necessary to rule out other possible explanations for the observed reductions in gun violence. Our rather extensive analysis of violent crime patterns in Massachusetts and other jurisdictions has convinced us that the Bartley-Fox law, and/or the publicity that attended its implementation, was indeed a highly effective deterrent—at least in the short run. The remainder of this article summarizes the evidence that has led us to this conclusion. We begin with an analysis of aggravated assault patterns, followed by robbery and then homicide. The discussion focuses on Boston, with only very brief synopses of our results for other jurisdictions in Massachusetts.

Armed Assault

A large proportion of assaults are the result of spontaneous arguments, which the antagonists are unlikely to have foreseen. Gun assaults may typically be committed by those who are carrying guns without criminal intent and find themselves provoked or threatened. A law that dramatically increases the punishment for illicit carrying may cause substantial proportion of these casual carriers to leave their guns at home, and thus may produce a substantial reduction in gun assaults.

To the extent that armed assault is situationally provoked rather than purposeful and preplanned, the removal of guns from the situations in which assault occurs cannot be expected to reduce the overall number of assaults. In assault-provoking situations, those involved will presumably resort to whatever weapons are available at the scene. Hence a reduction in the public's propensity to go armed with guns may increase the number of nongun assaults. Indeed, with fewer guns being carried into assault-prone situations, potential assaulters may feel less restrained, and hence the increase in nongun assaults could more than offset the decrease in gun assaults.

Our analysis of armed assault focuses on the complementary issues of deterrence and weapon substitution. The presentation of our results is organized into three parts: (1) an intervention point analysis, using Box-Jenkins techniques, to examine when and if the level of gun and nongun armed assaults change; (2) a control group comparison of changes in Boston against those in selected control jurisdictions; and (3) analysis of the impact of the law on citizen reporting.

Intervention Point Analysis

The analysis draws upon statistical techniques originally formulated by Box and Jenkins[9] and more recently elaborated by Deutsch.[10] These statistical techniques are used in conjunction with monthly crime data to model the pre-Bartley-Fox history of gun and nongun armed assaults in Massachusetts. * * * This information is then used to predict what future course of gun and nongun armed assaults would be if all factors affecting these two types of crime remained constant. We can test whether the actual observed crime trends after the gun law exhibit statistically significant departures from the predicted future of the crime time series based on its history prior to the policy intervention.

A major advantage of this method is that the techniques are capable of incorporating the type of seasonal cycles that is often found in crime data. This is particularly important because seasonal fluctuations can obscure or be mistaken for immediate or short-term effects of a policy intervention. * * *

For gun assault, we found that a statistically significant downward shift occurred in March 1975—the month prior to implementation of Bartley-Fox.[13] Since implementation was preceded by a vigorous publicity campaign of several months duration, it is not surprising to find evidence that the law began to influence behavior even before it was officially in effect. Our analysis found that the downward shift that occurred in March was sustained in subsequent months.

The same type of analysis yielded a statistically significant increase in nongun armed assaults in Boston, beginning in May 1975. We interpret this result as reflecting a tendency for people to substitute other weapons for guns in assault situations following implementation of the law.

A similar set of analysis for the remainder of Massachusetts demonstrated similar, though less pronounced, effects.[14]

Control Group Comparisons

As noted, intervention point analysis, by incorporating information on the pre-Bartley-Fox history of gun and nongun armed assaults, controlled for the effect of ongoing trends that might otherwise obscure or be mistaken for an impact of the law, or its publicity. These methods, however, do not control for those instances where exogenous events or socioeconomic factors intervene and result in departures from prior trends in crime. The Bartley-Fox law, of course, represents one such event, but the issue is to isolate the effects of the law from the effects of other possible factors.

To address this issue, we introduce control groups into our analysis. The importance of obtaining adequate control groups for this type of analysis is well articulated by H. Laurence Ross. He observes that "the literature of quasi-experimental analysis asserts that causal conclusions based only on the comparison of conditions sub-sequent to a supposed cause with those prior to a supposed cause are subject to a wide variety of rival explanations."[15] The control group design employed here allows us to compare the level of violent crime in Boston over time with the levels of crime in comparable jurisdictions over the same period.

The logic of this type of analysis is, of course, strengthened to the extent that an investigator can select control groups that are truly similar. That is, we want to be able to identify control jurisdictions that would be subject to the same exogenous factors or shocks—except for the Bartley-Fox law—as those in Boston, Massachusetts.

Since Boston's population has averaged approximately 600,000 inhabitants over the last decade, as control jurisdictions we have selected cities in two size categories: 250,000 to 500,000 inhabitants and 500,000 to 1,000,000 inhabitants for the United States, the North Central region, and the Middle Atlantic states. There are no cities in this population range in New England other than Boston; the Middle Atlantic states have no cities with 500,000 to 1,000,000 residents. In addition, we have drawn on the set of all cities within a 750-mile radius of Boston and that are equal to or larger than Boston in population: Washington, D.C.; Baltimore; Philadelphia; New York; Cleveland; and Detroit. The Eastern Seaboard cities are especially important because they represent a set of cities which are linked by a highway network that some previous work indicates may influence the flow of new firearms.[16] The North Central cities were selected because of their similarity to Boston as northern industrial cities.

In addition to these control groups, we also selected Chicago as a control jurisdiction. Chicago serves a dual purpose because (1) it is a northern industrial city, although somewhat farther away than the other individual cities selected; and (2) along with Boston and Washington, D.C., it was chosen by the Alcohol, Tobacco, and Firearms Commission to be one of the sites from the Project CUE, and experimental program designed to reduce the illegal sale of firearms. This program was initiated in Boston and Chicago in July 1976 and in Washington, D.C. in February 1976. Thus Chicago—and Washington, D.C., to a lesser extent—becomes a useful reference point for measuring the impact of an alternative intervention

(Project CUE) whose effects could be confounded with the Bartley-Fox law.[17]

Table 1 presents the comparison group analysis for Boston and its control jurisdictions. Three sets of annual statistics are presented in this table: (1) gun assaults per 100,000 inhabitants, (2) nongun armed assaults per 100,000 inhabitants, and (3) the percent of gun assaults of all armed assaults for the years 1974, 1975, and 1976. This last measure, because it combines both potential deterrent and displacement effects, is a particularly sensitive indicator of the law's impact.

Turning to the analyses of gun assaults in Boston, we first examine Boston's change in gun assaults between 1974 and 1975 compared with the changes occurring in the selected comparison jurisdictions.[18] Between 1974 and 1975, Boston showed a 13.5 percent decline in gun assaults, a decrease greater than that occurring in any of the central jurisdictions. Indeed, of the control jurisdictions, only Chicago showed a decline in gun assaults approaching that of Boston: 8.2 percent versus 13.5 percent. In the following year, 1975 to 1976, however, Boston showed a slight increase in gun assaults while a number of the control groups showed declines. Over the two-year period following Bartley-Fox—1974 to 1976—Boston showed an overall decline in gun assaults of 11.7 percent. Unlike the first year change, 1974 to 1975, where Boston showed the greatest decrease, 4 of the 13 control jurisdictions—Philadelphia, Washington, D.C., Cleveland, and Chicago—showed a two-year decline greater than that of Boston.

The pattern of these results—a one-year decline greater than that occurring in the control jurisdictions followed by a slight upturn in gun assaults—raises the question of whether the duration of the Bartley-Fox impact was short-termed, lasting perhaps less than a year. We do not, however, believe this is the case. First, we shall present evidence shortly that indicates that the Bartley-Fox law's effect on the actual incidence of gun assaults may have been particularly obscured by a concomitant effect of the law on citizens' reporting of gun assaults to police. Second, the remaining comparison group analysis for Boston, with regard to nongun armed assaults and the percentage of armed assaults in which guns were used, provides strong evidence for the proposition that the impact of Bartley-Fox extended through 1976, the final year of this analysis.

Table 1. Gun Assaults, Nongun Assaults, and Percentage of Gun Assaults of Armed Assaults in Boston in Comparison to Cities Grouped Regionally and for Selected Eastern Seaboard and North Central Cities

Regions	Gun Assaults per 100,000			Nongun Armed Assaults per 100,000			Percentage of Gun Assaults of Total Armed Assaults		
	Rate, 1974	1974-75, % Change	1974-76, % Change	Rate, 1974	1974-75, % Change	1974-76, % Change	1974	1974-75, % Change	1974-76, % Change
Boston	101.4	-13.5	-11.7	290.0	31.1	40.4	25.9	-27.6	-30.4
Comparison cities grouped regionally: 250,000-500,000 inhabitants									
United States without Massachusetts	108.1	6.7	3.1	181.3	9.3	17.5	37.4	-1.5	-8.7
North Central states	101.6	13.8	15.2	154.2	5.2	13.6	39.7	4.8	.8
Middle Atlantic states	57.4	4.8	-7.4	181.1	15.0	16.1	24.1	-6.9	-16.1
Comparison cities grouped regionally: 500,000-1,000,000 inhabitants									
United States without Massachusetts	111.7	1.9	-7.5	178.5	3.4	5.0	38.5	-.9	-7.7
North Central states	120.9	7.6	-1.4	131.6	8.5	12.0	47.9	-.4	-6.6
Selected eastern seaboard and north central cities									
New York	113.7	5.9	-.8	359.5	10.0	12.4	24.0	-2.8	-4.3
Philadelphia	80.3	-4.5	-21.3	158.7	-6.4	-17.3	33.6	1.3	-3.3
Baltimore	165.0	12.2	-5.2	493.2	-1.0	-7.5	25.1	9.3	1.9
Washington, D.C.	142.0	3.9	-16.1	233.6	-.5	6.5	37.8	2.7	-14.3
Detroit	139.9	11.3	15.6	318.9	-.9	-1.2	30.5	8.3	11.2
Cleveland	244.0	-3.4	-13.3	135.7	3.8	-13.6	64.3	-2.6	2.0
Chicago	123.5	-8.2	-26.0	249.6	2.3	-5.9	33.1	-7.1	-15.4

Looking at nongun armed assaults, we find that Boston shows a 31.1 percent increase between 1974 and 1975 and a 40.4 percent increase over a two-year period, 1974 to 1976. Importantly, these increases are more than twice those exhibited by any of the control jurisdictions. It should be noted that Boston's increase in nongun armed assaults may not have been entirely a function of displacement effects. Indeed as noted, some control jurisdictions showed increases in nongun armed assaults of 17 and 16 percentage points. Thus it is possible some of Boston's 40.4 percent increase in nongun armed assaults would have occurred as part of an ongoing increase in assaults. This also suggests, however, that Boston might have experienced an increase in gun assaults in 1975, rather than the decline that actually occurred following Bartley-Fox.

Examination of the measure that combines potential deterrent and weapon substitution effects shows that the weapon-related character of armed assaults in Boston changed following Bartley-Fox. Between 1974 and 1975—the first year following Bartley-Fox—the percent that guns represented of all armed assaults in Boston dropped from 25.9 percent to 18.8 percent. This decrease was almost four times greater than that shown by any of the control jurisdictions. In the two-year period—1974 to 1976—Boston showed a 30.4 percent decline in the percentage that gun assaults represent of armed assaults versus a maximum 16.1 percent decline occurring in the control group.

A similar analysis of the remainder of Massachusetts, not reported here, demonstrated qualitatively similar findings.[19]

Review of the impact on assault findings reveals a strong pattern of evidence supporting the hypothesis that the Bartley-Fox law reduced the likelihood of gun assault in Massachusetts. When the first year—1975—following the introduction of the law was examined, we found that relative to each of the control jurisdictions in both Boston and non-Boston, Massachusetts communities (1) gun assaults decreased, (2) nongun armed assaults increased, and (3) the percent that gun assaults represent of all armed assaults declined. In the two years following Bartley-Fox—1974 to 1976—this same pattern of results held up with one exception: between 1974 and 1976 gun assaults in 4 of Boston's 12 control jurisdictions showed larger declines than Boston had exhibited. Thus in 5 of 6 possible comparisons made, the results consistently indicate that the gun law affected the character of armed assault in Massachusetts.[20]

The statistics in Table 1 suggest the rather surprising conclusion that the weapon substitution effect of Bartley-Fox was larger than the deterrent effect—that is, the increase in nongun assaults more than compensated for the reduction in gun assaults. However, closer scrutiny of these data have convinced us that deterrent effects of the law are underestimated in Boston. Implementation of the Bartley-Fox law and its attendant publicity appears to have increased the likelihood of citizens' reporting gun assaults. We present the evidence for this conclusion in the next section.

Impact on Citizen Reporting: More Refined Measurement of Gun Assaults

As Richard Block has noted, the citizen's decision to notify the police of a crime is based, in part, on a victim's "calculation of the benefits derived from notification and the costs incurred."[21] For example, a victim may think he has something to gain by reporting an assault if he believes that the police can actually catch and punish an offender.

The Bartley-Fox law may have altered the likelihood that citizens will report gun crimes, particularly gun assaults, to the police. Compared with robberies or murders, assaults are a relatively ambiguous category of offenses. That is, in some cases it may not be altogether clear to the average citizen whether a legally punishable assault has actually occurred. Particularly in cases where a victim has been threatened with the visible display of a deadly weapon, but where no injury has occurred, the citizen may not be sure that such an action constitutes a criminal assault that the police and courts will take seriously. The Bartley-Fox law may have signaled the public that any crime involving a gun was serious and would be treated as such by the criminal justice system.

We would expect that any tendency of the law to increase citizen's reporting of gun assaults would be concentrated on the less serious forms of gun assault that involved threats rather than injuries. Empirical research bears out this observation. Richard Block found that assault victims who have been hospitalized or have received medical attention are significantly more likely to report the crime to the police than victims who were not injured.[22] Thus more accurate estimates of the deterrent effect of the gun law on assaultive behavior—unbiased by possible changes in citizens' reporting behaviors—could be obtained by isolating for analysis those gun assaults where an injury has been incurred.

This line of analysis cannot, however, be pursued using the FBI's Uniform Crime Reports (UCR) statistics because the UCR definition of an armed assault combines into one category: (1) assaults that involve only threats or attempts to inflict "bodily harm" on a victim and (2) assaults in which the victim actually has been injured. With statistics based on the UCR definition of assault, then, it is not possible to separate gun assaults that are threats from those that result in injury.

Fortunately, the Boston Police Department's (BPD) computerized crime statistics provide more refined categories of gun assaults than are available in the UCR data. Specifically, using BPD data, we can independently examine gun assaults with battery and gun assaults without battery. Under Massachusetts law, assault with battery indicates that some type of force has been used on the victim. In the case of a gun assault, this would mean that the victim had in some manner been struck with either a bullet or a gun. In contrast an assault without battery simply means that an offender has attempted to injure or has threatened to injure his victim, but has not inflicted any physical harm. Table 2 presents BPD statistics on gun assaults involving battery and those without battery.

The top row of figures in Table 2 presents the annual number of gun assaults with battery in Boston from 1974 through 1976. This is the category that research suggests should be less subject to changes in reporting behavior. Notably, while UCR Boston gun assault statistics (Table 1) show only a 11.7 percent decline between 1974 and 1976, BPD gun assaults with battery—that is, those most likely to involve injury—show a 37.1 percent decline over this same period. Thus the subcategory of gun assaults with battery showed a decrease in the two years following the introduction of the Bartley-Fox law more than three times the decrease exhibited by the UCR gun assault statistics, which groups gun assaults both with and without battery into one category.

Table 2. Gun Assaults With Battery and Without Battery in Boston
for the Period 1974 to 1976

	Number and Percentage Change	1974	1975	1976	1974-76, Percentage Change
Gun assaults involving battery	Number	329	289	207	—
	Percentage change	—	-12.2	-24.9	-37.1
Gun assault without battery	Number ·	266	236	339	—
	Percentage change	—	-10.3	+43.6	+27.4
Proportion of gun assaults which in- volved battery	Proportion	55.3	55.0	37.9	—
	Percentage change	—	-.5	-31.1	-31.5

Note further that in the two years after the introduction of the law, the number of gun assaults without battery actually increased and that the increase was concentrated between 1975 and 1976. Thus it would appear that the pattern of reported gun assaults in Table 1, especially the increase between 1975 and 1976 in Boston, occurs in the category of assaults without battery, which is more subject to reporting biases. Although the specific dynamic underlying the increase in incidence of less serious forms of gun assault in Boston is unclear, it seems likely that the increase is a result of some changes in citizens' willingness to report gun assaults.

If we rely on Boston's battery gun assault statistics for our estimate of the deterrent impact of the gun law in Boston, we find, as noted previously, that Boston showed a 37.1 percent decline in the level of gun assaults between 1974 and 1976. It is important to note that using this revised estimate of the gun law's impact, we find that Boston's two-year decline in gun assaults is 30 percent greater than exhibited by any of Boston's control jurisdictions in Table 1.

Conclusions of the Assault Analysis

The introduction of the Bartley-Fox gun law had a twofold effect on armed assaults in Massachusetts. First, the law substantially reduced the incidence of gun assaults in Boston and other Massachusetts communities. Importantly, the decline in gun assaults in Boston appears to have started one month prior to the introduction of the law—suggesting that offenders initially were responding to the publicity attendant with the gun law implementation. Second, the gun law also apparently resulted in a substantial increase in nongun armed assaults. Thus while the law appears to have deterred some individuals from carrying and/or using their firearm, it appears not to have encouraged these individuals to avoid assaultive situations.

The law also appears to have increased the likelihood of citizens reporting less serious forms of gun assaults to the police; at least in Boston this phenomenon tended to obscure the deterrent effect of the law on gun assaults.

Armed Robbery

As with our analysis of the Bartley-Fox law's impact on armed assaults, the armed robbery analysis will examine the dual questions of deterrence and weapon substitution. Specifically, we shall examine whether the gun law resulted in a reduction in gun robberies and whether this change was offset by corresponding increases in robberies with other types of weapons.

The analysis will also compare the relative magnitude of potential deterrence and weapon substitution effects for robbery with those observed in the assault analysis. To the extent that robbery is more often the result of planned purposeful action than is assault, we would expect a law like Bartley-Fox to have less deterrent impact on robbery because this law is specifically aimed at the carrying rather than the using of a firearm. Under these circumstances, individuals who carry firearms with a specific use in mind have relatively less to lose than offenders who are not planning to assault or to rob someone. Quite simply, although the costs are the same in terms of the gun law—a one-year prison term—the benefits of carrying a gun are less for the person who carries a gun, but who has no specific anticipated use for it.

Compared with assault, we also expect the magnitude of the displacement effects to be less. The logic behind this hypothesis is straightforward.[23] Robbery with a gun is generally a much easier task than robbery with other types of deadly weapons, unless an offender chooses to rob highly vulnerable targets. However, there is also a disincentive to switch to more vulnerable targets because these also tend to be much less lucrative, for example, a street robbery of an elderly person is generally much easier but also less lucrative than a robbery of a drug store.

Control Group Comparisons

Data restrictions prevent our conducting an intervention point analysis of gun and nongun armed robberies. The UCR program only began classifying armed robbery into gun and nongun categories in 1974. * * *

The available data are sufficient, however, for a comparison group analysis. As in the assault analysis, we examined the law's impact on (1) gun robbery, (2) nongun armed robbery, and (3) the percent that gun robbery represents of all armed robbery for Boston.

Table 3 represents annual statistics for Boston and its control jurisdictions on gun robberies, nongun robberies, and the percent that gun robberies represent of all armed robberies. When we initially examined Boston's first-year (1974 to 1975) post-Bartley-Fox change in gun robbery, there appeared to be little evidence of an immediate deterrent effect of the law. Indeed, between 1974 and 1975, gun robberies declined by only 1.8 percent in Boston. However, when Boston's first change in gun robberies—1.8 percent—is compared to the changes occurring in the control jurisdictions, we find that in 9 of the 12 sets of control jurisdictions, gun robberies increased more than they did in Boston. Thus, although the law failed to reduce the level of gun robbery in Boston between 1974 and 1975, it may have been responsible for suppressing what would have been a substantial increase.

Table 3. Gun Robberies, Nongun Robberies, and Percentage of Gun Robberies of Armed Robberies in Boston in Comparison to Cities Grouped Regionally and for Selected Eastern Seaboard and North Central Cities

Regions	Gun Assaults per 100,000			Nongun Armed Assaults per 100,000			Percentage of Gun Assaults of Total Armed Assaults		
	Rate, 1974	1974-75, % Change	1974-76, % Change	Rate, 1974	1974-75, % Change	1974-76, % Change	1974	1974-75, % Change	1974-76, % Change
Boston	363.4	-1.8	-35.5	319.7	32.4	+6.3	53.2	-14.0	-23.2
Comparison cities grouped regionally: 250,000-500,000 inhabitants									
United States without Massachusetts	194.2	4.9	-11.8	74.2	-.8	-3.9	72.4	1.5	-2.4
North Central states	181.1	4.0	-20.9	73.0	-18.0	-19.5	71.3	6.5	-.5
Middle Atlantic states	179.7	17.5	-5.5	145.4	6.7	-4.1	55.3	4.3	-.5
Comparison cities grouped regionally: 500,000-1,000,000 inhabitants									
United States without Massachusetts	249.9	7.3	-12.1	80.9	5.3	-4.1	75.5	.5	-2.2
North Central states	300.9	24.3	.1	83.6	18.5	-.8	78.2	1.0	.2
Selected eastern seaboard and north central cities									
New York	326.4	6.5	8.4	391.2	9.8	-4.9	45.5	1.6	1.8
Philadelphia	229.6	-5.1	-36.7	99.9	9.4	-17.9	69.7	-4.4	-8.3
Baltimore	422.1	-5.1	-30.0	184.0	-4.0	-15.1	69.9	-.3	-6.1
Washington, D.C.	570.4	12.1	-13.2	90.6	6.6	-10.9	86.3	.6	-.4
Detroit	767.6	22.3	32.4	38.7	19.6	32.3	95.2	.1	0.0
Cleveland	492.9	25.9	-2.0	59.8	16.9	5.5	89.2	.8	-.8
Chicago	414.9	-20.6	-43.5	136.6	0.0	-5.8	75.2	-6.1	-14.2

This impression is reinforced when the two-year (1974 to 1976) post-Bartley-Fox change in gun robbery is examined. Between 1974 and 1976, Boston showed a 35.5 percent decrease in gun robberies. Boston's two-year post-Bartley-Fox decline was exceeded by only 2 of the 12 control groups: Philadelphia, 36.7 percent, and Chicago, 43.5 percent.

The preceding interpretation, of course, remains quite tentative because several of Boston's control jurisdictions showed declines in gun robbery, similar to or greater than those exhibited by Boston. As in our armed assault analysis, however, we do not analyze the effect of the Bartley-Fox law on gun robberies from the analysis of the law's potential effect on nongun armed robberies.

Indeed, analysis of Boston's nongun robbery statistics (Table 3) reveals strong evidence indicating substantial first-year (1974 to 1975) displacement effects. In the first year following the Bartley-Fox law, we find nongun armed robberies in Boston increased by 35.4 percent between 1974 and 1975—an increase of 40 percent greater than that occurring in any of the control jurisdictions.

One measure—the fraction of robberies involving guns—incorporates both the potential deterrent and displacement effects of the law, and hence is an especially sensitive indicator of the gun law's impact. When this measure is examined, Boston unambiguously shows the greatest post-Bartley-Fox change in the weapon-related character of armed robbery. In the first year following Bartley-Fox— 1974 to 1975—the percent that gun robbery represents of all armed robbery declined in Boston by 14 percent—a decline twice that shown in any of the control jurisdictions. In the two-year period— 1974 to 1976—following Bartley-Fox, Boston showed a 23.3 percent decline versus a maximum 14 percent decline—Chicago—shown in any of the control jurisdictions.

Conclusions on Armed Robbery

The introduction of the Bartley-Fox law appears to have resulted in a short-term reduction in gun robberies throughout the city of Boston, Massachusetts. The decrease in gun robberies also appears to have been accompanied by an increase in nongun armed robberies. The magnitude of the displacement effect for armed robbery appears to be less than we observed for armed assault.

Finally, due to data contingencies and time limitations, our conclusions with regard to robbery are more tentative than they are for assault: (1) historical data on gun robbery is unavailable prior to 1974 and (2) a refined analysis of the impact of the Bartley-Fox law on the reporting of gun robbery using BPD data has not yet been conducted.

Criminal Homicide

To the extent that homicide is a function of an offender's premeditated willful intention to kill his victim, we would have little reason to expect that the Bartley-Fox law would deter gun-related homicides. The assumption is that an offender who is willing to risk the legal sanction for murder would also be willing to risk the sanction for a Bartley-Fox offense. On the other hand, if as Richard Block proposes, homicides occur not primarily as a result of an offender's planned determination to kill, but rather as something that sometimes happens as the unanticipated consequence of other criminal or life-style activities,[25] then the introduction of the gun law might have a derivative deterrent effect on gun homicide. That is, the gun law might prevent some gun-related homicides by affecting the decisions that potential offenders make regarding whether or not to carry a firearm, and/or whether or not to use a firearm to commit robbery or an assault.

Indeed, we have already observed that the Bartley-Fox law appeared to reduce gun-related assaults and robberies throughout Massachusetts. Thus we should not be surprised if gun-related homicides also show a decline following the Bartley-Fox law.

There also appears to have been an increase after the law in nongun armed assaults and, to a lesser extent, nongun armed robberies. However, for at least two reasons, we also do not expect to find similar displacement effects for criminal homicides: (1) we would expect to find that an increase in nongun armed assaults or robberies did not result in a proportionate increase in nongun criminal homicides because guns are likely to be more deadly than other types of weapons and (2) offenders who switch from guns to other deadly weapons may generally be those offenders who are least intent upon physically harming their victims. Thus an increase in the use of other deadly weapons by these offenders might very well not result in an increase in homicides.

Comparison Group Analysis

As in the robbery and assault analyses, we will compare homicide trends for Boston with those in selected control jurisdictions. We have selected as our control jurisdictions grouped into communities of 250,000 to 1,000,000 inhabitants for the Middle Atlantic states, the North Central states, and all United States cities, except Boston. In addition, we also included the selected Eastern Seaboard and North Central cities included in the assault and robbery analyses.

Criminal homicide statistics for Boston and the control jurisdictions are presented in Table 4. We first examine the impact of the Bartley-Fox law on gun-related homicide. In the first year—1974 to 1975—following the gun law's implementation, gun homicide in Boston declined by 21.4 percent—a decrease greater than any of the jurisdictions experienced except Baltimore. In the two years—1974 to 1976—after Bartley-Fox, gun homicides in Boston declined by 55.7 percent—a decrease greater than that exhibited by any of the control jurisdictions. Thus it appears that the Bartley-Fox law in the short-term prevented some gun-related homicides in Boston.

We, of course, want to address the issue as to whether the Bartley-Fox law also produced displacement effects similar to those observed for nongun armed assaults and to a lesser extent nongun armed robberies. However, when nongun criminal homicides for Boston are examined we find that in two years—1974 to 1976—following Bartley-Fox, nongun homicides actually dropped in Boston by 20.3 percent. Moreover, only one of the control jurisdictions—Washington, D.C.—exceeded this decline while several other jurisdictions experienced decreases in nongun criminal homicide ranging between 1.5 percent and 13.5 percent. Thus we find no evidence suggesting a displacement effect of the Bartley-Fox law on nongun criminal homicide.

Table 4. Gun Homicides, Nongun Homicides, and Percentage of Gun Homicides of All Homicides in Boston in Comparison to Cities Grouped Regionally and for Selected Eastern Seaboard and North Central Cities

Regions	Gun Homicides			Nongun Homicides			Percentage of Gun Homicides of All Homicides		
	Rate, 1974	1974-75, % Change	1974-76, % Change	Rate, 1974	1974-75, % Change	1974-76, % Change	1974	1974-75, % Change	1974-76, % Change
Boston	70	-21.4	-55.7	64	0.0	-20.3	52.2	-11.5	-27.6
Comparison cities grouped regionally: 250,000-500,000 inhabitants									
United States without Boston	3140	-6.5	-23.0	1379	+9.3	-0.7	69.5	-4.9	-8.2
North Central cities	470	-9.1	-26.1	139	+3.4	-5.7	77.2	-9.7	-9.1
Middle Atlantic cities	164	-0.6	-28.0	171	-1.3	-11.6	49.0	+6.9	-10.4
Selected eastern seaboard and north central cities									
New York	794	9.1	-2.5	822	0.2	3.0	49.1	4.3	-2.9
Philadelphia	248	-24.2	-32.7	171	-4.1	-13.5	59.2	-9.8	-10.5
Baltimore	204	-23.5	-45.6	90	15.6	-4.4	69.4	-13.5	-18.9
Washington, D.C.	170	-14.7	-30.6	106	-16.0	-33.0	61.6	0.6	1.3
Detroit	510	-14.7	-3.5	200	-13.5	-12.5	71.8	-0.4	2.8
Cleveland	254	-15.7	-34.6	52	42.3	-11.5	83.0	-10.5	-5.7
Chicago	668	-17.4	-25.0	301	-11.3	2.7	68.9	-2.2	-10.2

The pattern of impact where gun homicides appear to have been deterred while nongun homicides do not appear to have increased has important implications because it suggests that the Bartley-Fox law may have had an overall effect of reducing incidence of criminal homicides in Boston, at least in the short run. Indeed, if the gun homicide and nongun homicide statistics in Table 4 are added together, we can see that the overall level of criminal homicides showed a greater decline in Boston—38.8 percent—than in any of the control jurisdictions in the two years following the introduction of the gun law.

Finally, further evidence of the Bartley-Fox law's impact on criminal homicide in Boston is available when the percent of gun homicides (Table 4) is studied. Here we find that between 1974 and 1976, Boston showed a greater decrease in this measure than any of the control jurisdictions.

Criminal Homicide Conclusion

The Bartley-Fox law appears to have in the short run deterred some gun-related criminal homicides in Boston, but the law does not appear to have resulted in an increase in nongun criminal homicides. We conclude that the gun law caused an overall decline in the incidence of criminal homicide in the first two years of its implementation.

Conclusion

This analysis has focused on the Bartley-Fox law's impact on armed assault, armed robbery, and homicide. For each type of crime, we independently examined the law's impact on gun-related offenses and nongun-related offenses in Boston.

Introduction of the gun law had a twofold effect on armed assaults. First, the law substantially reduced the incidence of gun assaults. Second, it resulted in a substantial increase in nongun armed assaults. Thus while the law appears to deter some individuals from carrying and/or using their firearms, it did not prevent them from using alternative weapons in assaultive situations.

Introduction of the Bartley-Fox law also resulted in a short-term reduction in gun robberies, and a concomitant increase in nongun armed robberies. However, the magnitude of weapons substitution effect for armed robbery appears to be less than what we observed for armed assault.

The law also deterred some gun-related criminal homicides in Boston, but did not result in a corresponding increase in nongun criminal homicides. Thus the gun law produced an overall decline in the incidence of criminal homicide.

Our analysis also suggests that the law may have achieved its effect primarily through its "announced" intent, rather than its actual implementation. Importantly, in the assault analysis where the effects were most pronounced, we observed that the decline in gun assault in Boston started one month prior to the effective date of the law—suggesting that offenders, at least initially, were responding to the publicity attendant with the introduction of gun law rather than to mandatory imposition of its sanctions. Hence, we conclude that the observed reduction in gun crime was the result of an announcement effect,[26] rather than the product of sanctions actually imposed—the traditional definition of a deterrent effect. In research presently underway, we address the matter of separating the announcement and deterrent effects of the law.

For this reason, we draw no conclusions about the effect of the "mandatory" nature of the law. That is, the observed effects of the law do not depend on its having been applied in a mandatory fashion. At this point in our analysis, we simply know that it was advertised as imposing a "mandatory one-year prison term."

Notes

Note #1: The data for this article were provided by the Boston Police Department (BPD) and the Uniform Crime Reporting (UCR) branch of the Federal Bureau of Investigation (FBI). We wish to thank Philip J. Cook and Joe Garner for their critical insights.

Note #2: This article is a revised version of a report entitled *The Impact of the Bartley-Fox on Gun and Nongun Related Crime in Massachusetts* by the present authors released in April 1979 by the Center for Applied Social Research, Northeastern University, Boston, Massachusetts, and supported by the National Institute of Justice, Contract No. 76-NI-99-0100.

Footnotes

[1] The recent New York state gun law that became effective in 1980 is an exception that focuses on both carrying and use of a firearm.

[2] James Wright, "The Recent Weapons Trend and the Putative 'Need' for Gun Control" (Presented at the American Sociological Association, 1980).

[3] Colin Loftin and David McDowall, "'One With a Gun Gets You Two': Mandatory Prison Sentencing and Firearms Violence in Detroit," *The Annals* of The American Academy of Political and Social Science, 455:150-67 (May 1981).

[4] *Ibid.*

[5] James A. Beha, III, "And Nobody Can Get You Out: The Impact of a Mandatory Prison Sentence for the Illegal Carrying of a Firearm on the Use of Firearms and the Administration of Criminal Justice in Boston, Part I-Part II," *Boston University Law Review*, 57 (1977).

[6] Since the punishments imposed for aggravated assaults, armed robbery, and criminal homicide are, respectively, more severe in that order (quite apart from the use of a gun), a flat or constant increment in punishment when a gun is used may be expected to reduce gun assaults most, gun robberies next, and gun homicides least. The proportional addition to (marginal utility of) the additional punishment corresponds to this ordering of the three crimes. The fact that homicides are largely assault and robbery precipitated adds a derivative deterrent component for gun homicides. And, the fact that punishments for the nongun versions of assault, robbery, and homicide remain unaltered, adds a weapons displacement component for all three crimes, at least for potential offenders with a relatively high level of criminal intent. In effect, although punishments applied to carrying and to use may operate through different deterrence mechanisms, they lead, at least according to the logic of deterrence theory, to similar patterns of expected impact.

[7] Loftin.

[8] David Rossman, *The Impact of the Mandatory Gun Law in Massachusetts*. (National Institute of Law Enforcement and Criminal Justice, Law Enforcement Assistance Administration, United States Department of Justice, 1979).

[9] G.E.P. Box and G.M. Jenkins, *Time Series Analysis: Forecasting and Control* (San Francisco, CA: Holden-Day, 1977).

[10] S.J. Deutsch, "Stochastic Models of Crime Rates," *ISYE Report Series*, 77(15) (Atlanta: Georgia Institute of Technology, 1977).

* * *

[13] This is not at all a necessarily surprising result., The Bartley-Fox law was preceded by a dramatic, and not completely accurate, two-month publicity campaign, designed to educate the public concerning the new consequences citizens faced for violating the Massachusetts gun law. Under these circumstances, it is quite possible that this publicity preceding the gun law's introduction on 1 April 1975 resulted in what Zimring has termed an "announcement" effect by creating in the minds of citizens and potential gun offenders the impression that the new law was actually in force prior to its effective date. If this were so, we might indeed expect the gun law, or more accurately its publicity, to have affected gun and nongun related assaults as early as February 1975.

[14] Glenn Pierce and William Bowers, "The Impact of Bartley-Fox Gun Law in Massachusetts" (To be published in *Crime and Delinquency*, 1982).

[15] H. Lawrence Ross, "Deterrence Regained: The Cheshire Constabulary's Breatholyser Blitz," *J. Legal Studies* 4(L):244 (Jan. 1977).

[16] Franklin Zimring, critical review of Rossman et al., *The Impact of the Mandatory Gun in Massachusetts* (Office of Research and Evaluation Methods, National Institute of Law Enforcement and Criminal Justice, Law Enforcement Assistance Administration, 1980).

[17] Since CUE was an undercover operation explicitly directed at reducing illegal sale of guns, it, therefore, did not affect the existing pool of illegally owned firearms. It is somewhat doubtful that this program would impact gun-related crime in Boston during 1976. However, if CUE did have a fairly immediate impact, it ought to show results in both Boston and Chicago. Thus Chicago serves as a control for the potentially confounding of Bartley-Fox and Project CUE.

[18] Examinations of these changes on an annual basis potentially make the 1974 to 1975 change a conservative test because the Bartley-Fox law was implemented on 1 April 1975, with March as the empirically determined intervention point for gun assaults (Table 1).

[19] Pierce and Bowers.

[20] This refers to the comparisons made with each of three indicators we have examined for the gun law impact: (1) gun assault, (2) nongun assault, and (3) the percent that gun assault represents of all assaults in the first year (1974-75) and in the two years (1974-76) following the Bartley-Fox law.

[21] Richard Block, "Why Notify the Police: The Victims Decision to Notify the Police of an Assault," *Criminology*, 4(2):555 (Feb. 1974).

[22] Block.

[23] Philip J. Cook, "The Effect of Gun Availability on Violent Crime Patterns," *The Annals* of The American Academy of Political and Social Science, 455:63-79 (May 1981).

* * *

[25] Richard Block, *Violent Crime: Environment, Interaction and Death* (Lexington, MA: Lexington Books, 1977).

[26] It should be noted that if gun assault, gun robbery, and gun homicide rates for 1974 in Boston were abnormally high, the results shown in Table 2-5 would tend to exaggerate the deterrent effect of the Bartley-Fox law. That is, the subsequent reduction in these rates could be "a regression to the mean" or a return to levels more consistent with the previous history of these offenses. However, this appears not to be the case, at least for gun assaults and gun homicide. For example, linear projections of gun homicides and gun assaults based on the year 1970 through 1973 yield predicted 1974 levels of 81 and 97.1 for gun homicides and gun assaults, respectively, versus their observed levels of 70 and 101.4. A more detailed analysis of this issue will be presented in our subsequent work (Pierce and Bowers).

POLICIES TO ACHIEVE DISCRIMINATION ON THE EFFECTIVE PRICE OF HEROIN

Mark H. Moore

I. Opportunities for Discrimination on the Effective Price of Heroin

A. The Effective Price of Heroin

Traditional representations of demand curves assume that the dollar price of a good is the only significant element of the cost to the consuming individual. For most goods, other aspects of consumption such as transaction costs and uncertainty about quality are assumed to play a minor role. Not so with heroin.

Heroin is different because, first, users face significant transaction costs. Often they must search intently for an opportunity to "score." In addition, in any attempt to score they risk being arrested or victimized by other addicts. The consequences of these transaction costs include withdrawal symptoms, beatings, and jail. Second, users face quality uncertainties which may be even more significant. The amount of pure heroin and the toxicity of adulterants vary widely among street bags. The possible consequences include fraud and death.

Against these possible consequences of purchasing and using heroin, the dollar price may be relatively unimportant. Consequently, in describing the cost of consuming heroin, it is best to speak in terms of an effective price of heroin. The effective price is defined as an index including the following elements: dollar price, amount of pure heroin, toxicity of adulterants, access time, and threats of victimization and arrest. Many of these elements are uncertain quantities from the point of view of the consumer.

B. Elasticity of Demand for New and Old Users

The effective price to users may vary because: (1) the individual users place different weights on the elements of the price index; and (2) the market condition confronting individuals may be quite

"Policies to Achieve Discrimination on the Effective Price of Heroin," by Mark H. Moore, *The American Economic Review*, Vol. 63, No. 2, May 1973, is reprinted by permission of the author and the American Economic Association. © 1973 by the American Economic Association.

different. In general, these factors result in new users perceiving higher effective prices than experienced users. The disutility of a new user's first arrest is likely to be subjectively much larger than the disutility of an experienced user's eighth arrest. The expected access time for a new user who has no regular connection is likely to be longer (and have a larger variance) than for experienced users who have several regular connections.

The observation that new users face relatively higher effective prices gains added importance when one observes that at any given price the elasticity of demand for heroin is likely to be greater for new users than for experienced users. The reason is simply that new users are not yet addicted to heroin. Consequently, when tightening supplies boost prices, new users are the first to drop or be dropped from the market.

C. Why Discrimination on the Effective Price is Desirable

The possibility that the effective price of heroin differs systematically between new users and experienced users resolves a cruel dilemma in the design of the heroin policy. We would like a high effective price to new users to reduce the probability that they become regular users. We would like a low effective price to experienced users to reduce the pressure to commit crimes and to restore some dignity and comfort. Without the possibility of price discrimination, we would face a difficult tradeoff between the prevention objective and the crime-reduction objective. With price discrimination, we can pursue both objectives simultaneously.

Since virtually everyone wishes that fewer people became heroin users, we may assume that our utility increases monotonically as the effective price to experimental users increases. Since most people wish that experienced users would commit fewer crimes and suffer less harassment, we may also assume that our utility increases with decreases in the effective price to old users.

D. Factors Determining the Effective Prices to New and Experienced Users

Before turning to the analysis of policy alternatives, it is useful to analyze the factors which determine the effective prices to new and old users. The first factor is, of course, the aggregate supply of heroin. If the supply is large, effective prices to both new and experienced users will be driven down.

A second factor is the strength of the incentives which motivate suppliers to discriminate against new users. Doctors will be more or less strongly motivated to discriminate against new users depending on their beliefs about the evils of heroin addiction and the penalties they must accept if they prescribe heroin to nonaddicts. Illegal dealers will be more or less strongly motivated depending on their perception of the profits and risks associated with dealing to new users. The stronger the motivation of suppliers to discriminate, the greater the price differential that is established.

A third factor is the ability of the suppliers to distinguish new users from experienced users. If new users look very much like experienced users on the signals which dealers use in deciding which customers to accept, then dealers will make many Type I errors (identifying a person as an experienced user who is in fact a new user.) A Type I error results in experienced users facing higher effective prices than is desirable. The more frequently these errors occur, the less will be the price differential that is established.

A fourth factor is the extent to which old users can act as "brokers" for new users. The amount of "brokering" depends on the experienced users' ability to get more heroin than they need for their own consumption, their incentives to conceal their heroin use from nonusers in the society, and the extent to which they circulate throughout the society. The existence of brokers will reduce the price discrimination that results from successful discrimination by regular suppliers.

By looking at how these factors are influenced by different policy instruments, we can make tentative judgments about the impact of these policy instruments on the effective price to new and experienced users.

II. Policy Alternatives

A. The Choice Between Legal Prescription and Prohibition

The major policy alternatives are to continue the prohibition of heroin or to allow heroin to be legally prescribed. Variants within these major policies are created by different enforcement strategies and different levels of supervision over doctors and users.

Some observers argue that the legal prescription policy has a clear advantage compared to the prohibition policy in terms of achieving a sharp price discrimination. The doctors in the legal prescription system are assumed to have stronger incentives and greater ability to discriminate against new users than illegal dealers. Indeed, dealers under the prohibition system are sometimes assumed to prefer selling to new users in order to gain additional lifetime customers. Differences in the opportunities for established users to act as brokers are not usually analyzed.

However, illegal dealers *do* have strong incentives to discriminate. Illegal dealers wish to maximize a utility function which includes income and the probability of arrest as arguments. This utility function gives them clear preferences for certain kinds of customers; those known not to be undercover police, those known to be "stand-up guys" (i.e., nonsquealers), those who buy heroin regularly, and those who buy large quantities at each transaction. These customers yield higher incomes at lower risk. A marginal customer is one who has no solid reputation, who buys irregularly, and who buys little. The characteristics which dealers prefer in customers are positively correlated with duration of use. Consequently, although illegal dealers may be indifferent on the issue of selling to new or old users, they have incentives to discriminate on the basis of characteristics correlated with a customer's previous experience as a user. A *de facto* discrimination against inexperienced users and in favor of old users results.

Further, it can be argued that the opportunities for established users to act as brokers may be less under a prohibition policy than under a legal prescription policy. Under a prohibition policy, the user has some incentive to conceal his heroin use from strangers. In addition, since users in an illegal system depend on one anther for current information about good places to score for both heroin and money, they have an incentive to congregate in specific areas. Under a legal prescription policy, users would have weaker incentives to conceal their heroin use. In addition, the users under a legal prescription system would be more widely dispersed throughout the society. Thus, the opportunities for inexperienced users to encounter, discover, and persuade established users to act as brokers may be greater under a legal prescription policy than under the prohibition policy.

Given that regular dealers have incentives to discriminate in favor of experienced users and against inexperienced users under both policies, and that opportunities for established users to become brokers may be more numerous and more widely dispersed in a legal prescription system, there is no clear advantage for legal prescription.

B. Variants Under the Prohibition Policy

The prohibition policy can be enforced by a variety of police strategies, each with different targets and ploys. Four that are commonly employed or advocated are: (1) surveillance of known locations; (2) use of old addicts as informants; (3) use of young policemen as undercover agents to make purchases at street levels: and (4) attacks directed at intermediate or high levels of the industry.

Figure 1 shows the possible outcomes of employing the different tactics both alone and in combinations. The specific estimates are justified below.

(1) The surveillance of known locations gives users and dealers incentive to avoid those locations. Although this tactic has no effect on the regular dealer's desire to discriminate among his customers, it does affect the ease with which experimental users can locate suppliers and brokers. Consequently, the mean and the variance in the access time to new users increase. The access time for experienced users also increases. However, given their extensive

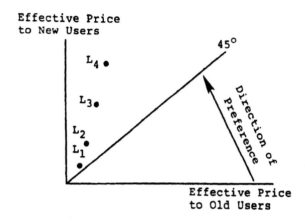

Figure 1. Outcomes of Different Police Strategies Under a
Prohibition Policy

leads, connections, and experience in finding junk, the increase is
less than for new users. The effect of this policy, then, is to raise the
effective price to both new and old users, but more for new users
than for old users.

(2) Using old addicts as informants increases the dealer's desire
to discriminate among his customers. Unfortunately, he begins to
discriminate *against* experienced users and in favor of new users. In
addition, the informants may be granted some immunity by the police. The immunity may not extend to serious dealing, but might
easily cover brokering. The proximate effects of this tactic, then,
are to encourage dealers to discriminate against experienced users
and to permit old users to become more brazen in their brokering
activities. This results in somewhat higher effective prices for both
old and new users and a reduction in the degree of discrimination
that is achieved.

(3) The use of young patrolmen as undercover agents again
gives dealers strong incentives to discriminate among their customers. However, with this tactic the regular dealer is motivated to
discriminate against people with characteristics associated with inexperience, i.e., in the direction that we prefer. Note that the worse

a policeman is in terms of his ability to imitate hardcore junkies (i.e., the more inexperience he reveals), the better is his performance in motivating dealers to avoid inexperienced users. This should relieve those who were worried about the ability of police to imitate the behavior and posture of real junkies. The effect of this tactic is to raise the effective price to new users by a large amount and to have only a minor effect on the effective price to old users.

(4) For regular street dealers the important effect of attacks directed at intermediate and high levels of the distribution system is that the attacks lead to a reduced aggregate supply. If the dealers were simply profit maximizers, they would exploit the situation by charging higher effective prices for all users. However, the dealers would also like to reduce their risk. Consequently, they are willing to take some of their gain in the form of actions designed to reduce their risk. This tactic alone does not suggest any specific ways that the dealer might reduce his risk. However, if the dealer judges that his risks could be reduced by reducing the number of transactions or discriminating among his customers, this tactic may result in new users facing relatively higher effective prices. If the dealer does not belive that reducing his transactions or cutting out marginal customers will reduce his risks, the outcome of this tactic will be simply to raise the effective price equally to new and old users.

(5) The analysis of attacks directed at intermediate and high levels hints strongly that combinations of tactics (given a constant budget) are more powerful than any one tactic pressed alone. The reason is simply that reduction in the aggregate supply of heroin will motivate dealers to look for ways of reducing risk as well as gaining more profits. In this situation dealers might respond to slight increases in the probability that young users could be undercover police with a dramatic increase in the extent to which they discriminate against young users. Thus, a combination of sufficient high-level arrests to keep inventories tight and a modest increase in undercover activities at the street level might achieve P_5 on Figure 1.

(6) The tactics aimed at dealers' incentives to discriminate can be complemented by policies aimed at reducing the incentives and opportunities for established users to act as brokers. The surveillance of known locations would accomplish this reduction in opportunities to encounter brokers. The effect would be to boost the price to new users above levels reached by strategy P_5. The price of

achieving this higher effective price to new users is an even larger increase in the effective price to old users. It is they who will bear the brunt of this tactic. The outcome of a three-pronged strategy involving the use of undercover police, attacks at intermediate levels, and the surveillance of known locations might lie in the vicinity of point P_6 in Figure 1.

C. Variants Under the Legal Prescription Policy

Legal prescription policies vary for several different reasons. Doctors can be more or less conservative in diagnosing addiction. In making their diagnoses, the doctors can use tests of varying quality. The dose provided to users can be more or less generous. The users who receive heroin can be vulnerable to varying degrees of supervision. Finally, the legal prescription policy can be combined with more or less aggressive enforcement against residual "unauthorized use." From the set of possible variants, we can distinguish four that are advocated or employed.

(1) Permitting doctors to prescribe heroin without close government supervision (the British policy until (1968).

(2) Permitting heroin to be prescribed by doctors serving in government-supervised clinics (the British policy from 1968 to the present).   .

(3) Permitting heroin to be prescribed only to be used under the supervision of the government.

(4) Prescription for use only under supervision and aggressive enforcement against unauthorized sales and use.

Figure 2 presents speculative estimates of the outcomes of these four different policies. These estimates are supported below.
(1) The policy of not supervising doctors allows them to do as they wish in diagnosing addiction and in prescribing maintenance doses of heroin. We can, of course, rely on a strong motivation to discriminate against new users and to avoid overprescription. Unfortunately, it is difficult for doctors to distinguish reliably between experienced users and new users and to calibrate "maintenance" doses of heroin. In diagnosing addiction doctors may look for

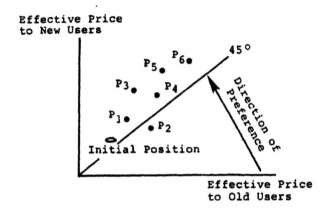

Figure 2. Outcomes of Variant Policies Under a Legal Prescription
Policy

track marks, perform urinalyses, require documented histories of addiction, or induce withdrawal symptoms. Of these tests only the last
is reliable—and it is expensive, both for doctors and patients. In deciding on the appropriate dose, the doctor can bargain with the addict or admit him to a hospital for a series of titrating experiments.
Again, only the expensive test is accurate.

In practice private doctors have been unwilling to invest in the
expensive but accurate tests. Further, they have used a relatively
liberal criterion in diagnosing addiction and in deciding on the appropriate dosage. The combination of crude tests and liberal criteria
implies that many Type II errors are made: nonaddicts are diag-
nosed as addicts; addicts receive substantially more heroin than
they need for their own consumption. Because doctors cannot reliably distinguish new users from old users, and because overprescrip-
tions subsidize extensive brokerage activity, the price differential
under this policy is small. Both new and old users face low effective
prices.

The government had two basic options to increase the price differential between new and old users. The first is to attempt to control the number of Type II errors in both diagnosis and prescription.
The second is to exercise some level of supervision over the estab-

lished users to reduce the extent of brokerage activities. Acting on these diverse fronts yields policies L_2 and L_3.

(2) The government can control the number of Type II errors by punishing doctors for Type II errors, or by gaining direct control over the diagnostic and prescription procedures. There is a strong argument for the government to gain direct control.

Private physicians can respond to punishment for Type II errors in two different ways. They can continue to use the same tests, but use a more conservative criterion. Or, they can shift to a more accurate test. Both moves reduce the frequency of Type II errors. However, the moves have much different implications for the frequency of Type I errors. Moving to a more accurate test secures a reduction in Type II errors without a large corresponding increase in Type I errors. Shifting to a more conservative criterion without changing the test secures a reduction in Type II errors only at the price of an increase in Type I errors. We care about Type I errors (which represent discrimination against experienced users and under prescription) for two reasons: experienced users face higher effective prices than is desirable; the experienced users who are excluded from the legal distribution system may support a residual illicit market in heroin which is relatively hospitable to new users. The difficulty of controlling the responses of doctors to punishment for Type II errors and the significant costs of increasing the number of Type I errors are strong justifications for the government to control the diagnostic and prescription procedures. They can guarantee the use of high quality tests.

However, even with the high quality tests, both Type I and Type II errors will occur in diagnosis and prescription. No matter what criterion we adopt in making diagnostic and dosage decisions, these errors will tend to reduce the price differential that might otherwise be established. If we adopt a conservative criterion, we will raise the effective price to old users by more than we would like (because of incorrect exclusions and underprescription), and we will fail to raise the effective price to new users by as much as we would like (because of the support our Type I errors provide for a residual black market). If we adopt a liberal criterion, we can keep a low effective price to old users, but risk a low effective price to new users as a result of extensive brokering by old addicts and successful penetration of the legal system by new users. Assuming the government chooses a conservative criterion, the outcome of this policy may be in the vicinity of L_2 on Figure 2.

(3) The problem with policy L_2 is that we do not adequately control the behavior of old users. It is their brokering or their support of an illicit market which causes us problems. Policy L_3 seeks to solve this problem by securing effective supervision of old users. There is a problem of how much supervision of the user's drug consumption and other activities is optimal. At one extreme is the policy of permitting users to take their week's supply out of the clinic. At another extreme is an inpatient program. One quickly discovers that neither of these extremes is a satisfactory policy for achieving price discrimination. With the weekly take-out system, one expects to encounter widespread brokering early in the week when users have excess supplies of heroin, and widespread purchases of illegal heroin late in the week when users have consumed or sold all of their legal heroin. With an inpatient system, one will fail to attract a large number of old users to the legal system. They will support a residual black market. The optimal level of supervision may be a program in which old users are obliged to consume all their prescribed heroin under government supervision. The problem with this program is that it is vulnerable to the charge that it is antitherapeutic. This charge is made on two different grounds. First, since heroin must be injected at the clinic several times a day, the user may be prevented from holding a regular job and be forced to associate frequently with other addicts. Both effects are considered antitherapeutic. Second, in order to attract addicts to the program and to guarantee that they do not supplement, the prescribed doses may have to be generous enough to give users a "rush" and allow them a lengthy "nod." In both England and the United States doctors resist such a program. To avoid the antitherapeutic charge, doctors are likely to compromise on both the generous dose requirement and the closer supervision requirement. If doses are not sufficiently generous, many users will supplement in illicit markets. If supervision is not sufficiently close, some brokerage activities will undoubtedly occur—particularly if the dose is generous. The outcome of this policy, then, will probably be to raise the effective price to new users (due to some reduction in both brokering and the size of a residual illicit

market), and to raise slightly the effective price to old users (due to less generous prescriptions and the difficulty of showing up at the clinics).

(4) A final step the government can take to achieve price discrimination under a legal prescription policy is to have effective law enforcement against remaining unauthorized use. The residual black market under a legal prescription policy is often overlooked on the assumption that legal competition will drive out illegal distributors. The arguments supporting this assumption are (1) that profits in the distribution systems will decrease by so much that dealers will turn to more attractive occupations, or (2) that there is a minimum economic size for the illegal industry which is larger than the demand that remains unsatisfied after the creation of a legal distribution system. Both these assumptions appear highly doubtful. Heroin dealers almost certainly have low opportunity costs. In addition, the minimum economic size of an illegal distribution firm is probably small. The residual demand composed of supplementing users, users who wish to stay out of the legal system, and experimenting users may be large enough to keep the illegal distributors in business.

Note that only a few of these illegal dealers need to remain in business for inexperienced users to confront *lower* effective prices than they confront under a prohibition policy. Suppose that 10 percent of users at any given time were inexperienced users. Because they were not particularly heavily addicted, they would constitute less than 10 percent of total heroin consumption—perhaps as little as 2-3 percent. Now suppose that a legal distribution system is developed. Many of the addicted people flock to the legal prescription system. Many illegal dealers decide to go out of business. However, if less than 97 percent of the former illicit supply capability disappears, inexperienced users will face *improved* supply conditions; the supply to them will be greater than under the prohibition policy. The small proportion of total consumption required to support large growth rates in the using population requires that one has to drive out nearly 100 percent of the illegal supply capacity.

These observations suggest that one must have a law enforcement strategy to attack the residual illicit market and that it must be very effective to reduce the aggregate supply to new users. The strategies available for enforcing narcotic laws have been previously analyzed. If the government used the most successful law enforcement strategy to control the residual black market, it might be able to achieve L_4 on Figure 2. The argument is that the law enforcement policy would disproportionately raise the effective price to new users who are solely dependent on the market for opportunities to score.

III. Conclusion

The purpose of this extremely speculative discussion of the impact of various policies toward the supply of heroin is not to demonstrate that one general policy or one specific variant is the most desirable policy. Rather, the purpose is to suggest that these policies could be usefully evaluated in terms of their impact on the effective price to new and old users. A secondary purpose is to identify the various factors which determine the level of the effective prices to the different consuming groups and to show that an analysis of these factors can facilitate the design and a priori evaluation of various policies.

References

I. Chein, et al, *The Road to H*, New York 1964.

Griffith Edwards, "The British Approach to the Treatment of Heroin Addiction," *Lancet*, 1969, 1, 768-772.

Seymour Fiddle, *Portraits from the Shooting Gallery*, New York 1967.

J. Larner, *The Addict on the Street*, New York 1964.

M. Moore, "The Economics of Heroin Distribution," *Policy Concerning Drug Abuse in N.Y. State*, 3, New York 1970.

Robert Schaste, "Cessation Patterns Among Neophyte Heroin Users," *Inter. J. of Addictions*, 1, 1966.

Alan Thalinger, "A Study of Deaths of Narcotic Users—1969," New York City Dept. of Health Research Training Program, 1970.

Richard Woodley, *Dealer*, New York 1971.

ECONOMICS AND CRIMINAL ENTERPRISE

Thomas C. Schelling

At the level of national policy, if not always of local practice, the dominant approach to organized crime is through indictment and conviction. This is in striking contrast to the enforcement of antitrust or food-and-drug laws, or the policing of public utilities, which work through regulation, accommodation, and the restructuring of markets. For some decades, antitrust problems have received the sustained professional attention of economists concerned with the structure of the markets, the organization of business enterprise, and the incentives toward collusion or price-cutting. Racketeering and the provision of illegal goods (like gambling) have been conspicuously neglected by economists. (There exists no analysis of the liquor industry under prohibition that begins to compare with the best available studies of the aluminum or steel industries, air transport, milk distribution, or public-utility pricing.) Yet a good many economic and business principles that operate in the "upperworld" must, with suitable modification for change in environment, operate in the underworld as well—just as a good many economic principles that operate in an advanced competitive economy operate as well in a socialist or a primitive economy.

In addition to the sheer satisfaction of curiosity, there are good policy reasons for encouraging a "strategic" analysis of the criminal underworld. Such an analysis, in contrast to "tactical" intelligence aimed at the apprehension of individual criminals, could help in identifying the incentives and disincentives to organize crime, in evaluating the costs and losses due to criminal enterprises, and in restructuring laws and programs to minimize the costs, wastes, and injustices that crime entails.

What market characteristics determine whether a criminal activity becomes "organized"? Gambling, by all accounts, invites organization; abortion, by all accounts, does not. In the upperworld, automobile manufacture is characterized by large firms, but not machine-tool production; collusive price-fixing occurs in the electrical-machinery industry, but not in the distribution of fruits and vegetables. The reasons for these differences are not entirely under-

T.C. Schelling, "Economics and Criminal Enterprise," is reprinted with permission of the author from *The Public Interest*, No. 7 (Spring, 1967) pp. 61-78. © 1967 by National Affairs, Inc.

stood, but they are amenable to study. The same should not be impossible for gambling, extortion, and contraband cigarettes.

How much does organized crime depend on at least one major market in which the advantages of large scale are great enough to support a dominant monopoly firm or cartel? Not all businesses lend themselves to centralized organization; some do, and these may provide the nucleus of capital and entrepreneurial talent for extension into other businesses that would not, alone, support or give rise to an organized monopoly or cartel. Do a few "core" criminal markets provide the organizational stimulus for organized crime? If the answer turns out to be yes, then a critical question is whether the particular market so essential for the "economic development" of the underworld is a "black market," whose existence is dependent on the prohibition of legal competition, or instead is an inherently criminal activity. Black markets always offer to the policymaker, in principle, the option of restructuring the market—of increasing legal competition, of compromising the original prohibition, of selectively relaxing either the law itself or the way it is enforced. If, alternatively, that central criminal enterprise is one that rests on violence, relaxation of the law is likely to be both ineffectual and unappealing.

Since one of the interesting questions is why some underworld business becomes organized and some not, and another, what *kinds* of organization should be expected, a classification of these enterprises has to cover more than just "organized crime" and to distinguish types of organization. A tentative typology of underworld business might be as follows.

Black Markets

A large part of organized crime is the selling of commodities and services contrary to law. In what we usually consider the underworld this includes dope, prostitution, gambling, liquor (under prohibition), abortions, pornography, and contraband or stolen goods. Most of these are consumer goods.

In what is not usually considered the underworld, black markets include gold, contraceptives in some states, rationed commodities and coupons in wartime, loans and rentals above controlled prices, theater tickets in New York, and a good many similar commodities that, though not illegal per se, are handled outside legitimate markets or diverted from subsidized uses.

In some cases (gambling) the law bans the commodity from all consumers; in others (cigarettes), some consumers are legitimate and some (minors) are not. In some cases what is illegal is that the tax or duty has not been paid; in some, it is the price of the transaction that makes it illegal. In some (child labor, illegal immigrant labor), it is buying the commodity, not selling it, that is proscribed.

Racketeering

Racketeering includes two kinds of business, both based on intimidation. One is *criminal monopoly*, the other *extortion*.

"Criminal monopoly" means the use of criminal means to destroy competition. Whether a competitor is actually destroyed or merely threatened with violence to make him go out of business, the object is to get protection from competition when the law will not provide it (by franchise or tariff protection) and when it cannot be legally achieved (through price wars, control of patents, or preclusive contracts).

We can distinguish altogether three kinds of "monopoly": those achieved through legal means, those achieved through means that are illegal only because of antitrust and other laws intended to make monopoly difficult, and monopolies achieved through means that are criminal by any standards—means that would be criminal whether or not they were aimed at monopolizing a business. It is also useful to distinguish between firms that, in an excess of zeal or deficiency of scruple, engage when necessary in ruthless and illegal competition, and the more strictly "racketeering" firms whose profitable monopoly rests entirely on criminal violence. The object of law enforcement in the former case is not to destroy the firm but to curtail its illegal practices. If the whole basis of success in business, though, is strong-arm methods that keep competition destroyed or scare it away, it is a pure "racket."

"Extortion" means living off somebody else's business by the threat of violence or of criminal competition. A protection racket lives off its victims, letting them operate and pay tribute. If one establishes a chain of restaurants and destroys competitors or scares them out of business, that is "monopoly"; if he merely threatens to destroy people's restaurant business, taking part of their profits as the price for leaving them alone, he is an extortionist and likes to see them prosper so that his share will be greater.

For several reasons it is difficult to distinguish "extortion" that, like a parasite, wants a healthy host, from "criminal monopoly" that is dedicated to the elimination of competitors. First, one means of extortion is to threaten to cut off the supply of a monopolized commodity—labor on a construction site, trucking, or some illegal commodity provided through the black market. That is to say, one can use a monopoly at one stage for extortion leverage at the next. Second, extortion itself can be used to secure a monopoly privilege: instead of taking tribute in cash, for example, a victim signs a contract for the high-priced delivery of beer or linen supplies. The results look like monopoly, but arose out of extortion.

It is evident that extortion can be organized or not, but in important cases it has to be. Vulnerable victims, after all, have to be protected from other extortionists. A monopolistic laundry service, deriving from a threat to harm the business that does not subscribe, has to destroy or to intimidate not only competing legitimate laundry services but other racketeers who would muscle in on the same victim. Thus, while criminal monopoly may not depend on extortion, organized extortion always needs an element of monopoly.

Black-Market Monopoly

Any successful black marketeer enjoys a "protected" market in the way a domestic industry is protected by a tariff, or butter is protected by a law against margarine. The black marketeer gets protection from the law against all competitors unwilling to pursue a criminal career. But there is a difference between a "protected industry" and a "monopolized industry." Abortion is a black market commodity but not a monopoly; a labor racket is a local monopoly but not a black market one; a monopoly in dope has both elements—it is a "black market monopoly."

Cartel

A "conspiracy in restraint of trade" that does not lead to single-firm monopoly but to collusive price-fixing, and that maintains itself by criminal action, gives rise to a cartel that is not in, but depends on, the underworld. If the garment trade eliminates competition by an agreement on prices and wages, hiring thugs to enforce the agreement, it is different from the monopoly racket discussed above. If the government would make such agreements legally enforceable (as it does with retail-price-maintenance laws in some states), the business would be in no need of criminally enforcing discipline on itself. Similarly, a labor union can use criminal means to discipline its members, even to the presumed benefit of its members, who may be better off working as a bloc rather than as competing individuals. If the law permits enforceable closed-shop agreements, the criminal means become unnecessary.

Organized Criminal Services

A characteristic of the businesses listed above is that they usually involve relations between the underworld and the upperworld. But as businesses in the upperworld need legal services, financial advice, credit, enforcement of contract, places to conduct their business, and communication facilities, so in the underworld there has to be a variety of business services that are "domestic" to the underworld itself. These can be organized or unorganized. They are *in* the underworld, but not because they exploit the underworld as the underworld exploits the legitimate world.

The Incentives to Criminal Organization

The simplest explanation of a large-scale firm, in the underworld or anywhere else, is high overhead costs or some other element of technology that makes small-scale operation more costly than large-scale. The need to keep equipment or specialized personnel fully utilized often explains at least the lower limit to the size of the firm.

A second explanation is the prospect of monopolistic prices. If most of the business can be cornered by a single firm, it can raise the price at which it sells its illegal services. Like any business, it does this at some sacrifice in size of the market; but if the demand is inelastic, the increase in profit margin will more than compensate for the reduction in output. Of course, decentralized individual firms would have as much to gain by pushing up the price, but without discipline it will not work; each will undercut its competitors. Where entry can be denied to newcomers, centralized price-setting will yield monopoly rewards to whoever can organize the market. With discipline, a cartel can do it; in the absence of discipline a merger may do it; but intimidation, too, can lead to the elimination of competition and the conquest of a monopoly position by a single firm.

Third, the larger the firm, and especially the larger its share of the whole market, the more will formerly "external" costs become costs internal to the firm. "External costs" are those that fall on competitors, customers, bystanders, and others outside the firm itself. Collection of all the business within a single firm causes the costs that individual firms used to inflict on each other to show up as costs (or losses) to the larger centralized firm now doing the business. This is an advantage. The costs were originally there but disregarded; now there is an incentive to take them into account.

Violence is one such external cost. Racketeers have a collective interest in restricting violence, so as to avoid trouble with the public and the police—but the individual racketeer has little or no incentive to reduce the violence connected with his own crime. There is an analogy here with the whaling industry, which has a collective interest in not killing off the whales although an individual whaler has no incentive to consider what he is doing to the future of the industry when he maximizes his own catch. A large organization can afford to impose discipline, holding down violence if the business is crime, holding down the slaughter of females if the business is whaling.

There are also "external economies" that can become internalized, to the advantage of the centralized firm. Lobbying has this character, as does cultivating relations with the police. No small bookie can afford to spend money to influence gambling legislation, but an organized trade association or monopoly among those who live off illegal gambling can. Similarly with labor discipline; the small firm cannot afford to teach a lesson to the labor force of the industry, since most of the lesson is lost on other people's employees, but a single large firm can expect the full benefit of its labor policy. Similarly with cultivating the market; if one cultivates the market for dope, by hooking some customers, or cultivates a market for gambling in a territory where the demand is still latent, he cannot expect much of a return on his investment if opportunistic competitors will take advantage of the market he creates. Anything that requires a long investment in cultivating a consumer interest, a labor market, ancillary institutions, or relations with the police, can be undertaken only by a fairly large firm that has reason to expect that it can enjoy most of the market and get a satisfactory return on the investment.

Finally, there is the attraction of not only monopolizing a market but achieving a dominant position in the underworld itself, and participating in its governing. To the extent that large criminal business firms provide a governmental structure to the underworld, helping to maintain peace, setting rules, arbitrating disputes, and enforcing discipline, they are in a position to set up their own businesses and exclude competition. Constituting a "corporate state," they can give themselves the franchise for various "state-sponsored monopolies." They can do this either by denying the benefits of underworld government to their competitors or by using the equivalent of their "police power" to prevent competition.

Market Structure

In evaluating crime, an accounting approach gives at best a benchmark as to magnitudes, and not even that for the distribution of economic and social gains and losses. The problem is like that of estimating the comparative incidence of profits taxes and excise taxes, or the impact of a minimum-wage law on wage differentials. Especially if we want to know who bears the cost, or to compare the costs to society with the gains to the criminals, an analysis of *market adjustments* is required. Even the pricing practices of organized crime need to be studied.

Consider the illegal wire service syndicate in Miami that received attention from Senator Kefauver's committee. The magnitude that received explicit attention was the loss of state revenues due to the diversion of gambling from legal race tracks, which were taxable, to illegal bookmakers, whose turnover was not taxable. No accounting approach would yield this magnitude; it depended (as was pointed out in testimony) on what economists call the "elasticity of substitution" between the two services—on the fraction of potential race track business that patronized bookmakers.

Similar analysis is required to determine *at whose expense* the syndicate operated, or what the economic consequences of the syndicate's removal would have been. The provision of wire-service was of small economic significance. It accounted, on a cost basis, for less than 5% of the net income of bookmakers (of which the syndicate took approximately 50%). And cheaper wire-service to the bookies might have been available in the absence of the syndicate, whose function was not to provide wire-service but to eliminate wire-service competitors.

The essential business of the syndicate was to practice *extortion against bookmakers*. It demanded half their earnings, against the threat of reprisals. The syndicate operated like a taxing authority (as well as providing some reinsurance on large bets); it apparently did not limit the number of bookmakers so long as they paid their "taxes."

How much of this tax was passed along to the customer (on the analogy of a gasoline or a sales tax) and how much was borne by the bookie (on the analogy of an income or profits tax) is. hard to determine. If we assume (a) that bookmakers' earnings are approximately proportionate to the volume of turnover, (b) that their customers, though sensitive to the comparative odds of different bookmakers, are not sensitive to the profit margin, (c) that they tend, consciously or implicitly, to budget their total bets and not their rate of loss, we can conclude that the tax is substantially passed along to the customer. In that case the bookmaker, though nominally the victim of extortion, is victimized only into raising the price to his customers, somewhat like a filling station that must pay a tax on every gallon sold. The bookmaker is thus an intermediary between an extortionate syndicate and a customer who pays his tribute voluntarily on the price he is willing to pay for his bets.

The syndicate in Miami relied on the police as their favorite instrument of intimidation. It could have been the other way around, with the police using the syndicate as their agency to negotiate and collect from the bookmakers, and if the police had been organized and disciplined as a monopoly, it would have been the police, not the syndicate, that we should put at the top of our organizational pyramid. From the testimony, though, it is evident that the initiative and entrepreneurship came from the syndicate, which had the talent and organization for this kind of business, and that the police lacked the centralized authority for exploiting to their own benefit the power they had over bookmakers. Presumably—though there were few hints of this in the hearings—the syndicate could have mobilized other techniques for intimidating the bookmakers; the police were the chosen instrument only so long as the police's share in the proceeds was competitive with alternative executors of the intimidating threats.

Any attempt to estimate the long-term effect on police salaries would have to take into account how widespread and nondiscriminatory the police participation was, especially by rank and seniority in service. Recruiting would be unaffected if police recruits were unaware of the illegal earnings that might accrue to them; senior members of the force who might otherwise have quit the service, or lobbied harder for pay increases, would agitate less vigorously for high wages if their salaries were augmented by the racket. One cannot easily infer that part of the "tax" paid by the bookmaker's customer subsidized the police force to the benefit of nonbetting taxpayers; mainly they supported a more discriminatory and irregular earnings pattern among the police—besides contributing, unwittingly, to a demoralization of the police that would have made it a bad bargain for the taxpayer anyway.

This is just a sketch, based on the skimpy evidence available, of the rather complex structure of "organized gambling" in one city. (It is not, of course, the gambling that is organized; the organization is an extortionate monopoly that nominally provides a wire service but actually imposes a tribute on middlemen who pass most of the cost along to their voluntary customers.) Similar analysis would be required to identify the incidence of costs and losses (and gains, of course) of protection rackets everywhere (e.g., monopoly-priced beer deliveries to bars or restaurants, vending machines installed in bars and restaurants under pain of damage or nuisance, etc.).

Institutional Practices

Institutional practices in the underworld need to be better understood. What, for example, is the effect of the tax laws on extortion? Why does an extortionist put cigarette machines in a restaurant or provide linen service? Do the tax laws make it difficult to disguise the payment of tribute in cash but easy to disguise it (and make it tax deductible) if the tribute takes the form of a concession or the purchase of high-priced services? Why does a gambling syndicate bother to provide "wire service" when evidently its primary economic function is to shake down bookies by the threat of hurting their businesses or their persons, possibly with the collusion of the police?

The Kefauver hearings indicate that the wire service syndicate in Miami took a standard 50% from the bookies. The symmetry of the 50% figure is itself remarkable. Equally remarkable is that the figure was uniform. But most remarkable of all is that the syndicate went through the motions of providing a wire service when it perfectly well could have taken cash tribute instead. There is an analogy here with the car salesman who refuses to negotiate the price of a new car, but is willing to negotiate quite freely the "allowance" on the used car that one turns in. The underworld seems to need institutions, conventions, traditions, and recognizable standard practices much like the upperworld of business. A better understanding of these practices might lead not only to a better evaluation of crime itself but also to a better understanding of the role of tax laws and regulatory laws on the operation of criminal business.

The role of vending machines, for example, appears to be that they provide a tax-deductible, non-discriminatory, and "respectable" way of paying tribute. Pinball and slot machines installed by a gang in somebody's small store may be only half characterized when identified as "illegal gambling"; they are equally a conventionalized medium for the exaction of tribute from the store owner. Effective enforcement of a ban on the machines will take care of the "gambling" part of the enterprise, what happens to the extortion racket depends than on how readily some other lucrative concession, some exclusive delivery contract, or some direct cash tribute can be imposed on the store owner.

Even the resistance to crime would be affected by measures designed to change the cost structure. Economists make an important distinction between a lump-sum tax, a profits tax, and a specific or ad valorem tax on the commodity an enterprise sells. The manner in which a criminal monopolist or extortionist prices his service, or demands his tribute, should have a good deal to do with whether the cost is borne by the victim or passed along by the customer. The "tax" levied by the racketeer uniformly on all his customers—monopoly-priced beer or linen supplies—may merely be passed along in turn to their customers, with little loss to the intermediate victims, if the demand in their own market is inelastic. A bar that has to pay an extortionate price for its beer can seek relief in either of two ways. It can try to avoid paying the extortionate or monopolized price; alternatively, it can insist that its supplier achieve similar concessions from all competing bars, to avoid a competitive disadvantage. An individual bar suffers little if the price of wholesale beer goes up; it suffers when competitors' prices do not go up.

Similarly, legal arrangements that make it difficult to disguise illegal transactions, and that make it a punishable offense to pay tribute, might help to change the incentives. In a few cases, the deliberate stimulation of competing enterprises could be in the public interest: loansharking, for example, might be somewhat mitigated by the deliberate creation of new and specialized lending enterprises. Loansharking appears to involve several elements, only one of which is the somewhat outmoded notion—outmoded by a few centuries—that people so much in need of cash that they'd pay high interest rates should be protected from "usury" even if it means merely that they are protected by being denied any access to credit at all. A second element is that, now that debtors' prison has been liberally abolished, people who cannot post collateral have no ready way to assure their own motivation to repay—attachment of wages has also been liberally made illegal—so that those without assets who need cash must pledge life and limb in the underworld. Thus when the law has no way of enforcing contract, the underworld provides it; a man submits to the prospect of personal violence as the last resort in contract enforcement. Finally, the borrower whose prospects of repayment are so poor that even the threat of violence cannot hold him to repayment is enticed into an arrangement that makes him a victim of perpetual extortion, one who cannot go to the law because he is already party to a criminal transaction. Evidently there is some part of this racket that thrives on a void in our legal and financial institutions.

Evaluating Costs and Losses

Crime is bad, as cancer is bad; but even for cancer, one can distinguish among death, pain, anxiety, the cost of treatment, the loss of earnings, the effects on the victim and the effects on his family. Similarly with crime. It is offensive to society that the law be violated. But crime can involve a transfer of wealth from the victim to the criminal, a net social loss due to the inefficient mode of transfer, the creation of fear and anxiety, violence from which nobody profits, the corruption of the police and other public officials, costs of law enforcement, and private protection, high prices to customers, unfairness of competition, loss of revenue to the state, and even loss of earnings to the criminals themselves who in some cases may be ill-suited to their trade.

There are important "trade-offs" among these different costs and losses due to crime, and in different ways that government can approach the problem of crime. There will be choices between reducing the incidence of crime and reducing the consequences of crime, and other choices that require a more explicit identification and evaluation of the magnitude and distribution of the gains and losses.

If there were but one way to wage war against crime, and the only question how vigorously to do it, there would be no need to identify the different objectives (costs and consequences) in devising the campaign. But if this is a continual campaign to cope with some pretty definite evils, without any real expectation of "total victory" or "unconditional surrender," resources have to be allocated and deployed in a way that maximizes the value of a compromise.

In the black-markets it is especially hard to identify just what the evils are. In the first place, a law-abiding citizen is not obliged to consider the procurement and consumption of illegal commodities inherently sinful. We have constitutional procedures for legislating prohibitions; the outvoted minority is bound to abide by the law but not necessarily to agree with it, and can even campaign to become a majority and legalize liquor after a decade of prohibition, or legalize contraceptives in states where they have been prohibited. Even those who vote to ban gambling or saloons or dope can do so, not because they consider the consumption sinful, but because *some* of the consequences are bad; and if it is infeasible to prohibit the sale of alcohol only to alcoholics, or gambling only to minors, we have to forbid all of it to forbid the part we want to forbid.

The only reason for rehearsing these arguments is to remind ourselves that the evil of gambling, drinking, or dope, is not necessarily proportionate to how much of it goes on. The evil can be greater or less than suggested by any such figure. One might, for example, conclude that the consumption of narcotics that actually occurs is precisely the consumption that one wanted to prevent, and that it is the more harmless consumption that has been eliminated; or one might conclude that the gambling laws eliminate the worst of gambling, that what filters through the laws is fairly innocuous (or would be, if its being illegal per se were not harmful to society), and that gambling laws thus serve the purpose of selective discrimination in their enforcement if not in their enactment.

The evils of abortion are particularly difficult to evaluate, especially because it is everybody's privilege to attach his own moral value to the commodity. Are the disgust, anxiety, humiliation, and physical danger incurred by the abortionists' customers part of the "net cost" to society, or are they positively valued as punishment for the wicked? If a woman gets an abortion, do we prefer she pay a high price or a low one? Is the black market price a cost to society, a proper penalty inflicted on the woman, or merely an economic waste? If a woman gets a safe cheap abortion abroad, is this a legitimate bit of "international trade," raising the national income like any gainful trade or is it even worse than her getting an expensive, more disagreeable, more dangerous abortion at home, because she evaded the punishment and the sense of guilt?

These are not academic questions. There are issues of policy in identifying what it is we dislike about criminal activity, especially in deciding where and how to compromise. The case of prostitution is a familiar example. Granting the illegality of prostitution, and efforts to enforce the law against it, one may still discover that one particular evil of prostitution is a hazard to health—the spread of venereal disease, a spread that is not confined to the customers but transmitted even to those who had no connection with the illicit commodity. Yet there is some incompatibility between a campaign to eradicate venereal disease and a campaign to eradicate prostitution, and one may prefer to legislate a public health service for prostitutes and their customers even at the expense of "diplomatic recognition" of the enemy. The point is that a hard choice can arise and ideology gives no answer. If two of the primary evils connected with a criminal activity are negatively correlated, one has to distinguish them, separately evaluate them, and then make up one's mind.

Similarly with abortion. At the very least, one can propose clinical help to women seeking abortion for the limited purpose of eliminating from the market those who are actually *not* pregnant, providing them the diagnosis that an abortionist might have neglected or preferred to withhold. Going a step further, one may want to provide reliable advice about post-abortion symptoms to women who may become infected or who may hemorrhage or otherwise suffer from ignorance. Still a step further, one may like to provide even abortionists with a degree of immunity so that if a woman needs emergency treatment he can call for it without danger of self-incrimination. None of these suggestions compromises the principle of illegality; they merely apply to abortion some of the principles that would ordinarily be applied to hit-and-run driving or to an armed robber who inadvertently hurt his victim and preferred to call an ambulance.

One has to go a step further, though, on the analogy with contraception, and ask about the positive and negative value of scientific discovery, or research and development, in the field of abortion itself. Cheap, safe and reliable contraceptives are now considered a stupendous boon to mankind. What is the worth of a cheap, safe and reliable technique of abortion, one that involves no surgery, no harmful or addicting drugs, no infection, and preferably not even reliance on a professional abortionist? Suppose some of the new techniques developed in Eastern Europe and elsewhere for performing safer and more convenient abortions become technically available to abortionists in this country, with the consequence that fewer patients suffer—but also with the consequence that more abortions are procured? How do we weigh these consequences against each other? Each of us may have his own answer, and a political or judicial decision is required if we want an official answer. But the questions cannot be ignored.

The same questions arise in the field of firearm technology. Do we hope that nonlethal weapons become available to criminals, so that they kill and damage fewer victims, or would we deplore it on grounds that any technological improvement available to criminal enterprise is against the public interest? Do we hope to see less damaging narcotics become available, perhaps cheaply available through production and marketing techniques that do not lend themselves to criminal monopoly, to compete with the criminally monopolized and more deleterious narcotics? Or is this a "compromise" with crime itself?

Should Crime Be Organized Or Disorganized?

It is usually implied, if not asserted, that organized crime is a menace and has to be fought. But if the alternative is "disorganized crime"—if the criminals and their opportunities will remain, with merely a lesser degree of organization than before—the choice is not an easy one.

There is one argument for favoring the "organization" of crime. It is that organization would "internalize" some of the costs that fall on the underworld itself but go unnoticed, or ignored, if criminal activity is decentralized. The individual hijacker may be tempted to kill a truck driver to destroy a potential witness—to the dismay of the underworld, which suffers from public outrage and the heightened activity of the police. A monopoly or a trade association could impose discipline. This is not a decisive argument, nor does it apply to all criminal industries if it applies to a few; but it is important.

If abortion, for example, will not be legalized and cannot be eliminated, one can wish it were better organized. A large organization could not afford to mutilate so many women. It could impose higher standards. It would have an interest in quality control and the protection of its "goodwill" that the petty abortionist is unlikely to have. As it is, the costs external to the enterprise—the costs that fall not on the abortionist but on the customer or on the reputation of other abortionists—are of little concern to him and he has no incentive to minimize them. By all accounts, criminal abortion is conducted more incompetently and more irresponsibly than illegal gambling.

Compromising With Organized Crime

It is customary to deplore the "accommodation" that the underworld reaches, sometimes , with the forces of law and order, with the police, with the prosecutors, with the courts. Undoubtedly there is corruption of public officials, bad not only because it frustrates justice but also because it lowers standards of morality. On the other hand, officials concerned with law enforcement are inevitably in the front line of diplomacy between the legitimate world and the underworld. Aside from the approved negotiations by which criminals are induced to testify, to plead guilty, to surrender themselves, or to tip off the police, there is always a degree of accommodation between the police and the criminals—tacit or explicit understandings analogous to what in military affairs would be called the limitation of war, the control of armament, and the delineation of spheres of influence.

In criminal activity by legitimate firms—such as conspiracy in restraint of trade, tax evasion, illegal labor practices, or the marketing of dangerous drugs—regulatory agencies can deal specifically with the harmful practices. One does not have to declare war on the industry itself, only on the illegal practices. Regulation, even negotiation, are recognized techniques for coping with those practices. But when the business itself is criminal, it is harder to have an acknowledged policy of regulation and negotiation. For this involves a kind of "diplomatic recognition."

In the international field, one can cold-bloodedly limit warfare and come to an understanding about the kinds of violence that will be resisted or punished, the activities that will be considered nonaggressive, and the areas within the other side's sphere of influence. Maybe the same approach is necessary in dealing with crime itself. And if we cannot acknowledge it at the legislative level, it may have to be accomplished in an unauthorized or unacknowledged way by the people whose business—law enforcement—requires it of them.

The Relation of Organized Crime to Enforcement

We have to distinguish the "black market monopolies," dealing in forbidden goods—gambling, dope, smuggling, prostitution—from the racketeering enterprises. It is the black market monopolies that depend on the law itself. Without the law and some degree of enforcement, there is no presumption that the organization can survive competition—or, if it could survive competition once it is established, that the organization could have arisen in the first place in the face of competition.

There must be an "optimum degree of enforcement" from the point of view of the criminal monopoly. With no enforcement—either because enforcement is not attempted or because enforcement is not feasible—the black market could not be profitable enough to invite criminal monopoly (at least not any more than any other market, legitimate or criminal). With wholly effective enforcement, and no collusion with the police, the business would be destroyed. Between these extremes, there may be an attractive black market profitable enough to invite monopoly.

Organized crime could not, for example, possibly corner the market on cigarette sales to minors. Every 21-year-old is a potential source of supply. No organization, legal or illegal, could keep a multitude of 21-year-olds from buying cigarettes and passing them along to persons under 21. No black-market price differential, great enough to make organized sale to minors profitable, could survive the competition. And no organization, legal or illegal, could so intimidate every adult that he would not be a source or supply to the youngsters. Without there being any way to enforce the law, organized crime would get no more out of selling cigarettes to children than out of selling them soft drinks.

The same is true of contraceptives in those states where their sale is nominally illegal. If the law is not enforced, there is no scarcity out of which to make profits. And if one is going to try to intimidate every drugstore that sells contraceptives, in the hope of monopolizing the business, he may as well monopolize toothpaste, which would be more profitable. The intervention of the law is needed to intimidate the druggists with respect to the one commodity that organized crime is trying to monopolize.

What about abortions? Why is it not "organized"? The answer is not easy, and there may be too many special characteristics of this market to permit a selection of the critical one. The consumer and the product have unusual characteristics. Nobody is a "regular" customer the way a person may regularly gamble, drink, or take dope. (A woman may repeatedly need the services of an abortionist, but each occasion is once-for-all.) The consumers are more secret about dealing with this black market, secret among intimate friends and relations, than are customers of most banned commodities. It is a dirty business, and too many of the customers die; and while organized crime might drastically reduce fatalities, it may be afraid of getting involved with anything that kills and maims so many customers in a way that could be blamed on the criminal himself rather than just on the commodity that is sold.

Black Markets and Competition

I have emphasized that a difference between black market crimes and most others, like racketeering and robbery, is that they are "crimes" only because we have legislated against the commodity they provide. We single out certain goods and services as harmful or sinful; for reasons of history and tradition, and for other reasons, we forbid dope but not tobacco, gambling in casinos but not on the stock market, extramarital sex but not gluttony, erotic stories but not mystery stories. We do all this for reasons different from those behind the laws against robbery and tax evasion.

It is policy that determines the black markets. Cigarettes and firearms are borderline cases. We can, as a matter of policy, make the sales of guns and cigarettes illegal. We can also, as a matter of policy, make contraceptives and abortion illegal. Times change, policies change, and what was banned yesterday can become legitimate today; what was freely available yesterday, can be banned tomorrow. Evidently there are changes under way in policy on birth control; there may be changes on abortion and homosexuality, and there may be legislation restricting the sale of firearms.

The pure black markets reflect some moral tastes, economic principles, paternalistic interests, and notions of personal freedom in a way that the rackets do not. And these tastes and principles change. We can revise our policy on birth control (and we are changing it) in a way that we could not change our policy on armed robbery. The usury laws may to some extent be a holdover from medieval economics; and some of the laws on prostitution, abortion, and contraception were products of the Victorian era and reflect the political power of various church groups. One cannot even deduce from the existence of abortion laws that a majority of the voters, even a majority of enlightened voters, oppose abortion; and the wise money would probably bet that the things that we shall be forbidding in fifty years will differ substantially from the things we forbid now.

What happens when a forbidden industry is subjected to legitimate competition? Legalized gambling is a good example. What has happened to Las Vegas is hardly reassuring. On the other hand, the legalization of liquor in the early 1930s swamped the criminal liquor industry with competition. Criminals are alleged to have moved into church bingo, but they have never got much of a hold on the stock market. Evidently criminals cannot always survive competition, evidently sometimes they can.

The question is important in the field of narcotics. We could easily put insulin and antibiotics into the hands of organized crime by forbidding their sale; we could do the same with a dentist's novocaine. (We could, that is, if we could sufficiently enforce the prohibition. If we cannot enforce it, the black market would be too competitive for any organized monopoly to arise.) If narcotics were not illegal, there could be no black market and no monopoly profits; the interest in "pushing" it would not be much greater than the pharmaceutical interest in pills to reduce symptoms of common colds. This argument cannot by itself settle the question of whether (and which) narcotics (or other evil commodities) ought to be banned, but it is an important consideration.

The greatest gambling enterprise in the United States has not been significantly touched by organized crime. That is the stock market. (There has been criminal activity in the stock market, but not monopoly by what we usually call "organized crime.") Nor has organized crime succeeded in controlling the foreign currency black markets around the world. The reason is that the market works too well. Federal control over the stock market, designed mainly to keep it honest and informative, and aimed at maximizing the competitiveness of the market and the information of the consumer, makes it a hard market to tamper with.

Ordinary gambling ought to be one of the hardest industries to monopolize. Almost anybody can compete, whether in taking bets or providing cards, dice, or racing information. "Wire services" could not stand the ordinary competition of radio and Western

Union; bookmakers could hardly be intimidated if the police were not available to intimidate them. If ordinary brokerage firms were encouraged to take horse-racing accounts, and buy and sell bets by telephone for their customers, it is hard to see how racketeers could get any kind of grip on it. And when any restaurant, bar, country club or fraternity house can provide tables and sell fresh decks of cards, it is hard to see how gambling can be monopolized any more than the soft-drink or television business, or any other.

We can still think gambling is a sin, and try to eliminate it; but we should probably try not to use the argument that it would remain in the hands of criminals if we legalized it. Both reason and evidence seem to indicate the contrary.

The decisive question is whether the goal of somewhat reducing the consumption of narcotics, gambling, prostitution, abortion or anything else that is forced by law into the black market, is or is not outweighed by the costs to society of creating a criminal industry. The costs to society of creating these black markets are several.

First, it gives the criminal the same kind of protection that a tariff gives to a domestic monopoly. It guarantees the absence of competition from people who are unwilling to be criminal, and an advantage to those whose skill is in evading the law.

Second, it provides a special incentive to corrupt police, because the police not only may be susceptible to being bought off but can even be used to eliminate competition.

Third, a large number of consumers who are probably not ordinary criminals—the conventioneers who visit prostitutes, the housewives who bet on horses, the women who seek abortions—are taught contempt, even enmity, for the law by being obliged to purchase particular commodities and services from criminals in an illegal transaction.

Fourth, dope addiction may so aggravate poverty for certain desperate people that they are induced to commit crimes, or can be urged to commit crimes, because the law arranges that the only (or main) source for what they desperately demand will be a criminal (high-priced) source.

Fifth, these big black markets may guarantee enough incentive and enough profit for organized crime so that large-scale criminal organization comes into being and maintains itself. It may be—this is an important question for research—that without these important black markets, crime would be substantially decentralized, lacking the kind of organization that makes it enterprising, safe, and able to corrupt public officials. In economic-development terms, these black markets may provide the central core (or "infrastructure") of underworld business.

A good economic history of prohibition in the 1920s has never been attempted, so far as I know. By all accounts, though, prohibition was a mistake. It merely turned the liquor industry over to organized crime. In the end we gave up, probably because not everybody agreed drinking was bad (or, if it was bad, that it was anybody's political business), but also because the attempt was an evident failure and a costly one in its social by-products. It may have propelled underworld business in the United States into what economic developers call the "take-off" into self-sustained growth.

A DEFENSE OF ORGANIZED CRIME?

James M. Buchanan

I. Organized Crime as Monopoly Enterprise

Monopoly in the sale of ordinary goods and services is socially inefficient because its restricts output or supply. The monopolist uses restriction as the means to increase market price which, in turn, provides a possible source of monopoly profit. This elementary argument provides the foundation for collective or governmental efforts to enforce competition. Somewhat surprisingly, the elementary argument has rarely been turned on its head. If monopoly in the supply of "goods" is socially undesirable, monopoly in the supply of "bads" should be socially desirable, precisely because of the output restriction.

Consider prostitution. Presumable this is an activity that is a "bad" in some social sense, as witness the almost universal legal prohibitions. (Whether or not particular individuals consider this to be an ill-advised social argument is neither here nor there.) For many potential buyers, however, the services of prostitutes are "goods" in the strict, economic sense of this term: these buyers are willing to pay for these services in ordinary market transactions. From this, it follows that monopoly organization is socially preferable to competitive organization precisely because of the restriction on total output that it fosters. It is perhaps no institutional accident that we observe organized or syndicated controls of that set of illegal activities that most closely fits this pattern (prostitution, gambling, smuggling, drug traffic). In journalistic discussions, the concentration of organized crime's entrepeneurs in these activities is explained by the relatively high profit potential. The supplementary hypothesis suggested here is that monopoly is socially desirable and that this may be recognized implicitly by enforcement agencies who may encourage, or at least may not overtly and actively discourage, the organization of such industries.

The monopolization thesis can be extended and developed. Significantly, elements of the analysis can be applied to those criminal activities that involve nonvoluntary transfers. In this paper, I

Reprinted with permission of the American Enterprise Institute for Public Policy Research from *The Economics of Crime and Punishment*, edited by Simon Rottenberg. © 1973 by American Enterprise Institute for Public Policy Research.

shall present first the simple geometry of the relationships between law enforcement and criminal effort. This allows me to discuss, in abstract and general terms, the social advantages that may be secured from effective monopolization of criminal activities. Following this, I shall discuss some of the possible objections to implications of the simple economic argument.

II. The Geometry of Crime and Law Enforcement

The geometry of crime and law enforcement may be presented in a model that is familiar to economists. We may apply a reaction curve construction quite similar to those that have been developed in several applications such as international trade theory, duopoly theory, voting theory, or public-goods theory.[1] Consider Figure 1. On the horizontal axis we measure resources devoted to the enforcement of law. On the vertical axis we measure resources devoted to criminal activities. We want to develop two separate and independent functional relationships between these two variables. If there were no criminal, if no resources were devoted to criminal activities, society would not find it useful or advantageous to apply resources that might be used to produce goods of value in wasteful law enforcement effort. If no one breaks the law, there is no need for policemen, who could be trained instead as plumbers or carpenters.[2] This establishes the origin as the base point for one of the two functional relationships, the one that we may call the "enforcement response" or reaction curve. As resources are observed to be applied in criminal activity, society—that is, the collectivity of citizens acting though organized political units, governments—will find it advantageous to invest resources in law enforcement. Passive acquiescence to crime is rarely advocated, even among Quakers.[3] Furthermore, there are acknowledged to be major advantages from organizing law enforcement publicly rather than through private and independent action.[4] We should, therefore, expect to find the enforcement-response curve sloping upward and to the right from the origin in geometrical representation, as indicated by the curve L in Figure 1. The precise shape of this curve or relationship need not concern us at this point. The general upward slope indicates only that the public will desire to devote more resources to law enforcement as the observed input of resources into criminality increases.

A second relationship, independent of the first, exists between criminal activity and law enforcement effort, with the first now being the dependent and the second the independent variable. To derive the L curve, we made the enforcement response depend on the observed level of resources in criminality. To develop the separate "criminal response" relationship, drawn as the C curve in Figure 1, we make criminal resource input depend on the level of law enforcement that is observed. It is reasonable to hypothesize that the C curve slopes downward and to the right throughout the range of enforcement effort. If no resources were devoted to enforcement, if there were no policemen, we should predict a relatively large investment in criminal activity. This locates the left-hand intercept high on the vertical axis. As more resources enter enforcement levels, it seems reasonable to think that a minimal level of criminality would be realized and that further enforcement would have little or no effect. This is indicated by the flattened portion of the C curve in its rightward extremities in Figure 1.

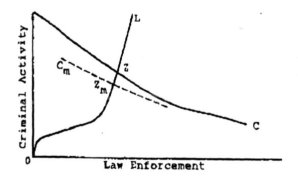

Figure 1. Relationship of Resources Devoted to Criminal Activity and Law Enforcement

Some care must be taken to define just what the C curve represents. For any observed level of law enforcement effort, a level of investment in criminality will be generated. This will be the result or outcome of the private and independent behavior of many persons, potential criminals all, and there is no implication that the response is deliberately controlled by anyone or by any group. Hence, we may qualify or restrict the C curve by the adjective "competitive" if we assume that entry into criminality is open and that the industry is not centrally controlled, not cartelized or monopolized.

Given the two independent relationships as depicted, we can readily demonstrate convergence of the system to a stable equilibrium position at Z, provided that the L curve exhibits a steeper absolute slope value over relevant adjustment ranges than the C curve.[6] Given any starting point, under these conditions the two response or reaction patterns will lead through a succession of adjustments to Z. At such point, no further responses will be forthcoming unless the system is shocked by external forces. At Z, the public demand for inputs into law enforcement is adjusted properly to the level of input into a criminality that is being observed, while at the same time, the criminal industry finds itself in equilibrium under the law enforcement effort that it confronts. There is no observed net entry into or net egress of resources from either criminality or law enforcement. Furthermore, as noted, the equilibrium is stable; if an external force shifts the system from Z, a response mechanism will come into play to return the system to a new equilibrium.

III. The Predicted Effects of Criminal Monopoly

We may now move beyond this elementary adjustment model and consider the effects to be predicted from the effective replacement of a fully competitive criminal industry by a monopolized industry. For this purpose, it will be necessary to distinguish two types of activity. The first, referred to initially in the introduction, covers those activities that are deemed "socially bad," but which involve the sale of goods and services that are considered to be economic "goods" by some potential buyers. Prostitution is the example used before, and it may be taken as a typical case. In the absence of legal prohibition, activities of this sort would amount to nothing more than ordinary exchange or trade, with mutual agreement among contracting parties. Journalistic discussion often labels these as "victimless crimes," although this terminology seems misleading.

The second type of criminal activity involves no such mutual agreement, even in the complete absence of legal prohibition. We may think of burglary as an example of these so-called "crimes with victims." Here the legal structure prescribes involuntary transfers of "goods" among persons rather than the voluntary transfers proscribed under activities of the first type. As the analysis below will indicate, there are three possible sources of an argument for monopolization or cartelization of criminal industries fitting the first category, but only two of these remain applicable to those criminal industries falling within the second category.

Consider a "Type I" industry, exemplified here by prostitution. Initially, we may assume that inputs are available to this industry at an invariant supply price that is determined by the resource returns in alternative employment. Under competitive organization of the industry, there will be tendency for each productive service to be employed so long as this exogenously fixed input price (or wage) falls below marginal value product, MVP, of this input. The necessary condition for competitive equilibrium in the employment of a particular input, I, is:

$$W_I = MVP_I = MPP_I \cdot P_0. \tag{1}$$

As noted in equation (1), the marginal value product is made up of two components, the value of the output, represented by the price, P_0, and the actual change in total quantity of output consequent on the change in the supply of inputs, MPP_I. Elementary price theory suggests that when we replace competition by monopoly, the necessary conditions become:

$$W_I = MVP_I = MPP_I \cdot MR_0. \tag{2}$$

Marginal revenue replaces output price as a component of marginal value product of input. The reason for the change is that, under monopoly, rational decision making (profit-maximizing behavior) will take into account the fact that price varies with total output placed on the market Even if the monopolist acts as a pure price-taker in the market for inputs, as he does under our assumptions, he cannot assume the role of price-taker in the output market. In setting output, he also sets price. Hence, he will take into account not only the actual price that an incremental unit of output can command but also the effects that this addition to supply will exert on the potential selling price of all inframarginal units. Total revenues are a multiple of price times quantity, and it is the change in this total that is relevant to the monopolist's decisions.

From this element alone it is clear that a monopolist will find it profitable to reduce total output in the industry to some level below that which would be observed under competition. This straightforward, price-induced output effect may be identified as the first of the three parts of an argument for the effective monopolization or cartelization of a Type I criminal industry,[7] provided, of course, that the legal prohibition of this type of activity is itself a welfare-increasing policy rule.[8]

This effect is not directly applicable to industries embodying the second type of criminal activity, that which involves no potential contractual agreements or arrangements among willing buyers and sellers. Monopoly control in these "Type II" industries, exemplified by burglary, could not exploit a price-induced, output effect. This requires us to look more carefully at the basic economic model for a Type II activity, again taking burglary as an example.

Output here is presumably measured by the value of the loot that is stolen. Since, however, this material is not different in kind from that which remains in the possession of legal owners, modifications in the rate of supply of loot by the burglary industry will not affect price significantly. In this respect, a potential monopolist of this industry would remain in the same position as the single member among the many members in an openly competitive structure. This point can be seen clearly if we treat the theft of money as an illustration. Units of money are indistinguishable, and the price of a dollar is invariant at a dollar.[9]

In this initial model, there is no incentive for the monopolist to restrict output in a Type II activity because of the effects on output price. But there may exist an *input-output effect*, applicable for both Type I and Type II activities, that would offer the monopolist an incentive to restrict total supply below that which would be observed under open competition. Initially, we assumed that resource inputs were available to the industry in question at constant supply prices. This amounts to assuming that the resources are unspecialized, that criminality generates no differential rents. If we drop this assumption and allow for this possibility, then an expansion in output of the industry may increase the prices of inputs. If a monopolist (monopsonist) is unable to discriminate among different owners of specialized inputs, he will have an incentive to reduce total inputs hired (and hence total output produced) below that generated under competitive organization.[10]

There remains the third source of the argument for monopolization, and this part also carries over for both Type I and Type II criminal activities. Note that in our discussion of either the output-price or input-price effect, we did not find it necessary to introduce law enforcement effort or investment as a determining variable. Regardless of the public's attitudes toward law enforcement and the total investment in enforcement determined by such attitudes, if the conditions described are present, monopolization will tend to reduce total social investment in criminality below that which would be forthcoming under competitive structure. This conclusion holds when society does nothing at all toward law enforcement as well as when society expends a major share of its annual treasure to this end. Furthermore, the shape of the relationship between law enforcement and the level of criminal activity, the enforcement response or L curve, in Figure 1, is not relevant. Indeed, we could have dispensed with any L curve to this point in the analysis.

Things become different when we examine the third part of the monopolization argument. Here the ability of a potential monopolist to observe the *shape* of the enforcement-response relationship distinguishes the monopoly outcome from the competitive one. If the L curve should be vertical, indicating that there is no enforcement response to changes in the level of investment in criminality, the monopoly situation becomes identical to the competitive. For almost all other configurations, however, strategic behavior by the monopolist in recognition of anticipated enforcement response will generate lower levels of criminality than those predicted under competitive organization.

In order to isolate this effect, which we may call the "internalization of externality" effect, we shall assume that the output of the criminal industry is marketed in a fully competitive setting, and, furthermore, that inputs are available to the industry at constant supply prices.[11] This means that producers must remain price-takers in both output and input markets whether the industry is organized along competitive of monopolistic lines. Despite the invariance in input prices, however, average cost of engaging in criminality would increase with an expansion in the output of industry. This increase in the costs would be directly caused by the shape of the L curve in Figure 1, that is, by society's expressed response to the aggregate level of criminality. The effect is to increase the average cost of a unit of criminal output, or, to state the same thing differently, to decrease the marginal (and average) productivity of an input into criminality. The supply curve for the criminal industry would slope upward, despite our assumption that input prices are invariant.

The individual firms in a competitive organization of the industry will not recognize the effects of expanded industry output on average costs. The enforcement response generated by expanded industry output acts to place such firms in a position of imposing reciprocal external diseconomies, one on the other. In considering its own output decision, the individual firm will act as if it has no influence on total industry output and, hence, on the change in costs as industry expands. In making a decision to produce an additional unit, the competitive firm will impose costs on other firms in the industry.

It is precisely the existence of this enforcement-induced external diseconomy that provides the third argument for monopolization. The replacement of competition by monopoly has the effect of internalizing the diseconomy. The monopolist can take into account the relationship between aggregate industry output and the predicted enforcement response, and he can control total industry output so as to increase profits above those forthcoming under competition.

Both the price-induced and the enforcement-induced effects work in the same direction; both provide opportunities for the rational monopolist to secure gains from reducing output below competitive levels. For any given enforcement level, we could, therefore, predict that monopoly output would fall short of the competitive. We may return to Figure 1 and depict monopoly output as a function of enforcement effort, as indicated by the curve C_m in the diagram. This curve falls below C at all points. The equilibrium toward which the system converges under monopoly or cartel control of the industry is shown at Z_m.

If the enforcement-response depicted in Figure 1 is assumed to be socially efficient, then a position at Z_m is clearly preferable to one at Z. The level of criminality is lower, and this must be evaluated positively unless crime itself is somehow considered to be "good." Furthermore, at Z_m, the total amount of enforcement effort is lower than that at Z. Resources involved in enforcement may be freed for the production of alternative goods and services that are positively valued; the taxpayer has additional funds that he may spend on alternative publicly provided or privately marketed goods and services.

IV. Possible Objections to Criminal Monopolies

We should examine possible counterarguments or objections to the monopolistic organization of criminal industries. Are there effects of monopolization that are socially undesirable and which have been obscured or neglected in our analysis?

Distributional objections may be considered at the outset. Monopolization offers opportunities for profits in crime over and above those forthcoming under competition, and this, in itself, may be deemed socially "bad." It must be noted, however, that profits are made possible only because of the reduction in total criminal activity below fully competitive levels. Furthermore, the possible monopoly profits do not represent transfers from "poor deserving criminals." Under open competition, in the absence of specialization, owners of inputs into crime secure returns that are roughly equivalent to those that could be earned in legitimate, noncriminal activities. Monopolization has the effect of shifting a somewhat larger share of these inputs into noncriminal pursuits. For some of these services, transfer rents may be reduced, but these reductions are offset by increased transfer rents received by other owners of services. It seems difficult to adduce strictly distributional objections to the monopolization of crime.

A second possible objection may be based on the presumed interdependence of the several types of criminal activities. In the analysis below, I have implicitly assumed that the separate criminal industries are independent from one another. If we should assume that potential criminals constitute a noncompeting group of persons, distinct and apart from the rest of society, monopolization of one or a few areas of criminality may actually increase the supply of resources going into remaining and nonorganized activities. This sort of supply interdependence provides an argument for the extension of monopolization to all criminal activities. It does not, however, offer an argument against monopolization per se. Under full monopolization or effective cartelization, the allocation of resources among the separate criminal activities may not be equivalent, in the proportional sense, to that which would prevail under competition. The crime syndicate that effectively controls all criminal activities will equalize the marginal return on its resources in all categories, but the returns captured will include portions of "buyers' surplus" not capturable under effective competition. The mix among crimes will probably be different in the two cases; there may be more burglars relative to bank robbers under one model than the other. There will, however, be fewer of both under monopoly except under exceptional circumstances.

A third possible objection to the whole analysis must be considered more seriously and discussed in more detail. To this point, I have implicitly assumed that resource inputs are transformed into criminal output with equal efficiency in competitive organization and in monopoly. This assumption may not be empirically appropriate. It seems plausible to argue, at least under some circumstances, that a monopolized or cartelized criminal industry can be more efficient than competition. For any given output, the monopoly may require fewer resource inputs. If this is the case, the C curve of Figure 1 cannot be allowed to represent resource input and/or criminal output interchangeably as we have implicitly done in the discussion. The nonstrategic monopoly-response curve will not be coincident with the competitive C curve if the former is defined in terms of output. The nonstrategic monopoly-response curve will lie above that which describes competitive criminal response. The strategic monopoly-response function will be below the nonstrategic function, as depicted, but there is no assurance that it need lie below the competitive-response function as shown in Figure 1. To the extent that there are significant economies of large scale in crime, monopoly organization will tend to be relatively more efficient. Even if this hypothesis is accepted, however, the advantages of competitive criminal organization are not clear. Consider an example in which a fully strategic monopoly response, given a predicted enforcement-response function, generates a criminal output valued at X dollars, which is the same as the output that would be generated under competition. Assume, however, that the latter industrial organization uses resources valued at X dollars in alternative uses, whereas the monopoly uses up only X/2 dollars in generating X. The social "bad" represented by crime is identical in the two forms: law enforcement investment is the same. But resources valued at X/2 are freed for the production of valued "goods" under monopoly whereas these "goods" cannot be produced under competition.[12]

A possible misunderstanding of the whole analysis rather than an explicit objection to it may emerge. Emotions may be aroused by the thought that one implication of the whole analysis is that governments should "deal with the syndicate," the law enforcement agencies should work out "accommodations" or "arrangements" with those who might organize central control over criminal effort. I should emphasize that there is nothing of this sort implied in the analysis to this point. In its strictest interpretation, the analysis carries no policy implications at all. It merely suggests that there may be social benefits from the monopoly organization of crime. Policy implications emerge only when we go beyond this with a suggestion that governments adopt a passive role when they observe attempts made by entrepreneurs to reduce the effective competitiveness of criminal industries. In practice, this suggestion reduces to an admonition against the much-publicized crusades against organized crime at the expense of enforcement effort aimed at ordinary, competitive criminality.

I do not propose that explicit "arrangements" be made with existing or potential criminal syndicates. If this approach were taken, the solution to the system depicted in Figure 1 would not be at Z_m, but would, instead, be located to the southwest of Z_m, embodying even less criminal output and less enforcement effort. At Z_m, "gains from trade" between a monopoly syndicate and the community may be exploited only by moves in the general southwesterly direction.[13] There are compelling arguments against this approach. In the first place, even if the persons in potential control of criminal activity could be identified in advance and a bargain struck with them, the governmental agency involved would find that the "trading" solution lies off the community's enforcement response, or L, curve. This would bring pressure on politicians to break the agreement. A government agency, precisely because it acts on behalf of, and is thereby subject to review by, the whole community, cannot readily behave monolithically, whether this behavior is unilateral strategic response to, or explicit bilateral dealing with, a syndicate. The community enforcement-response function necessarily describes outcomes generated by the interaction of many behavioral components; in many respects such responses are more closely analogous to competitive, than to monopoly, behavior.

Perhaps an equally important technical difficulty with this approach involves the question of identification itself. Even if the enforcement agencies could act monolithically, independent from community political pressures, the question would remain: If the criminal syndicate could be identified with sufficient predictability to allow bargains to be struck, why should "trade" be necessary? The community's preferred position is the reduction of criminal activity to zero, allowing for a comparable reduction in enforcement effort. The enforcement-response function, shown by the L curve in Figure 1, is based on the implicit assumption that there are technological limits to the productivity of police effort. These limits may rule out the full identification of the organizers of crime, even if monopoly is known to exist and to be effective. Passive acquiescence in the syndication of crime is a wholly different policy stance from active negotiations with identified leaders.

If "arrangements" are ruled out on technological, ethical, or contractual bases, however, a subsidiary question arises concerning appropriate policy norms to be followed when and if positive identification of the monopolists becomes possible, either fortuitously or as a result of search effort. Suppose, for example, that a municipality that is initially in a Z_m equilibrium finds it possible to identify leaders of the local syndicate. Should the community prosecute these leaders and break up the monopoly? Failure to prosecute here is quite different from the arrangement of explicit trades or deals. Breakdowns of an existing control group may loose a flood of entrants and the competitive adjustment process might converge toward a new equilibrium at Z. If such a pattern is predicted, attempts at breaking up even those criminal monopolies whose leaders are positively identified should be made with caution.

The law enforcement response that this analysis implies is no different in detail from that which might be followed under competitive organization of the criminal industries. Enforcement units and agencies are presumed to make normal efforts to apprehend criminals of all sorts, and community or public pressures will insure that these efforts are bounded from both sides. Indeed, the monopolist's response function has been presumed to be based on the expectation that community response would be as noted. The analysis does nothing toward suggesting that enforcement agencies should not take maximum advantage of all technological developments in crime prevention, detection and control. To the extent that new technology increases the cost of criminal output, the relevant C curve, competitive or monopolistic, is shifted downward. To the extent that court rulings increase the expected productivity of investment in criminality and/or reduce the productivity of enforcement effort, the relevant C curve is shifted upward. The whole analysis had been presented on the assumption that the public's "tastes" for enforcement remain unchanged. This is merely a convenient expository device, and there is no difficulty in incorporating shifts toward the right or left in the L function.[14]

V. Criminal Self-Interest as a Social "Good"

The genius of the eighteenth-century social philosophers, notably Bernard Mandeville, David Hume, and Adam Smith, is to be found in their recognition that the self-interests of men can be made to serve social purpose under the appropriate institutional arrangements. The sought reform in the organization or the institutions of society is an instrumental means of accomplishing more specific social objectives. The philosophical foundations of competitive economic organization are contained in Adam Smith's famous statement about the butcher whose self-interest, rather than benevolence, puts meat on the consumer's supper table. So long as attention is confined to the production, supply and marketing of pure "goods," both as evaluated by direct purchasers, and by the members of the community in their "public" capacities, competition among freely contracting traders, with entry into and egress from industry open, furthers the "public interest" in a meaningful sense of this term. There is no argument for monopolistic restriction in this setting, whether this be done via governmental agencies, as in Smith's era (and, alas, all too commonly in our own) or by profit-seeking private entrepreneurs. The preservation of free entry and egress, the prohibition of output-restricting, price-increasing agreements among sellers, the control of industries or groups of industries by one or a small number of persons and/or firms—all of these are genuinely "public goods" and, as such, their provision warrants the possible investment of governmental resources.

Things become somewhat different, however, when it is recognized that "goods," which individuals value positively in their private capacities, may be mixed variously with "bads," which individuals value negatively in their capacities as members of the community. To the extent that the "goods" element is isolated, restrictions on competitive supply are socially undesirable. If the "bads" necessarily accompany the production-sale of the "goods," however, some balance must be struck and some reduction in the output of "goods" below openly competitive levels may be in the social interest. If the "bads" are internal to an industry, monopolization will cause these to be internalized and taken into account in decision making. In this case, profit-seeking behavior of the monopolist will reduce the output of "goods" below socially optimal levels. In this case, it becomes impossible to determine, a priori, which of the two organizational forms, competition or monopoly, is socially more efficient. If the "bads" are external to an industry, wholly or partially, monopolization will at least shift the total supply of "goods" in the direction indicated by social optimality criteria, but profit-induced restriction may fall short of or overshoot the mark. Aside from this, there may also be highly undesirable distributional consequences of monopolization. In general, no straightforward organizational or institutional principles can be deduced for the cases where "goods" and "bads" are mixed. The choice between competitive and monopoly organization, if these are the only effective alternatives, must be made on the basis of pragmatic considerations in each case.[15]

Unambiguous organizational-institutional guidelines re-emerge, however, when we examine activities that are unambiguously "bads" in the social or public sense. Here the argument advanced by Mandeville and Smith becomes applicable in reverse. If it lies within the self-interest of men to produce "bads" without accompanying and compensating "goods," this same self-interest may be channeled in a socially desired direction by encouraging the exploitation of the additional private profit opportunities offered in explicit restraint of trade. Freedom of entry, the hallmark of competition, is of negative social value here, and competitiveness is to be discouraged rather than encouraged. These principles become self-evident once we recognize, with the eighteenth-century philosophers, that institutional structures are variables that may be used as instruments for achieving social purpose in this case, the reduction in the aggregate level of criminality along with the reduction in resource commitment to law enforcement. It is not from the public-spiritedness of the leaders of the Cosa Nostra that we should expect to get a reduction in the crime ratio but from their own self-interests.[16]

Footnotes

[1] For an application that perhaps comes closest to this paper, see my "Violence, Law, and Equilibrium in the University," *Public Policy*, vol. 19 (Winter 1971), pp. 1-18. Also see Gordon Tullock, "The Welfare Costs of Tariffs, Monopolies, and Theft," *Western Economic Journal*, vol. 5 (June 1967), pp. 224-232.

[2] For a generalized account of the "social dilemma" that law enforcement represents, along with numerous applications, see Gordon Tullock, *The Social Dilemma* (forthcoming).

[3] At minimal levels of criminal activity, acquiescence may be the efficient course of action. The formal properties of an efficient or optimal position will take into account both the amounts of criminal activity and the costs of enforcement activity. See Winston Bush, *Income Distribution in Anarchy* (forthcoming) for an attempt to specify these formal properties.

[4] Law enforcement qualifies as a genuine "public good" in that there are major efficiency gains from joint, as opposed to individual, provision. All persons secure benefits from the same policeman on the beat simultaneously. This need not, of course, imply that private supplements to public law enforcement may not also be advantageous. And there is nothing in the argument for public organization of law enforcement that suggests explicit governmental production. A collectivity may well secure efficiency gains from hiring the services of a private policing firm, as opposed to hiring its own municipal policemen.

5 For those who adopt a pathological interpretation of crime, the C curve would be horizontal. This would indicate that the number of criminals and the amount of criminal effort are not influenced by enforcement at all.

6 If the society's law enforcement reaction to changes in the level of criminality should be highly elastic relative to the converse reaction of criminal effort to enforcement, the simple system depicted in Figure 1 would generate an explosive cycle. One implication of this suggests that the enforcement response, that which is under society's collective control, should not be overly sensitive. On this, see my paper, "Violence, Law, and Equilibrium in the University."

7 The argument holds so long as anything less than perfect discrimination is available to the monopolist. If perfect discrimination were possible, the output under monopoly would be identical to that under competition. Note particularly that the complete absence of discrimination is not required for the argument, and, in fact, some less-than-perfect discrimination might be expected to take place in industries of Type I. Buyer's information about alternatives would presumably be significantly higher.

8 The welfare of participants in the voluntary exchanges, considered as a subset of the total population, would be maximized by an absence of legal prohibitions. In the presence of such prescriptive rules, furthermore, restrictions on industry output would be welfare-reducing. Hence, for this subset of the population, monopoly control is less desirable than competition. For the inclusive community, this welfare-decreasing effect of monopolization must be more than offset by welfare gains of nonparticipants if the legal prescriptions are, themselves, socially desirable. There is, of course, no means of determining by simple observation whether or not this condition is fulfilled. For purposes of analysis here, I shall assume that it is.

9 When we consider the theft of real goods, such as items of clothing, jewelry, plate, and automobiles, some elements identified as characteristic of Type I industries may enter. The value of stolen items here is determined by the ability to market them through indirect and illegal channels. To the extent that the supply of "fence"

services is not, itself, highly elastic, the monopolist might face a downsloping curve of effective "demand price." In this case, the argument developed above would, of course, hold and marginal revenue would fall below price. My purpose is not to deny the real-world relevance of this situation, but to develop a pure Type II-model in which, by assumption, final purchasers do not distinguish stolen from nonstolen goods and in which there are no institutional or supply barriers to resale.

[10] Discrimination among suppliers of inputs may be considerably easier to accomplish than discrimination among purchasers of outputs. See Footnote 7 above.

[11] These assumptions are not fully consistent with a general equilibrium setting. They may be made plausible by assuming that the industry is small relative to the total economy. They are made here, however, solely for purposes of exposition.

[12] The media sometimes becomes confused in assessing the comparative efficiency of organized and unorganized crime. In June 1971, attention was focused on the theft of stock certificates from brokerages. On consecutive evening news broadcasts, one TV network reported (1) organized crime *exploits* the actual thieves by giving them only 5 percent of the face value of the stolen certificates, and (2) the increase in theft is facilitated because organized crime provides a *ready market* for the securities.

[13] Economists familiar with ridge-line or reaction-curve constructions will recognize that the C_m curve depicts the locus of vertical points on the series of indifference contours representing the preferences of the monopolist. Similarly, the L curve is the locus of horizontal positions on the community's set of indifference curves, assuming away all difficulties in interpersonal amalgamation. The preferred position of the monopolist lies high along the ordinate, and the preferred position of the community lies at the origin.

---

[14] The situation in the United States in the early 1970s may be interpreted in terms of the analysis of this paper. Adverse court rulings since the middle 1950s have continually shifted the relevant C curves upward. This has created a disequilibrium in the whole system that is reflected in the observed increases in enforcement effort.

[15] Economists, in their roles as social reformers, constantly search for alternatives that will accomplish the explicit objectives more directly without basic modifications in organizational structure. For example, witness the current popularity of schemes to correct for "public bads" exemplified in air and water pollution by placing charges or fees on the production and sale of marketable goods and services, while maintaining competitive structure as the organizational form.

It will be recognized that the content of this paragraph covers, in extremely brief form, many parts of modern welfare economics. Earlier works of my own have discussed some of the points made. See my "Private Ownership and Common Usage: The Road Case Re-examined." *Southern Economic Journal*, vol. 22 (January 1956), pp. 305-16; "External Diseconomies, Corrective Taxes, and Market Structure," *American Economic Review*, vol. 59 (March 1969), pp. 174-76; and "Public Goods and Public Bads," in *Financing the Metropolis*, ed. John P. Crecine (Beverly Hills: Sage Publications, 1970), pp. 51-71.

[16] Only upon reading another paper delivered at the conference did I see the reference to the paper by Thomas Schelling on the economics of organized crime. Upon subsequent examination, I find that Schelling explored some of the issues touched upon in my paper, but that he did not explicitly discuss the central principle that I have emphasized. See Thomas C. Schelling, "Economic Analysis of Organized Crime," Appendix D in *Task Force Report: Organized Crime* Annotations and Consultants' Papers, Task Force on Organized Crime, The President's Commission on Law Enforcement and the Administration of Justice (Washington D.C.: Government Printing Office, 1967).